1990

D1124229

NARRATIVE THOUGHT
and
NARRATIVE LANGUAGE

NARRATIVE THOUGHT
and
NARRATIVE LANGUAGE

Edited by
Bruce K. Britton
A. D. Pellegrini
University of Georgia

A publication of the
Cognitive Studies
Group and the
Institute for
Behavioral Research
at the University
of Georgia

LEA LAWRENCE ERLBAUM ASSOCIATES, PUBLISHERS
1990 Hillsdale, New Jersey   Hove and London

Lawrence Erlbaum Associates, Inc., Publishers
365 Broadway
Hillsdale, New Jersey 07642

Library of Congress Cataloging in Publication Data
Narrative thought and narrative language / edited by Bruce K. Britton.
A. D. Pellegrini.
    p.   cm.
Includes index.
ISBN 0-8058-0099-9
    1. Narration (Rhetoric) 2. Discourse analysis—Psychological
aspects. 3. Psycholinguistics. 4. Thought and thinking.
5. Consciousness. I. Britton, Bruce K. II. Pellegrini, Anthony D.
PN212.N38 1989
401.41—dc19   89–1612
                                                            CIP

Printed in the United States of America
10 9 8 7 6 5 4 3 2 1

Contents

vi

Preface

This volume is the product of the conference on Narrative Thought and Narrative Language, held February 12, 1987 at the University of Georgia, organized by the Institute for Behavioral Research Cognitive Studies Group, and jointly sponsored by the Institute for Behavioral Research, the College of Education, the Department of Psychology, and the Department of Speech Communication. The participants in the conference were Jerome S. Bruner, Wallace Chafe, and David R. Olson. The other authors represented here were selected from nominations solicited from the three participants.

1

Narrative Comprehension

Carol Fleisher Feldman
Jerome Bruner
Bobbi Renderer
Sally Spitzer
New York University

Basic cognitive processes for understanding the physical world have been at least well studied if not altogether well elucidated in recent decades. We now know a good deal about how experience of that world is organized—the classes and relations used, the propositions and operations employed, and so forth. But the world we inhabit has more than things in it. It also includes cultural products, among which are written poems, stories, and novels, and oral stories that we tell each other. Although these are symbolic objects, we strive to understand them too, and we probably succeed at it as well as we do with the physical world. But how do we do it? What cognitive processes are engaged? Are they the same as the ones we employ in understanding the world of things? And if different, what are they like?

To construe stories, may, of course, require the use of cognitive processes used for other purposes, but there are other processes that are unique to the story domain and to the world of narrative products. Other students of narrative have amply noted the applicability of non-unique processes to the comprehension of simple narratives: Trebasso and Sperry (1985) for moral parables and folk tales, Nelson (1986) and others for a restaurant tale that reports a sequence of events, and Mandler (1984) for goal-directed action patterns analyzable as schemas. But narrative products in any culture are typically more richly patterned than that. One source of this richer patterning in more literary stories—say in Modern Western literature or in Indian oral poetry—is the presence of a dual patterning: They contain both a landscape of consciousness and a landscape of action (Bruner, 1986).

Narrative forms can exist, of course, with only a landscape of action. Propp's (1986/1968) famous study of the morphology of the folktale describes a sequence of action functions as types, where many tokens can fulfill the type in order to structure the plot as a whole. For such folktales, the landscape of action is a temporally patterned sequence of action events reported in the third person with minimal information about the psychological states of the protagonists. Even when accounts of this kind are in the first person, as in *The Travels of Marco Polo*, the narrative is dominated by the landscape of action, and events are reported as they might have appeared to anyone who had been present, to an omniscient observer. In such a landscape, it is not of concern how things are perceived, felt, intended, or imagined. So, in the landscape of action, things happen or they don't. It is not concerned with how they are perceived.

In contrast, the landscape of consciousness (as in modern and postmodern fiction) is devoted precisely to how the world is perceived or felt by various members of the cast of characters, each from their own perspective. Whereas in folktales the verbs are verbs of action, in stories that include the landscape of consciousness, the language is marked by a heavy usage of mental verbs—of thinking, supposing, feeling, and believing. Indeed, the purpose of such stories is to explore the nature of the mental perspectives of characters rather than to report omnisciently on events encountered. Indeed, some forms (as in Joyce, Beckett, or Robbe-Grillet) may be largely dedicated to sketching a landscape of consciousness with virtually no landscape of action. But most modern narrative uses both a landscape of consciousness and a landscape of action and puts them into an ambiguous relation to each other. The modern reader, then, must interpret both sides of this dual landscape.

Whereas interpretation of the landscape of action may require only the use of the familiar cognitive processes that are used to explain the physical world, the landscape of consciousness may call into play cognitive processes not familiar from studies of our understanding of that world. A good deal has been written about the philosophical difference between explanation and interpretation (see, for example, Morton, 1980). In narratives having merely a landscape of action, the actions are given *causal* organization, and forms of processing (explanation) designed to unpack causality must be used to understand them. Narratives having a landscape of consciousness impose a different problem. By virtue of their events being mental, organized in terms of human agency and intentionality, they require processes of interpretation to deal with intentionality and its vicissitudes. Although we know very little about such processes of interpretation, fortunately they are not entirely unfamiliar. For the study of interpretation is as old as literary theory, which, after all, had its roots in Biblical exegesis. What we need to know better is the cognitive psychology of these processes.

No doubt the cognitive processing that we use to interpret human intentionality in stories is related to the processes we use to understand human intentionality in life encounters with other people. We might think of them both as derived from general cognitive procedures for interpreting intentionality. But literature is not quite life, and the procedures for interpretation of intentionality in texts and in human interaction may differ in some important ways. In other words, when we say that an action means such and such and that a text means such and such we invoke two different notions of meaning—and it is not yet clear how different they are.

In particular, the interpretation of intentionality in texts requires particular attention to two sorts of strictly linguistic phenomena: tropes and mental state terms. By tropes, we mean such devices as metaphor, metonym, synecdoche, and irony. Tropes can convey implicitly or in compressed form someone's point of view about an event (the neutral or metaphorically sympathetic "His mother was upstairs taking her medicine" vs. the pejorative and ironic "His mother was upstairs swallowing a pill.") An example of a mental state expression is "She dreaded his arrival." Both tropes and mental state terms play an important role in conveying human intentionality in stories, whereas the interpretation of intentionality in human action and interaction must depend largely on such other stance conveying mechanisms as facial expression, tone of voice, gesture, and posture. Each, then, depends on a very different tool kit of cues.

The studies reported here have the explicit purpose of trying to explore the cognitive processes people use to understand or unpack story texts that comprise a dual landscape typical of modern storytelling—both a landscape of consciousness and a landscape of action. What distinctive cognitive procedures do people bring to bear in order to interpret the landscape of consciousness; how do these differ from those used to understand the landscape of action; and how do people handle the combination of the two in the dual landscape? In order to explore these questions, we designed a procedure for manipulating the richness of the landscape of consciousness in literary story texts. We sought an experimental procedure to help us tease apart the two landscapes.

In order to manipulate the landscape of consciousness, or the richness of information about human intentionality in the texts, we created two versions of the same story. We selected, for the first study, two stories that had both a landscape of action and a landscape of consciousness. We then tried to diminish the landscape of consciousness in each story by neutralizing or deleting its mental state descriptions. Both versions of each story were used in the experiment. One version was the published version as written with its rich landscape of consciousness—called here *the conscious version*. The other was the version with many of the mental state verbs deleted or replaced with action language—called hereafter *the nonconscious version*. This made the nonconscious versions shorter than the conscious versions of both stories. Note that though the nonconscious versions have a much reduced language of consciousness, they still have an inferrable pattern of human consciousness—at least to modern readers who expect to know what their protagonists are thinking and will make inferences about it on minimal information.

We expected the nonconscious version to be understood at least in part by means of the familiar hypothetico-deductive processes that Bruner (1986) has called *paradigmatic thinking*, with some new wrinkles due to the fact that the material is text rather than physical states. We hoped to learn something of the nature of those wrinkles, and we also hoped to discover the nature of any unique cognitive processes of interpretation that these same subjects used to understand the stories in their conscious versions.

We conducted two studies of this kind to explore the cognitive procedures people use for interpreting stories. In each study, different stories were used, but both studies followed the same pattern. In each study, 12 adult subjects were individually read two short stories. One was read as published—the conscious version. The other contained a reduced landscape of consciousness—the nonconscious version. In each study, 6 of the 12 subjects got Story 1 in the conscious version, and Story 2 in the nonconscious version; 6 got Story 2 in the conscious version and Story 1 in the nonconscious version. The order of presentation was counterbalanced, and the counterbalanced pattern was preserved across the two experimenters who interviewed the subjects. Subjects were all young adults living in New York City.

Before we start, however, we must say a word about the place of this study in the general scheme of things. To begin with, it falls midway between literary "reader response" approaches to comprehension of narrative literature and the experimental study of "made up" stories of the kind mentioned earlier. It uses as its input genuine literary products (although it uses artificial variants of them as well), and attempts to use an "experimental" procedure to determine how people interpret "real" stories. Although it is motivated by theoretical concerns, it attempts, nonetheless, to maintain an "empirical innocence" in the sense of letting subjects give their own accounts of what stories "mean." We do not, moreover, attempt a sociolinguistic analysis in the sense of comparing our subjects' cultural background or analyzing closely the social context in which their interpretation were given. Our subjects were young, middle-class, educated adults who were occasional readers of novels.

We say all this not in apology, but to indicate that this was an exploratory study designed to give us a sense of how a group of literate subjects go about "interpreting" or "understanding" a small collection of literary works. In subsequent work, we have addressed more directly the kinds of issues mentioned. But the present pilot study nonetheless can contribute to an appreciation of the kinds of interesting reactions one obtains when one asks people what they make of a story that is unfolding before them.

STUDY 1

In the first study, the stories were Brendan Gill's "Truth and Consequences" and Henrich Böll's "Nostalgia or: Grease Spots." The stories, as written and as amended, appear in Appendix A. We strongly urge the reader to turn now to the Appendix and read the stories, for the findings are difficult to grasp for the reader unfamiliar with the stories.

As the story was read to the subject, the reading was interrupted at four fixed points. Before we were one quarter of the way into the story, we asked "What's the most important thing I've told you so far? Why?" Then, before one third of the way, we asked these questions again. Before we were three quarters of the way in, we asked "What are the directions this could be going? Which way do you think it will go? Why?" These questions were repeated again just before the end. The locations of the interrupting questions in each version are marked in Appendix A. After each story reading was over, the experimenter asked "Tell me some things about this character I haven't told you—what is he like?" Following this, subjects were asked to retell the story: "I'd like you to tell me the story now." Some 2 to 3 months later we returned to our subjects and asked them to tell us the gist of the story.

We were aware, of course, that the inserted questions may, themselves, be a trigger to interpretation and may affect the pattern of responses that we obtained. Unfortunately, there was no way of finding out how subjects would interpret the story without asking them to do so, and no way of asking them to do so that might not also cause them to begin interpreting. This unfortunate but inevitable complementarity may bar us from attributing any differences in interpretive approach to version differences alone. A more conservative approach to differences is to attribute them to version difference plus interpretive questions. Indeed, a similar point can be made about the effect of reading the story aloud. We read aloud because we didn't want to introduce the possibility of variable exposure—that some subjects reading it to themselves might skip portions or go back over the story and others not—and because we thought their responses to our questions would feel more natural if we had been talking too. So any interpretive differences evoked by different versions might best be attributed to version situation in a procedural context—with the use of questions, a live speaker, and so on, all included.

We intended, when we diminished the landscape of consciousness in the nonconscious versions, to leave the landscape of action unaltered. Leaving the basic plot unaffected by our manipulation was extremely important to our understanding of any differences that might be evoked by different versions. So, our first analysis concerns the accuracy of report of the basic plot line in the retellings.

Analysis of Plot-Line Reconstruction

To get at plot line, we identified 12 basic propositions (e.g., "Charles is going to be a priest") in each story that, when taken together, give a plot summary. Each proposition was present in the retellings of at least 50% (but never 100%) of our subjects. The 12 basic propositions comprising the plot of each story are given in Appendix B. Interrater reliability[1] for identifying the basic propositions in the subjects' retellings was $K = .77$. In order to be sure that there were no differences in basic plot understanding, recall for the 12 basic propositions was compared for the two versions of both stories. And, in fact, the 12 basic propositions were recalled equally well in response to the conscious versions and the nonconscious versions. Both groups, with $n = 12$ in each case, have a mean recall of 8.8 of the 12 basic propositions. We felt safe, then, in concluding that version did not affect subjects' understanding of the basic story line. We concluded that because basic comprehension of story line was unaffected by the version manipulation, any interpretive differences between versions could not be due to differences in comprehension or retention of the plot itself. Any effect of the version manipulation, therefore, could reasonably be attributed at least in part to the role of the landscape of consciousness in evoking interpretive processes.

The order in which the 12 basic propositions were retold by our subjects provides a first indication that there is more reconstruction going on in response to the conscious version than in response to the nonconscious version. We asked whether the order of the propositions in retelling generally conforms to their order in the story as read or whether the order was reorganized. Both stories in both their versions begin at an initial moment in time, then go back to an earlier point (the Gill to background, the Böll to the past), and then carry forward from the initial point. This pattern could easily tempt subjects to reorder the story into a linear temporal order, with the analeptic flashback in the story "straightened out." Subjects responding to the conscious version more often reordered the propositions (eight reordered retellings vs. four retellings in the order of the story read), whereas subjects given the nonconscious version were equally likely to give the story in a reordered form as in the order told (six responses of each kind). The difference is not statistically significant, but we note it nonetheless because later we discuss scanning the direction of such differences over many measures.

As a next step in analysis, 12 other propositions were extracted from each story; this time they were detail items not crucial to the plot but, rather, relevant as color or tone (e.g., "The girl had blond hair.") The 12 detail propositions are also given in Appendix B. The mean number of detail items recalled is smaller overall than for the

---

[1]This interrater agreement, and those for all subsequent codes developed here, is reported in Appendix C. All measures reported have interrater agreements exceeding $K = .76$.

basic propositions, and slightly larger for the conscious version *(M = 4.1)* than for the nonconscious version *(M = 3.4).* Of course, the conscious version is somewhat longer than the nonconscious version and, correspondingly, the retellings are somewhat longer: a mean of 47 lines for the conscious version and 36 for the nonconscious version. We might expect, therefore, that a bit more detail would appear in them.

This may be a good moment to stop and make some general observations. We shortly report a great many other differences found between the two versions in this first study. Nearly all of them have to do with greater amounts of and more interesting kinds of reconstruction or going beyond the information given evoked by the conscious versions of the stories. Bartlett's (1932) classical study of memory for stories demonstrated beyond any doubt that narrative pattern as found in his tale "The War of the Ghosts" triggered massive reconstruction in memory, a reconstruction following certain patterns—such as the amplification of the strange. The interesting question about narrative memory turned out to lie not in the extent of its accuracy but in its generative rules of reconstruction. Here, too, the interesting findings lie in the patterns of reconstruction. Both versions, and especially the conscious version, elicited massive reconstruction, and the two versions produced distinctive and different patterns of reconstruction.

Because the patterns of reconstruction are of such central interest here, we had first to identify instances of responses that did not merely report material in the story we told, but that went beyond the information given in the story. We coded the retellings first for units of information that were *given* in the story told and second for units of information *beyond the given* in the story told. The criteria used for this code, and all others subsequently discussed here, are found in the coding manual in Appendix C. Given information was greater in response to the conscious version (293 vs. 224), as one would expect because the conscious version is actually longer. There was also a difference between the two versions in information beyond the information given, with the conscious version evoking more (210 vs. 143). Thus, the conscious version presents more information, and subjects learn more from it. They also tend to create more, but not significantly more *(t = 1.43, df = 11, p < .1)* or relatively more than subjects receiving the nonconscious version.[2]

---

[2]All *t* tests were computed as one-tailed tests, and this should be borne in mind in interpreting them. The use of one-tailed tests is justified by our initial hypothesis that "conscious versions" of the stories would produce more interpretive and more psychological responses than "nonconscious versions."

For if we look at information beyond the given as a percentage of total information units, we find essentially the same percentage for the conscious version (42%) and for the nonconscious version (39%). Both versions, then, lead subjects to create or construct a great deal of new information that is not actually given in the stories read to them. Any interesting differences between the versions, then, should lie in differences in the generative rules with which information beyond the given is created for each of them.

We analyzed the information beyond the given into three categories: psychological (e.g., "He did realize in the end that he was fond of the girl. Uh, which he hadn't admitted to himself before"), action (e.g., "The only way she gets known is by acting like the boys do in many ways and stuff"), and trait (e.g., "She's a very honest creature").

Table 1.1 suggests that the patterning of responses to the two versions was quite different, with information beyond the given for the conscious version tending to be psychological, and for the nonconscious version tending to be about both psychology and actions. A t test finds a significant version difference in psychological responses $(t = 2.21, df = 11, p < .05)$, but not in action responses $(t = .51, ns)$. It is clear that the generative pattern of thinking about the conscious version includes considerations about the psychology of the protagonist, and it is clear that the nonconscious version evokes reasoning on some other basis—perhaps a basis connected in some manner with actions.

We can summarize the results from the retellings as follows: Basic plot propositions are reported with equal fullness for the two versions. Getting the basic propositions right seems to be unaffected by the version manipulation. Slightly more plot details are reported in response to the conscious version than the nonconscious version. Although the basic plot propositions are not differently reported for the two versions, the sequence of propositions is somewhat more often reordered by subjects receiving the conscious version. Information beyond the given is not reported more often in response to the conscious version than to the nonconscious ver-

TABLE 1.1
Information Beyond the Given in the Retellings

	Psychological		Action		Trait		TOTAL
	#	%	#	%	#	%	
Conscious	92	43.8	77	36.7	41	19.5	210
Nonconscious	44	30.7	64	44.7	35	24.4	143

sion, and it constitutes the same percentage of responses for the two versions. More important is that the nature of that new information tends to be of different kinds: psychological for the conscious version; something else, possibly something related to action, for the nonconscious version.

Analysis of Subject Responses

We turn now to the questions we asked our subjects while we were reading them the stories. Did their answers distinguish between the conscious and nonconscious versions? Consider some of the suggestive findings.

First, we analyzed replies to all questions for the number of mental verbs used and found that more such verbs were given in response to the conscious version (119) than to the nonconscious version (83; $t = 1.85$, $df = 11$, $p < .05$). This suggests that the two versions were in fact perceived by the subjects congruently with the manner of their actual textual construction. More specifically, mental verbs were attributed to protagonists in the conscious version twice as often (22) as in the nonconscious version (11), reflecting actual differences between the versions, though this difference was not significant ($t = 1.25$, $df = 11$ ns).

But an interesting finding emerged. For, in fact, only a very small percentage of the mental verbs used by our subjects were attributed to characters (18% for the conscious version and 13% for the nonconscious version). A far larger percentage are used to convey our subjects' mental states ("I think") than the characters' mental states ("he believes") in both versions. For both versions, then, subjects were highly reflective, and their reflections were constitutive of their interpretations of the story. But responses to the conscious version were more reflective in this sense, for a greater number of mental verbs conveying subjects' mental states were produced in response to the conscious version (97) than to the nonconscious version (72; $t = 1.89$, $df = 11$, $p < .05$).

Why? As a working hypothesis, we might say that the task of interpreting a story about the more reflective protagonist of the conscious version causes the subjects to be more reflective and to treat their reflections as part of what they make of the story, in a manner not unlike the way the protagonist's reflections are part of what he or she makes of the story. This suggests that the conscious version engages our subjects' subjectivity more than does the nonconscious version—an interesting finding. We return to it again later after we explore other results that are consistent with it.

The first question asked was this—"What is the most important thing I've told you so far? Why?" We analyzed these responses for the kind of event cited—whether it was psychological (a protagonist realizing something, for example) or an action (a protagonist going to see an old friend). We expected to see the more psychological responses among conscious version responses, but we did not— both the conscious and nonconscious versions received twice as many action responses as psychological responses, and the number of both kinds of responses was equal for the two versions. We mention this now despite the negative findings because we return to it when we report Study 2.

The same responses can be looked at another way—is the reply temporal or static? An extract from a temporal response is, "But that's an actual thing that's really going to happen and that sounds like it's going to have the greatest impact on what's to follow." Another is, "If he wasn't going to be entering a seminary, then things could go along smoothly, it seems to me." In contrast, the following responses were considered static: "There seems to be some kind of tension between Walter and the Narrator concerning Erica," and "It's like he's being tempted, you know, by what he's supposed to not be tempted by and by what he's supposed to sort of close his eyes to, you know."

Responses to the conscious version tended to be temporal (16) rather than static (8), whereas responses to the nonconscious version tended to be static (17) rather than temporal (7; $x^2 = 5.34$, $df = 1, p < .05$). This finding suggests that the well-marked landscape of consciousness found in the conscious version induces subjects to perceive a distinctively temporal, dynamic organizational pattern. Put together with the earlier reported finding that information beyond the given evoked by the conscious version is psychological whereas that for the nonconscious version is about action, we see that the conscious version interpretation is a dynamic one that is principally organized around expected changes in the inferred psychological states of the protagonists. Conversely, the organizational pattern extracted from the story by subjects hearing the nonconscious versions is a static organization of actions.

An interesting way of interpreting the temporal/static difference is to suppose that the temporal interpretations of the story represent a greater degree of engagement in ongoing narrative process, an engagement induced (as already suggested) by the subjective material in the conscious version. If this notion were right, there should also be a shift toward more temporal responding as subjects are exposed to more of the narrative and asked for their interpretations later in the story. We can test this hypothesis by comparing responses on the two occasions when the question was asked—the earlier (Round 1) and later (Round 2) posing of the same questions. When both versions are combined, earlier questioning yields 9 temporal and 15 static responses, whereas in later questions these numbers are reversed and there are 14 temporal and 10 static responses.

When we look at the two rounds of questioning separately for the two versions (see Table 1.2), we find that both versions show an increase in temporal responses from the earlier exposure of Round 1 to the later exposure of Round 2. Temporal responses to the conscious version increase from seven in Round 1 to nine in Round 2, whereas those for the nonconscious version increase from two in Round 1 to five in Round 2. This suggests that temporal interpretations are a measure of narrative involvement and essential to the interpretive process regardless of version or mode of interpretation. Eventually, after a certain length of exposure, the temporal–static difference between the versions might be washed out.

We checked to see whether the aforementioned result occurred for both stories. In fact, the increase in temporal interpretations from Round 1 to Round 2 turned out to be entirely due to Story 2 (the Böll). That story increased from 3 temporal interpretations in Round 1 to 10 in Round 2, and decreases from 9 static interpretations to 2. Amount of exposure, then, might tend to overwhelm version differences eventually, but only for one story. This was our first hint that although there may be some basic patterns of narrative response attributable to the dual-landscape patterning of narrative, the details of those patterns may not be universal but may rather be specific to particular stories, or to certain kinds of stories or genres. This raises questions that our first study was not designed to answer, but to which we turn more fully in Study 2.

Returning to the question of the narrative engagement of subjects in the two versions and how it changes from Round 1 to Round

TABLE 1.2
Temporal and Static Responses to Most Important Thing Question

	Temporal			Static		
	Round 1	Round 2	Total	Round 1	Round 2	Total
Conscious	7	9	16	5	3	8
Nonconscious	2	5	7	10	7	17

2, we did a more fine-grained, subject-by-subject analysis to see whether version effects and the effects due to the passage from Round 1 to Round 2 could be further clarified. Some seven subjects did not differentiate at Round 1 between the conscious and the nonconscious version, interpreting both as static or both as temporal. At Round 2, five subjects of those seven discriminated between them. Of those five, four do so in the expected direction; that is, the nonconscious story elicits a static response and the conscious story a temporal one.

In summary, it seems that there is a general disposition to interpret the conscious version dynamically and to interpret the nonconscious version statically. But, with increasing narrative exposure, stories become more dynamically interpreted—although, as we saw, this varies with type of story, a question to which we return later.

We turn now to an analysis of responses to the next set of questions: "What are the directions this could be going? Which way do you think it will go? Why?"

First we analyzed answers to the question "What are the directions this could be going?" First we looked at the number of possibilities. If the nonconscious version evokes paradigmatic thinking, in that case we might expect the two versions to differ on this question in some crucial ways. The nonconscious version might lead subjects to produce fewer possibilities. That result is not obtained. The conscious version yields 23 possibilities in the first Round and 16 in the second; the nonconscious version yields 24 and 17.

On the other hand, if we think of both versions as exemplifying a kind of interpretive thinking that differs from the hypothetico-deductive mode of scientific thinking, then we might expect subjects receiving both versions to be uncomfortable with the task of coming up with a single prediction. For, in Bruner's (1986) sense, prediction is typical of the paradigmatic rather than the narrative mode of thinking. In Morton's (1980) view, prediction is the essential task for scientific deductive thinking. We should not be surprised that it was difficult for our subjects to predict in this narrative context. Anecdotal evidence supports this view. Subjects in both conditions seemed to be caught off guard by the question. There was a moment of discomfort, and it seemed as if they were trying to change mental gears. It seemed as if the question itself had perhaps forced them away from an interpretive stance induced by both versions into an scientific (paradigmatic) stance. This was the first indication that both the conscious and nonconscious versions might be evoking forms of thought distinctive to narrative interpretation.

Next we looked at the question "Which way do you think it will go?" This question actually asks for a single prediction about where the action in the plot is leading. Any discomfort the subjects feel in coming up with a prediction might be further confirmed by the hedging of predictions. We coded as hedged the following kinds of responses (the hedges are in italics): "Oh, *likely* he'll *probably just* go off and become a priest" and "So that's how I *see it sort of* ending. You know, him *kind of* wondering what could have been." An example of an unhedged prediction is: "He's going to fall in love with her and not become a priest," and "I predict that he'll go out with her and that he'll have second thoughts about the seminary." The two versions did not differ in the number or percentage of hedged predictions, but nearly half the responses to both versions were hedged (11 of 24 for the conscious version, 10 of 24 for the nonconscious). See Table 1.3.

What were our subjects doing, then, when they predicted? If they were not using the normal causal deductive reasoning of paradigmatic thinking, what kind of thinking had they been led to by the narrative context? We undertook further analyses based on subjects' answers to the entire set of questions—"What are the directions this could be going; Which way do you think it will go; Why?"—to help us with this question. A great deal of what subjects said in response to these questions was an inferential going beyond the information given. We attempted to analyze these inferences for the form of thinking that lay behind them and was used to generate them.

A first finding was that there were nearly twice as many such inferences beyond the information given in responses to the conscious version (51) as to the nonconscious version (20; $t = 3.80$, 11 df, $p < .01$). Evidently, then, the conscious version evokes more inferential thinking than the nonconscious version. Moreover, in responses to this question (but not, as we saw in the retellings) it also evokes relatively more inferential thinking. When we count propositions beyond the given as a percentage of total number of

TABLE 1.3
Hedged and Nonhedged Predictions to "Which Way Do You Think
It Will Go?"

	Hedged			Nonhedged		
	Round 1	Round 2	Total	Round 1	Round 2	Total
Conscious	9	5	11	6	7	13
Nonconscious	5	5	10	7	7	14

propositions (given plus beyond the given), information beyond the given constitutes 72% of the total for the conscious version and 59% for the nonconscious version. Though there is more in the conscious version, both versions plainly evoke a great deal of information beyond the given.

The difference between earlier and later reactions in the rounds confirms the basic findings. Round 2, when subjects have become more engaged in the narrative of the story, evokes more information beyond the given than Round 1, and this is true of both the conscious version and the nonconscious version. However, even at Round 2, responses to the conscious version contain more information beyond the given (30) than those to the nonconscious version do (13); see Table 1.4. Perhaps it is essential to narrative interpretation that however it is done, it always involves drawing inferences that go beyond the given, and this pattern is triggered still more both by conscious versions and by longer exposure.

The new information may be about mental states, about action, or about personality features. Accordingly, they were coded in three categories: metacognitive or *psychological* (e.g., "He realizes that Walter and the girl are going to go through with it and there's nothing he can do to stop it"), *actions* (e.g., "She's just toying with him"), and *traits* (e.g., "He's a mama's boy").

Combining both rounds, psychological responses dominate over actions and traits in the responses to both versions (see Table 1.4). This is the case as well for each round. The only difference between the versions is that for the conscious version there is a dramatic and distinctive increase in psychological responses from Round 1 to Round 2, whereas the change between rounds for the nonconscious version is rather evenly distributed across the three categories.

We can now put several pieces of the puzzle together and get a picture of what happens when subjects process conscious and nonconscious versions of stories. From the retellings we learn the following:

TABLE 1.4
Psychological, Action, and Trait Subcategories of Information
Beyond the Given for Directions This Could Be Going Question

	Round 1			Round 2			Total		
	Psy	*Act*	*Trt*	*Psy*	*Act*	*Trt*	*Psy*	*Act*	*Trt*
Conscious	9	4	8	21	6	3	30	10	11
Nonconscious	4	1	2	7	2	4	11	3	6

1. They extract and recall the same basic plot events, but conscious version subjects reorder them.
2. The conscious version evokes more detail and more lines of retelling.
3. The conscious version evokes more given information and more information beyond the given, but not relatively more, and the information beyond the given tends to be of two different kinds—psychological for the conscious version, possibly action for the nonconscious version.

For the "*most important thing*" question, subjects reacting to the conscious version more often organize their responses in a temporal-dynamic manner, whereas the responses to the nonconscious version are static.

For the whole set of questions "*What are the directions this could be going? Which way do you think it will go? Why?*" subjects exposed to the conscious version offer more inferences beyond the given.

For the entire set of questions, subjects receiving the conscious version frame their responses with more mental verbs.

Up to this point, it appears that we have found two modes of thought—one that is psychological, temporal, and evokes metacognitive activity in the subjects, and another that is about actions and is static. But in both modes, subjects report a great deal of information beyond the given, and in neither are they comfortable with prediction. What these findings suggest, then, is that both modes are narrative modes, and that even the thinking evoked by the nonconscious version is not the same as the paradigmatic thinking applied to the world of things. One challenge now is to become clearer about the nature of the narrative reasoning pattern that is evoked by the nonconscious version.

A closer reading of the responses revealed that some subjects more often accounted for the directions they saw the story taking by alluding to matters of writing style—to the tone or mood of the piece (e.g., "It's got a gloomy atmosphere"); to genre (e.g., "It's one of those stories where my life and the meaning of my life isn't how I remember it and now it's going to be different and I'm a fool"); and to authorial intentions (e.g., "The writer is emphasizing. . . ."). We decided, consequently, to recode these data in a new three-category scheme: psychology of the protagonist, writing style, and plot. Note that whereas psychological responses refer to an intentional actor, both writing style and plot responses draw inferences by referring to aspects of the story itself or of the form in which it is told—plot responses consider causal necessities of actions; writing style responses invoke the intentions of the author. In contrast, psychological references extract the protagonist from the story and then draw inferences about him or her as a person one might have encountered.

Examples of reference to the psychology of the protagonist are, "He seems to have doubt. If he didn't have doubt, I don't think he'd be concerned with his mother," and "He's afraid to express himself." Examples of references to writing style are, "I say that because the tone of the piece—there's sort of a—sort of an existential, sort of a very objectified point of view, you know—like an omnipotent sort of critical look," and "Just because of the pace in which the story is moving." References to plot include, "Because there seems to be some rivalry between them, you know, in terms of the status of his wife," and "The characters have taken up such strong positions somehow so far that for the story to develop they've got to be budged from it in some way."

References to the plot differ little for the conscious and nonconscious versions—six in the former case, seven in the latter. But in the conscious version, more responses are couched in terms of the psychology of the protagonist (12) than in terms of writing style (6), as indicated in Table 1.5. For the nonconscious version, the results are just the reverse—more responses refer to writing style (10) than to the psychology of the protagonist (7; $x^2 = 2.71$, $df = 1$, $p < .10$). The results suggest that psychological states provide the underlying logic of inference for the conscious version, whereas writing style provides the logic of inference for the nonconscious version. By underlying logic we mean the subject's preferred basis of response, whether or not he or she is able to use it—occasionally subjects complain that they cannot answer because they haven't sufficient information about something. We take that something, then, to be the underlying logic of their response. A response of this kind with a psychological underlying logic would be "I don't know

TABLE 1.5
Psychology, Writing Style, and Plot Analysis for Directions This
Could Be Going Item

	Round 1			Round 2			Total		
	Psy	Ws	Plot	Psy	Ws	Plot	Psy	Ws	Plot
Conscious	4	3	5	8	3	1	12	6	6
Nonconscious	2	5	5	5	5	2	7	10	7

enough about this guy," with a writing style logic "I can't see what the author is trying to do," and a plot logic "I can't figure out where this romance is going."

This conclusion is further supported by the analysis by round, which is also reported in Table 1.5. In Round 2, with greater narrative exposure, both conscious and nonconscious responses move toward the pattern associated with conscious version: They are more often psychological, and less often about writing style. It seems as if longer story exposure functions in the same way as the added subjective matter in the conscious version. Thus, as we noted earlier, with greater exposure to the story, responses to the nonconscious version might move toward the pattern associated with the conscious version. The impression this gives is that eventually both versions might produce the same (namely, psychological) form of interpretation. If this is so, it can probably be attributed to the way modern, educated readers process stories. They are, so to speak, *set* for psychological explanation, for a dual landscape.

If conscious version responses are generated from the logic of mental states, what, we may ask, are subjects actually doing when they interpret a nonconscious version? How are the interpretations organized?

Most important, we have seen that the mode of construal for conscious versions is organized psychologically, and that for nonconscious versions it revolves around writing style or authorial intent. It is as if all interpretation required the discovery of an intentionality to be interpreted. Because subjects receiving the nonconscious version of stories having a landscape of action see its protagonist as driven from without rather than from within, the protagonist is an almost unwitting actor. In these cases, then, intentionality is attributed to the *constructor* of the landscape of action. A partial answer to the question of what organizes the interpretations of nonconscious versions, then, is that the features that compose our measure of writing style—tone, mood, and genre give the form of construal. That the focus of nonconscious versions is on story rather than on character is consistent with their focus on actions rather than psychology, and, if the protagonist is seen in this manner as a mere agent of the plot or the writer, that could explain the static and nondevelopmental character of the accounts as well.

In summary, then, we seem to have found two narrative modes of thinking. The first, associated with the conscious version, is psychological, temporal, and evokes metacognitive thinking. The second mode of narrative thinking, more often evoked by the nonconscious version, is about actions that are static. We can conjecture that if the underlying logic for inference in the conscious version is the psychological patterning of constituent conscious states, then the corresponding underlying logic for inference in the nonconscious version is a pattern of literary form organizing constituent actions. The first appears to be about a character who is pulled out of the story and is taken as real; the second about the story with its agents of plot. The author is transparent in the first mode but visible in the second.

After the story was read and just before the subject was asked to tell it back to us, we asked our subjects, "Tell me some things about the character I haven't told you—what is he like?" This question differed from the aforementioned ones in that it asked the subject to go beyond the information given. It literally invited subjects to use whatever generative patterns or rules of reasoning they had been able to mobilize up to this point.

We hoped, by asking this question, to get further insight into the way people built their concepts about the psychology of protagonists, and what, particularly, they could tell us about the development of the protagonist over time. Accordingly, we coded the replies as to whether or not they told us something developmental. Here are two examples of replies coded as developmental: "His crying for her probably represents a certain crying for the past that he's given up," and "He's sort of like a mama's boy—mainly because his father died." Two nondevelopmental, atemporal responses are the following: "He's lost more than just his girlfriend; he's lost a friend, too," and "He's very conflicted about his relationship with Erica."

There were twice as many total propositions (developmental and nondevelopmental) evoked by the conscious version (137) than by the nonconscious (73; $t = 2.41$, $df = 11$, p $< .05$). In both versions, there were far more nondevelopmental than developmental responses (conscious version, 84, nonconscious 57). There were more developmental responses given to the conscious version (53) than to the nonconscious version (16; $t = 2.66$, $df = 11$, $p < .05$), and they constituted a larger percentage of the total for the conscious version (39%) than the nonconscious version (22%). Moreover, more of these developmental responses are psychological (as opposed to action or trait) for the conscious version (33) than for the nonconscious version (9; $t = 2.60$, $df = 11$, $p < .05$).

These findings may help to explain the otherwise counterintuitive finding that temporal patterning is associated with the conscious version. The function of the temporal pattern that we have seen in the conscious version seems to be connected with its psychological pattern. Specifically, these accounts apparently include a time line at least partly because the past is invoked to explain the protagonist's present psychological states. For the moment, this interpretation should be taken as provisional, for the larger number of developmental responses in the conscious version resulted not only in more psychological responses, but also in more action characterization. However, it was confirmed by the results in Study 2.

Some time after the experiment proper (between 8 and 12 weeks later), we asked our subjects to tell us the gist of the stories they had heard. Memory for the stories was generally poor, the gists were short, and there were some subjects who could not remember at all, but there were interesting variations nonetheless. We established a priori a concluding interpretation for each story: for the Gill that Charles has a conflict; and for the Böll, that the narrator is regretful about his past. We coded all gists according to whether they included the relevant concluding interpretation. One gist illustrating each concluding interpretation follows, with the concluding interpretation in italics:

> He found some sort of physical sensation that he couldn't reconcile with his moral place through this girl that had a short leg, which created a conflict in him and uh, challenged his committment to his mother and his desire to be a young individual, uh, and follow his impulses. So it created a conflict—*the sexual vs. the pious young priest.*

> He's left all the comforts and greasy marks and wrappers and trappings of his old class affiliations behind him, but *evidently he's longing for it* because he cries in the elevator as he's leaving.

Seven of the nine subjects who gave a gist of the conscious version (78%) included a concluding interpretation, but only 4 of the 11 subjects who gave gists of the nonconscious version (36%) did so. Evidently, the ability to make sense of the story and/or to retain its meaning was greater for the conscious version.

This result, a happy confirmation of other aforementioned results, suggests that subjects hearing the conscious version made a greater effort to construct an interpretation. One possible explanation for their interpretive gists may be that they make use of the richer subjective material present in the conscious version to construct more digested interpretations. It is also possible that richer subjective material in the conscious version evokes in the subjects a more metacognitive stance. This finding seems consistent with the other finding of greater metacognition—that subjects hearing the conscious version use more mental verbs in answering all of our interpretive questions.

We may suppose then that we have found two kinds of narrative thinking. The first is triggered by the conscious version. It is meta-cognitive as well as interpretive and is organized in a temporal pattern around the psychological state of the protagonist. The second is triggered by the nonconscious version, is also interpretive, and is organized in a static pattern around matters of literary form. The first seems to be a psychologically richer form of narrative thinking; the second seems more richly literary. Both modes are generative in permitting subjects to go beyond the information given, but the mode triggered by the conscious version is more generative.

Both kinds of stories do not always produce pure patterns of either kind. And, rather disturbingly, the two stories used for creating conscious and nonconscious versions did not produce quite the same results. At times we had to temper our reports of findings by noting that the distinctive pattern reported applied particularly to one story, and there were story effects on other measures that we do not report here. The findings, we feared, might be genre specific or even story specific. We therefore turned our attention at once to a new set of data, using new stories.

STUDY 2

Our 12 subjects were all new. As before, each one individually heard both stories, one in the conscious version, the other one in the nonconscious version. We used exactly the same format for the two rounds of questions during the reading of the stories, but modified the questions asked after the story was completed. At the end, these questions were asked of each subject:

What happened at the end of the story?
Tell me some things about this character I haven't told you. What's she like?
What was the author trying to say?
What kind of story is this. It's not a mystery, a folktale. . . . What would you call it?
Tell me the story now, the same story I told you but in your own words.
What was the gist of the story?

[After both stories were read] How would you compare the two stories?

The stories used in this study were James Joyce's "Eveline" and Kate Chopin's "A Respectable Woman." The stories as written and as modified to create the nonconscious version are in Appendix D. The locations of the two rounds of "*most important thing*" questions and "*directions this could be going*" questions are marked.

The selection of stories in Study 1 had been governed by our wanting to study the difference between dual landscape and primarily landscape of action stories. Recall that we deleted descriptions of the protagonist's conscious mental states from the dual landscape stories used to create the nonconscious versions. This meant that the original stories had to be such that (a) they had a sufficient landscape of consciousness to permit a good deal of deletion, and (b) they had a sufficiently developed landscape of action to make sense in the nonconscious version. Because we hoped in the second study to replicate the first, we looked again for stories that met these same criteria.

But we also had another purpose in conducting Study 2. We wanted to vary genre or story type as well. This meant that we might have to choose two stories that differed as much as possible within the constraints imposed by the two aforementioned criteria. This created interesting problems.

The Chopin story, "A Respectable Woman," is much like those in Study 1 in that there is a temporal development in the landscape of action. The Joyce story differs, however, in that although it has an important plot feature, (organized, as it is, around the question of whether the protagonist will finally go off with her fiance), there is no overt action leading up to that moment—only thought, a Joycean stream of consciousness. Chopin's story, then, is of a genre that mixes action and consciousness in a dual landscape in a manner much like the stories in Study 1, whereas Joyce's, though still a story with a dual landscape, has a very limited landscape of action; it is principally played out on a landscape of consciousness. Better to appreciate the difference, read the two stories, found in Appendix D.

That our subjects were able to perceive the difference between the stories is revealed by their responses to the last question, asking them to compare the stories. Eleven of 12 subjects answered. Two said the stories were not differentiable. But, interestingly, both of them heard the more psychological story ("Eveline") in the less psychological (nonconscious) version, and the less psychological story ("A Respectable Woman") in a more psychological (conscious) version. Of the nine remaining replies, conscious versions were described six times as more differentiated or psychologically richer. But there was a large story effect: "Eveline" (regardless of version) was described this way seven times, "A Respectable Woman" twice. Subjects, in short, distinguished between the stories much as we had. We could then expect bigger effects to be produced by the story this second time out.

For all that, we could still ask about the effects produced by version (much as we had in Study 1), and test to see which version effects (found in Study 1)

1. would generalize across the stories—that is, would hold across the two stories used in Study 2 as they had in Study 1. These findings would be attributable to version.

2. If Joyce's "Eveline" did not conform to our earlier findings, would the dual-landscape Chopin study conform to the findings of Study 1? This would allow us to make inferences about the role of genre.

Consider first the retelling of the basic events of the stories. As before, we constructed a set of 12 basic propositions that comprise the events of the story. They are given in Appendix E. The retellings of the conscious versions and the nonconscious versions were virtually indistinguishable: 8.8 for the former, 8.2 for the latter ($t = 1.12$, $df = 11$, ns). So, as before, we anchor the ensuing discussion on the assurance that there are no version differences for basic comprehension of story line.

What of the order of report of the basic propositions in the retellings? Was it the same or different from the order in the story as told? Recall that in the first study the conscious version evoked somewhat more reordering than the nonconscious version. This time, neither of the stories lent itself to reordering. Neither had the analeptic pattern of the stories in Study 1, so there was no need to put the flashback into proper temporal order. Chopin is written in a straight temporal order that doesn't lend itself to this kind of linear reordering. And few instances of reordering were found. Joyce, in contrast, typically and repeatedly moves backward and forward many times. And subjects retold it in a seemingly infinite variety of ways: There simply was no single and obvious way of reordering it. So reordering must be thought of as related to specific patterns within a story—for example, analepsis and prolepsis—

and where the out of order pattern is not in the story, subjects will not reorder propositions.

As before, however, subjects reported slightly more of the extraneous details contained in the conscious versions. The 12 detail propositions for the two stories are reported in Appendix E. The mean number of details recalled for the conscious version was 4.0; for the nonconscious version 2.8. The mean number of lines in the retelling was again slightly greater for the conscious version (39) than for the nonconscious version (34.)

Consider matters in the retellings that were given and those that represented inferences beyond the information given. In the retellings, as before, the number of given details reported was greater in the conscious versions (341) than in the nonconscious (246) as one would expect because the conscious version is longer. We found the same pattern as was obtained in Study 1 for information beyond the given. The conscious version has more (171) than the nonconscious version (153), but not significantly more $(t = 1.08, df = 11, ns)$. or relatively more—conscious version 33%, nonconscious version 38%. So, as before, we can expect to find interesting differences between the versions, not in their amount of reconstruction but rather in the form of reconstruction they evoke.

As for possible differences between the versions in the reconstructive rules they elicit, we looked again at inferences beyond the given and divided them as before into psychological, action, and trait. The results are given in Table 1.6. Once again, the preferred category for the conscious story was psychological, and the preferred category for the nonconscious story was action. As before, a t test of the differences between the versions in psychological responses was significant $(t = 2.78, df = 11, p < .01)$, but not the contrasts between the groups in either actions $t = -.78)$ or traits $(t = .40)$.

Consider the replies to the questions we asked subjects in the course of reading them the stories. First, we look at the use of mental verbs attributable either to the reader or to character. As before, the conscious version produces more in toto (134) than the

TABLE 1.6
Information Beyond the Given in the Retellings, Study 2

	Psy		Act		Trt		Total
	#	%	#	%	#	%	
Conscious	84	49	71	42	16	9	171
Nonconscious	57	37	84	55	12	8	153

nonconscious version (122), but this time the t value was not even of borderline significance $t = .74$, $df = 11$, ns). And there were not a larger number of character-related mental verbs for the conscious version (13) than the nonconscious (17; $t = -.54$, $df = 11$, ns). This finding is not due to the difference between the two stories, for the same pattern of distribution of mental verbs across versions characterizes both the Chopin and the Joyce, though the Joyce accounts for two thirds of the mental verbs.

There were somewhat more reader-related mental verbs in the conscious version (121) than the nonconscious version (105), but the difference was not significant $(t = 1.02$, $df = 11$, ns). This is congruent, if not significantly so, with the main mental verb finding reported in Study 1: that a version where the characters' thinking is more often reported makes readers report their own thinking more and perhaps evokes in them a more metacognitive stance.

The first questions were about the most important thing in the story. We first looked at whether subjects chose a psychological state or an action. Unlike in Study 1, this time we did find the expected difference: the conscious version evokes more psychological responses than the nonconscious version (16 to 5) and fewer actions (8 to 19; $x^2 = 8.46$, $df = 1$, $p < .01$).

Next time we looked at temporal versus static patterning. The overall temporal versus static patterns found here were the same as in Study 1, though they were weaker and nonsignificant: Conscious stories evoke more temporal (19) responses than nonconscious stories (16); nonconscious stories evoke more static responses (8) than conscious (5) stories; $x^2 = .42$. There were virtually no differences between the versions in Round 1, but expected patterns were obtained for Round 2 where the conscious version outnumbers the nonconscious version in temporal responses by 11 to 7, and the nonconscious version outnumbers the conscious version in static responses by 5 to 1 ($x^2 = 3.56$, $df = 1$, $p < .06$). It may simply have taken longer for this tendency to assert itself in the new stories (see Table 1.7).

We turn now to an analysis of responses to the next set of questions: "What are the directions this could be going? Which way do you think it will go? Why?"

First we analyze answers to the question, "What are the directions this could be going?" and look at the number of possibilities. If the nonconscious version evokes paradigmatic thinking, it might lead subjects to produce fewer possibilities—something more like a prediction. Once again, this result was not obtained; there was no difference at all between the groups.

TABLE 1.7
Temporal and Static Responses to Most Important Thing Question,
Study 2

	Temporal			Static		
	Round 1	Round 2	Total	Round 1	Round 2	Total
Conscious	8	11	19	4	1	5
Nonsconscious	9	7	16	3	5	8

Next we look at the hedging pattern for answers to the question, "Which way do you think it will go?". The hedging results were different this time. This time the conscious version evoked significantly more hedged predictions (18) than the nonconscious version (11), and correspondingly fewer unhedged predictions (6 vs. 13; x^2 = 4.26, df = 1, p < .05). In light of other aforementioned results, especially the lack of a version difference for possibilities and the obtained version differences for mental verbs and concluding interpretations, it no longer seems reasonable to infer from nonhedged responding that the nonconscious version evokes paradigmatic thinking. The hedges, rather, seem to be part of a larger pattern of metacognition associated with the conscious version, because they make explicit the subjects' conscious processes as much as do mental verbs and concluding interpretations. The difference in the hedge effect in Studies 1 and 2 may be due to the unusually rich landscape of consciousness in the stories of Study 2.

Do readers base their inferences on psychological cues, on writing style, or on plot? In the first study, conscious versions evoked a preference for psychological cues, nonconscious versions for writing style cues. This pattern was obtained here, but it was not significant. Conscious version subjects gave more psychological responses (9) than nonconscious version subjects (5), and they gave fewer writing style responses (11) than nonconscious version subjects (14; x^2 = 1.45, df = 1, ns).

Comparing Study 1 and Study 2

Up to now, our new findings seem to be going in the same directions as those found in the first study. That is, there seem to be some general differences in how people interpret narratives with a dual landscape and those where the consciousness is reduced. It is helpful to pause here and see what Studies 1 and 2, taken together, permit us to surmise about these two interpretive modes.

First, the two modes evoke the same reporting of basic plot elements, but the conscious version yields somewhat more detail and somewhat more information beyond the given. The conscious version elicits an equally accurate but a more richly exemplified report. Information beyond the given in the retellings tends to be psychological in reaction to the conscious versions and relatively more action-oriented for nonconscious versions, as do the answers to the question about "what is the most important thing I've told you." Conscious versions are patterned around psychological states of the protagonist. In contrast, nonconscious versions seem to get their pattern from writing style and authorial craft. Conscious versions elicit more mental verbs, more concluding interpretations, and more hedged predictions—more metacognition. Conscious versions evoke more temporal patterning, whereas nonconscious versions evoke more static patterning. This is probably because, as we will see when we consider the character question, conscious versions generally induce subjects to think developmentally about the protagonist more than nonconscious versions do.

We have, then, suggested a picture of two modes of cognitive processing for narratives that have some (but not great) generality across genre type, subjects, and stories. The first, which is more readily evoked by the conscious version, is organized around the psychology of the protagonist and evokes a metacognitive (or perspectival) stance in the reader. It is temporally patterned and sees the protagonist as developing. The second, evoked more readily by the nonconscious version, is organized around writing style and narrated action, is nonperspectival, is statically patterned, and attributes less development to the protagonist.

What of the use of developmental and nondevelopmental approaches to the interpretations of characters in the stories? In Study 1, there were twice as many total propositions (developmental and nondevelopmental) evoked by the conscious version than by the nonconscious. Here, the numbers for the two versions were the same—conscious version (110), nonconscious (105; $t = .22$). As before, in both versions, there were far more nondevelopmental than developmental responses (conscious version 82%, nonconscious 88%). There were more developmental responses given to the conscious version (20) than to the nonconscious version (12), although the difference was not significant this time ($t = 1.08$, $df = 11$, ns), and as before they constituted a larger percentage of the total for the conscious version (18%) than for the nonconscious version (11%). Moreover, the pattern we observed before in the pattern of the developmental responses was again obtained: The conscious version evokes more that are psychological (14) than the nonconscious version (5; $t = 1.47$, $df = 11$, $p < .1$); and this time, the pattern is clearer, for there are actually fewer action responses for the conscious version (0) than the nonconscious version (6; $t = -2.17$, $df = 11$, $p < .05$). Trait responses were, as before, slightly greater in the conscious version (6) than the nonconscious version (1; $t = 1.60$, $df = 11$, $p < .1$), but it is difficult to know what to make of this.

The results reported hereafter confirm the Study 1 pattern, but only for the Chopin story. There, a dual landscape rich in action as well as in consciousness makes it possible for nonconscious version responses to differentiate by organizing themselves around action instead of psychology. The Joyce story is of a different genre, with a very diminished landscape of action. Joyce (and most post modernists) presented the world not as freestanding, to be recounted by a neutral narrator, but made it, rather, a world that exists in the mind of the protagonist. Whatever you delete, it is still consciousness that constitutes the focus of the story. So when one deletes anything from a Joyce story (as we did), the reader is forced all the more into making further inferences about consciousness by virtue of our having forced him or her to give a more complete account (in this case) of Eveline's mind. This is not a new observation about Joyce's technique and postmodernism (e.g., see Bruner's, 1986, discussion of readers' responses to Joyce's "Clay").

So, we turn to the genre-specific findings. First, an analysis of responses to, "What are the directions this be going; Which way do you think it will go; Why?" We found last time that more going beyond the information given was produced by the conscious than the nonconscious versions. This time we did not. There were 52 out of 79 total responses to conscious versions, constituting 65.8% of their responses, and 57 of 86 for the nonconscious, constituting 66.3% of theirs. Could this be due to genre? The dual landscape Chopin story has the old pattern. Joyce does not. For Chopin, there are 41 such instances for the conscious version, constituting 80.4% of their responses, whereas there are only 29 for the nonconscious version, constituting 65.9% of theirs. The Joyce story gives a quite contrary result: 11 units for the conscious versions and 28 for the nonconscious.

Other bits of the Study 1 pattern are also found in Chopin. When we examine psychological, action, and trait subcategories of these responses, we find again a preponderance of psychological explanation for both versions. The clear difference between the versions obtained in Study 1 was that conscious versions increased dramatically in psychological explanations from Round 1 to Round 2. In Study 2, the same pattern of results emerges (see Table 1.8). However, the nine added responses turn out on inspection to be attributable to the Chopin. We have, then, confirmed the finding that conscious versions evoke more psychological reasoning later in the story than they do earlier, but with as genre effect—that is, only in dual landscape stories with a well-delineated landscape of action do conscious versions move readers toward more psychological construal as they progress.

Because we asked subjects to tell us the gist of a story soon after they heard it, rather than weeks later, the gists given were much longer and more detailed than in the first study. We found it inappropriate to apply the same measures to the gist data, and we had to use a different approach. The approach we took was to distinguish between responses that summarized the particular events of a story from those that gave a timeless moral or theme. Two story responses are: "A woman who was deciding between eloping and staying to care for her family was unable to leave," and "A girl who never had much of a childhood of her own has to decide whether to leave her family and responsibilities or stay. She decides to stay." These gists seem to be in search of timeless truths of a kind—perhaps archetypes of human plight. At other times, subjects gave theme responses. These gists were often given as moral parables—for example, "Young love is not true love"; "You're a dead duck if you don't do what you think you should do"; "The body of history that is yours informs you, but the gist is in the going." It seems, then, that two kinds of gists were given.

There is no version difference in the kind of gist given, whether it is a theme or a story. In fact, all 12 subjects gave the same kind of gist for both of the stories that they heard. The patterns that we uncovered in this way of looking at the data are independent of version and therefore of actual genre. They are, however, somewhat related to the genre the subjects see in the stories—what might be thought of as conceived genre.

TABLE 1.8
Psychological, Action, and Trait Subcategories of Information
Beyond the Given for Directions This Could Be Going Item, Study 2

	Round 1			Round 2			Total		
	Psy	*Act*	*Trt*	*Psy*	*Act*	*Trt*	*Psy*	*Act*	*Trt*
Conscious	12	7	6	21	4	2	33	11	8
Nonconscious	15	3	12	15	3	9	30	6	21

At least for story gists, gist seems to be related to genre. The gist, "A woman who was deciding between eloping and staying to care for her family was unable to leave," was given by a subject who said that the genre was a "love story"; and the gist, "A girl who never had much of a childhood of her own has to decide whether to leave her family and responsibilities or stay" was given by a subject who said the genre was "a slice of life." In these cases, the way the genre is conceived seems to affect the gist. This suggests the possibility that beyond actual genre, as manipulated here with version differences, there might be another factor of perceived genre that provides a central organizing principle for the interpretation of narratives. What one is left wondering is whether, or to what degree, these perceived genre patterns affect the manner in which our subjects actually heard or took the stories we read them.

What can we say of these gists? Whatever function they may fill for the teller, they all seem to be in search of some more or less abstract mythic or moral form of which the story in some measure can be treated as an instantiation. Extracting a gist seems to be a bit like trying to dig out a Jungian archetypal form that can give a more universal sense to the story. Many centuries ago, Nicholas of Lyra, discussing how Bible stories might be interpreted, noted four levels: the literal, the moral, the allegorical or historical, and the anagogic or mythical. Our subjects seem not much different from Nicholas' description. The mythical, perhaps, has become domesticated as vaguely psychodiagnostic and internal. The allegorical or historical sounds more sociological now, telling about differences in social class rather than about the likeness of the story to great events of the past. And the moral is there in the homily like parables.

In the pair of studies reported, we have tried to discover something about the cognitive processes that are used to interpret complex narratives—narratives having a landscape of consciousness as well as of action. A good deal has been reported in the literature about the interpretation of simple action narratives, but almost nothing is known about the manner in which complex narratives are understood.

The dually patterned narrative is important to study for a variety of reasons. First, it is our form of self-understanding—autobiographies are never just about action. Second, it is *the* form of modern literature—the cultural expression of our understanding of others. Third, in nonliterate cultures, it is the form of those special kinds of talk that are used, roughly, for reflection rather than for the ordinary transactions of everyday life—Ilongot oratory, Wana Kiyori, and Indian poetry (see Feldman, in press, for a discussion of these forms of oral metalanguage in nonliterate cultures).

The results reported here are at most suggestive, and are presented in that spirit. They indicate that interpretations are highly patterned, and are of two types. One is based on an analysis of the psychological states of protagonists, and is metacognitive. It tends to be temporal in organization, probably because it is concerned with the development of protagonists in time. The other is based on action and is organized by considerations of writing style. It is static in its depiction, probably because it is not much concerned with the development of the protagonist. Stories with a rich landscape of consciousness joined with a rich landscape of action can evoke either form of interpretation. With consciousness played down, and action dominant, the second mode is more likely to be evoked. With consciousness played down, and action thin, responses are generated that cannot be described as fitting either form.

The form of interpretation seems to be affected not just by psychological richness, but also by richness in the landscape of action, and, finally, possibly by conceived or attributed genre. Psychological richness was explicitly varied in both the designs here, and for it we have the most elaborate findings. Many of them, however, are weak. If we should believe them, it is only because the same pattern appeared in both of the two studies. Even so, psychological richness plainly does not account for a great deal of the variance. The landscape of action was varied across stories in Study 2, and we saw that choice of form of interpretation sometimes requires the presence of a well-defined landscape of action. Attributed genre emerged as the merest suggestion for a third factor contributing to the form of interpretation.

Our sample size in both studies was small. One further possible source of variance that we have not discussed is subject differences. We retested both groups of subjects with the stories from the other study and are in the process of coding the results.

In the end, one wonders whether the two modes of textual interpretation found here (the inner and the outer, to oversimplify) do not in some way constitute the base of two protogenres: one a classical plot structure where actions provide the constituents as in the folklore tales analyzed by the Russian folklorist, Vladimir Propp (1986); the other more inward-looking, more premised on the reality of perspective and of a psychological world in which action is converted into subjective meaning. The first is, perhaps, more closely connected to our ways of understanding people as actors in the external world. The second is perhaps impelled by a need to understand the conscious, reflective states of human actors.

APPENDIX A: STORIES USED IN STUDY 1

Story 1: "Truth and Consequences" (Gill, 1961)

1C—Conscious Version

She had straight blond hair and a red mouth, and she was lame. Every day she played golf and went swimming in the center of a crowd of boys. Charles, sitting with his mother on the hotel porch, watched her and nodded while his mother repeated, "Isn't it extraordinary, a girl like that? I wonder what in the world they see in her." Charles took to walking past the pool in the morning as the girl and boys lay there side by side, laughing. He listened carefully to her voice. It was low, unhurried, forceful. So, he thought, was her language. Every other word seemed to him to be "damn," "hell," and worse. She spoke of God, to whom Charles was preparing to dedicate his life, as if He were a friend in the next block. "I swear to God," the girl said. "I must have told you this one, for God's sake." Charles walked out of range of the jokes that followed. He was eighteen and he was spending this last vacation with his mother before entering a seminary. In eight more summers he would be a priest.

    Q1a: What is the most important thing I've told you so far?
    Q1b: Why?

One night after dinner, while his mother was upstairs swallowing a pill, the girl sat down beside him on the hotel porch. Her lips were smiling, her eyes the color of her blue, open blouse. "We ought to know each other," she said. "You ought to join the rest of us at the pool."
    "I'm with Mother."
    The girl covered his hand with hers. "Well, for God's sake, you're old enough to swim by yourself, aren't you?"
    Charles felt that he ought to explain before it was too late, before she said something he could never forget. "I'm going to be a priest," he said.

The girl kept smiling. "A priest? With a turn-around collar and everything?"

He nodded.

"So you can't come swimming with the gang?"

"That has nothing to do with it. I just thought I ought to tell you. I always do tell people."

Q2a: What is the most important thing I've told you so far?

Q2b: Why?

"You can still come dancing with us if you want to?"

"Certainly."

"Could you take me to a movie if you wanted to?"

"Yes."

"I never met a boy who was going to be a priest. Could you take me out for a ride tonight if you wanted to?"

He said, in relief, "We didn't bring our car."

"Oh, hell. I mean in my car. I mean just for example. I didn't say I'd go with you. It would be funny, with a boy who was going to be a priest."

Fortunately, Charles thought, his mother would be coming downstairs at any moment now. She would make short shrift of the girl. "You oughtn't to keep swearing like that," he said.

He expected her to laugh, but she didn't. She ran her hand up and down the bare brown leg that was shorter than the other. "Like what?" she said.

"Like 'for God's sake.' That's taking the name of the Lord in vain. That's one of the Ten Commandments."

"I'm an awful damn fool," the girl said. "I talk like that to keep people from thinking about my leg. But I didn't know you were going to be a priest."

Q3a: What are the directions this could be going? (If subject responds with only one or two directions, prompt, "Are there any other possibilities?")

Q3b: Which way do you think it will go?

Q3c: Why?

Charles wanted to get rid of her, but he didn't know how. He stood up and said, "I don't think you ought to worry about things like that. I hadn't even noticed."

She stood up beside him. Her eyes shone in the mountain light.

"Oh, damn you, please don't lie to me," she said. "Of course you've noticed. But does it bother you? Does it make you want to stay away from me?"

"No," he said. "Oh, no."

She slipped her hand under his arm. "Thanks for saying that so nice and hard. I haven't asked anybody that in a long time."

Without having willed it, stupidly, Charles found himself walking the length of the porch beside the girl. Her blond hair touched the shoulder of his coat. It was difficult to tell, looking down at her, that she was lame. He bent his head to smell her perfume. "Tell me what you do," he said.

"You mean, bang, just like that, what do I do?"

"Not that you have to tell me."

"But I do. It's just that there aren't any surprises in me. I'm not beautiful or tormented—or not much tormented. I don't do anything. I got out of Walker's and I had a party and now I guess I'll be on the loose like this for a couple of years. Finally somebody may ask me to marry him, and quick like a fish I will. I hope I'll have sense enough for that. And I'll be terribly glad when I've done it. I'll try to let him win most of the arguments we'll have. I'll try to be good about satisfying him, the way all those awful books say, and about having good kids for him, and all that."

Charles felt himself stumbling. She had told him everything about herself. She had told him the truth, which he hadn't wanted. They reached the end of the porch and stood facing the valley between the mountains. Two old men were playing croquet in the gathering darkness, the wooden mallets and balls knocking softly together, the white trousers moving like disembodied spirits across the lawn. Charles and the girl could hear, below them in the kitchen, the clatter of dishes being washed and the high, tired voices of the waitresses.

Q4a: What are the directions this could be going? (If subject responds with only one or two directions, prompt, "Are there any other possibilities?")

Q4b: Which way do you think it will go?

Q4c: Why?

"Now talk about you," the girl said. "You think you want to be a priest?"

"Why—yes."

"It isn't just a vow your mother made while she was carrying you?"

Charles laughed, and was surprised as how easily he laughed. "Well," he said, "I guess Mother's always wanted me to be a priest, especially after Dad died. We went abroad then, Mother and I. We spent the summer in Rome. We had an audience with the Pope— the old one, a little man with thick glasses and a big ring. We got so we were going to Mass and even to Communion every day. When we came back to this country I started in at a Catholic school. I liked it. I graduated this year. I'm going down to the seminary in the fall. I guess I'll like that, too."

"But isn't there more to it than that?" the girl said. "I'm not a Catholic—I'm not anything—but don't you have to have some kind of a call, bells ringing, something like that?"

"You mean a vocation. Yes. Well, I guess I have a vocation all right."

"But what is it? How can you be sure?"

Charles gripped the railing of the porch. He had never been able to answer that question. He remembered kneeling beside his mother's bed, month after month, year after year. "Don't you feel it, darling?" his mother had whispered. "Don't you feel how wonderful it will be? Don't you feel how God wants you?" Charles had told himself finally that he was able to answer that question. The next day his mother, dabbing her eyes, had said, "Here's my boy, Father Duffy. I'm giving him to you." And Father Duffy had said, "Ah, you're an example to Irish mothers everywhere. Are you sure you want to come with us, boy?" "Yes, Father, I do," Charles had said, watching his mother. He had spoken an answer, written an answer, lived an answer, but he had never believed it. He had been waiting to believe it. Now he heard himself saying, for the first time, "No, I can't be sure."

The girl said, "Then you're not going to be a priest. You mustn't be. Why are you so damned afraid to face the truth?"

Charles saw his mother walking heavily along the porch. He studied her as if she were a stranger. What an enormous old woman she was, and how strong she was, and how she had driven him! He took the girl's hand. It was cool and unmoving. He felt the porch floor trembling under his mother's approach.

END

Q5: Tell me some things about this character that I haven't told you. What is he like?

Q6: I'd like you to tell me the story now—the same story I told you, but in your own words.

INC—Nonconscious Version

She had straight blond hair and a red mouth, and she was lame. Every day she played golf and went swimming in the center of a crowd of boys. Charles, sitting with his mother on the hotel porch, watched her and nodded while his mother repeated, "Isn't it extraordinary, a girl like that? I wonder what in the world they see in her." Charles often walked past the pool in the morning as the girl and boys lay there side by side. He heard her voice. It was low, unhurried, forceful. So was her language. He often heard "damn," "hell," and worse. "I swear to God," the girl said. "I must have told you this one, for God's sake." Charles' path took him out of range of the jokes that followed. He was eighteen and he was spending this last vacation with his mother before entering a seminary. In eight more summers he would be a priest.

Q1a: What is the most important thing I've told you so far?
Q1b: Why?

One night after dinner, while his mother was upstairs swallowing a pill, the girl sat down beside him on the hotel porch. She smiled, and her eyes were blue. "We ought to know each other," she said. "You ought to join the rest of us at the pool."

"I'm with Mother."

The girl covered his hand with hers. "Well, for God's sake, you're old enough to swim by yourself, aren't you?"

"I'm going to be a priest," Charles said.

The girl kept smiling. "A priest? With a turn-around collar and everything?"

He nodded.

"So you can't come swimming with the gang?"

"That has nothing to do with it. I just thought I ought to tell you. I always do tell people."

Q2a: What is the most important thing I've told you so far?
Q2b: Why?

"You can still come dancing with us if you want to?"

"Certainly."

"Could you take me to a movie if you wanted to?"

"Yes."

"I never met a boy who was going to be a priest. Could you take me out for a ride tonight if you wanted to?"

"We didn't bring our car."

"Oh, hell. I mean in my car. I mean just for example. I didn't say I'd go with you. It would be funny, with a boy who was going to be a priest."

"You oughtn't to keep swearing like that," he said.

She ran her hand up and down the bare brown leg that was shorter than the other. "Like what?" she said.

"Like 'for God's sake.' That's taking the name of the Lord in vain. That's one of the Ten Commandments."

"I'm an awful damn fool," the girl said. "I talk like that to keep people from thinking about my leg. But I didn't know you were going to be a priest."

Q3a: What are the directions this could be going? (If subject responds with only one or two directions, prompt, "Are there any other possibilities?")

Q3b: Which way do you think it will go?

Q3c: Why?

Charles stood up and said, "I don't think you ought to worry about things like that. I hadn't even noticed."

She stood up beside him. Her eyes were bright in the light. "Oh, damn you, please don't lie to me," she said. "Of course you've noticed. But does it bother you? Does it make you want to stay away from me?"

"No," he said. "Oh, no."

She slipped her hand under his arm. "Thanks for saying that so nice and hard. I haven't asked anybody that in a long time."

Charles walked the length of the porch beside the girl. Her blond hair touched the shoulder of his coat. He bent his head. "Tell me what you do," he said.

"You mean, bang, just like that, what do I do?"

"Not that you have to tell me."

"But I do. It's just that there aren't any surprises in me. I'm not beautiful or tormented—or not much tormented. I don't do anything. I got out of Walker's and I had a party and now I guess

I'll be on the loose like this for a couple of years. Finally somebody may ask me to marry him, and quick like a fish I will. I hope I'll have sense enough for that. And I'll be terribly glad when I've done it. I'll try to let him win most of the arguments we'll have. I'll try to be good about satisfying him, the way all those awful books say, and about having good kids for him, and all that."

They reached the end of the porch and stood facing the valley between the mountains. Two old men were playing croquet in the gathering darkness, the wooden mallets and balls knocking together, the white trousers moving across the lawn. Below them in the kitchen was the clatter of dishes being washed and the voices of the waitresses.

> Q4a: What are the directions this could be going? (If subject responds with only one or two directions, prompt, "Are there any other possibilities?")
>
> Q4b: Which way do you think it will go?
>
> Q4c: Why?

"Now talk about you," the girl said. "You think you want to be a priest?"

"Why—yes."

"It isn't just a vow your mother made while she was carrying you?"

Charles laughed. "Well," he said, "I guess Mother's always wanted me to be a priest, especially after Dad died. We went abroad then, Mother and I. We spent the summer in Rome. We had an audience with the Pope—the old one, a little man with thick glasses and a big ring. We got so we were going to Mass and even to Communion every day. When we came back to this country I started in at a Catholic school. I liked it. I graduated this year. I'm going down to the seminary in the fall. I guess I"ll like that, too."

"But isn't there more to it than that?" the girl said. "I'm not a Catholic—I'm not anything—but don't you have to have some kind of a call, bells ringings, something like that?"

"You mean a vocation. Yes. Well, I guess I have a vocation all right."

"But what is it? How can you be sure?"

"No, I can't be sure," he answered.

The girl said, "Then you're not going to be a priest. You mustn't be. Why are you so damned afraid to face the truth?"

Charles saw his mother walking along the porch. He took the girl's hand as his mother approached.

END

    Q5: Tell me some things about this character that I haven't told
          you. What is he like?

    Q6: I'd like you to tell me the story now—the same story I told
          you, but in your own words.

Story 2: "Nostalgia: or Grease Spots"
(Böll, 1986)

2C—Conscious Version

The night before Erica's wedding I changed my mind and did drive
to the hotel to have another talk with Walter. I had known both
him and Erica, his fiance, for a long time; after all, I had lived with
Erica for four years, in Mainz, while working on a construction job
and at the same time going to night school. Walter had been working on the same construction site and also going to night school. It
wasn't a pleasant period. I recall it without nostalgia: the arrogance
of our teachers, who were more critical of our accents than of our
performance was so insidious that it was more painful than wordy
abuse would have been. Apparently most of them couldn't bear
the idea that, with our unabashed dialect, we might eventually
acquire a university degree, and they forced us to speak in a way
that we used to call "night-school German."

    Q1a: What is the most important thing I've told you so far?
    Q1b: Why?

    When I came off shift—sometimes at the same time as Walter—
the first thing was always a shower, then fresh clothes and a general
sprucing up. Yet we still had lime under our fingernails, traces of
cement in our eyelashes. We slogged away at math, history, Latin
even, and when we actually did pass our exams, our teachers behaved as if it were some sort of canonization. After we'd gone on to
university there were still—for a while—traces of lime in our hair,
of cement behind our ears, sometimes in our nostrils, in spite of
Erica's careful inspection of me, after which she would shake her
head and whisper in my ear, "You'll never get rid of it, that proletarian background of yours." I felt no regret for my construction job
when I won a scholarship and eventually obtained a degree, a
B.Comm., with a correct accent, quite good manners, a reasonably

decent job in Koblenz, and the prospect of being granted leave of absence to work toward my master's degree.

I was never quite sure whether Erica had left me or I her: I couldn't even remember whether it had been before or after I got my B.Comm. I only remember the bitter half sentences with which she reproached me for having become too stuck up for her, and I reproached her for having remained too vulgar, a word I still regret; over the years her vulgarity had lost its naturalness, it had become deliberate, especially when she came out with details about her job in a lingerie shop, or teased me when I asked her to help me look for traces of cement behind my ears long after I had given up my construction job. To this day, although I haven't set foot on a construction site for eight years (not even my own—we're building a house, Franziska and I), I sometimes catch myself carefully inspecting my eyelashes and eyebrows in the mirror. This prompts a gentle headshake from Franziska: not knowing the reason for my concern, she ascribes this behavior to an excess of vanity.

Q2a: What is the most important thing I've told you so far?
Q2b: Why?

In Mainz, Walter had often joined us for supper in our cramming days: on the table a package of margarine, hastily ripped open, potato salad or chips from the store, mayonnaise in a cardboard container; if we were lucky, two fried eggs prepared on the hotplate that never worked properly (Erica was genuinely scared of that hotplate: a thread of egg white had once given her an electric shock); also a loaf of bread from which we hacked off thick slabs—and my perpetual fear of grease spots on books and notebooks lying on the table between mayonnaise and margarine. And I was constantly confusing Ovid with Horace, and of course grease spots did appear on the books, and I happen to loathe grease spots on printed paper, even on newspapers. Even as a child I used to be disgusted when I had to take home pickled or kippered herrings wrapped in newspaper. My father would turn to my mother and say with a note of mockery, "What makes him so fastidious, I wonder? He doesn't get it from me, and certainly not from your family."

It was already quite late, nearly ten, when I reached the hotel. On the eighth floor, as I walked along the corridor looking for Walter's room, I tried to estimate from the distances between doors whether he had a single or a double room: I couldn't face an encounter with Erica. In those seven years I had heard from her only once, a postcard from Marbella on which all she had written was "Boring, boring, boring—and not even any grease spots!"

It was a single room; even before I saw Walter I saw his dark suit on a hanger outside the clothes closet, black shoes underneath, a silver-gray tie on the crossbar of the hanger. My next glance was through the open bathroom door and took in a wet cigarette in a puddle of bathwater: the shreds of tobacco dyed the puddle yellow. Walter had evidently misjudged the size of hotel bathtubs and put in too much bath oil. I saw the glass of whiskey and soda on the plastic stool, before I discovered him behind clouds of foam.

"Come right in!" he said. "I imagine you've come to warn me." He wiped the foam from his face and neck and laughed at me.

"Only don't forget our difference in rank: after all, I do have my Ph.D., and you don't—I wonder whether, if it came to a duel, you'd be qualified to challenge me— and don't kid yourself that you can talk me out of marrying her! There's just one thing you should know, just one: In Mainz there was never anything between us, never."

Q3a: What are the directions this could be going? (If subject responds with only one or two directions, prompt, "Are there any other possibilities?")

Q3b: Which way do you think it will go?

Q3c: Why?

I was glad he didn't laugh as he said that. I closed the bathroom door, sat down on his bed, and looked at the dark suit: That was how, the night before our wedding, my own suit had hung outside a hotel clothes closet in Koblenz, and my tie had also been silver-gray.

I watched Walter come out of the bathroom, rub himself down in his bathrobe, put on his pajamas, throw the bathrobe onto the floor, and, with a laugh, run the silver-gray tie through his hands. "Believe me," he said, "I only met her again a year ago, quite by chance, and—well, now we're getting married. Will you be there tomorrow?"

I shook my head and asked, "In church too?"

"Yes, in church too, because of her parents, who love a good cry at weddings. The civil ceremony alone isn't enough for the tear ducts—and she's still vulgar, but already we're using a butter dish."

"Cut it out," I said, taking the glass of whiskey he held out to me.

"I'm sorry," he said, "I really am. Let's have no old-timers' reminiscences, no explanations, no confessions—and no warnings."

I thought of what I had intended to tell him: what a tramp she really was; that she couldn't handle money; that sometimes I had found hairs in the margarine and always those goddamn grease spots, on books, newspapers, even on photos; how hard it had been to get her out of bed in the morning, and her naive/proletarian ideas of breakfast-in-bed being the acme of luxury, and the resulting jam spots on the sheets and brown coffee stains on the quilt; yes, and she was lazy, too, and not even clean, I had literally had to force her to wash: sometimes I had actually grabbed hold of her and dumped her in the tub, bathed her the way one bathes a child, with much screaming and spluttering; yes, and that sometimes she had got mad yet had never been in a bad mood, no, never in a bad mood. At that point I remembered the house we were building, to which I never went, leaving it all to Franziska and the architect.

"And just imagine," said Walter, "she doesn't want us to start building a house, and I've always looked for a wife who didn't want that. Now I've found her, at last—she hates building and construction."

I was just about to say, "So do I," but all I said was, "Give her my regards. I suppose it's quite final, is it?"

"Final," he said, "in fact, irrevocable if only because of those parental tears. We can't do that to them, we can't deprive them of that."

"As for tears," I said, "they could also shed those if it didn't come off."

"But those wouldn't be the kind of tears they're after, they want the genuine kind, the real kind, with organ music and candles and all that—and they want the barely audible 'I do.' No. And the honeymoon—where d'you think we're going?"

"Venice?"

"Right—gondolas and color photos. Go ahead and cry a bit on your way down in the elevator."

Q4a: What are the directions this could be going? (If subject responds with only one or two directions, prompt, "Are there any other possibilities?")

Q4b: Which way do you think it will go?

Q4c: Why?

I finished my whiskey, shook his hand, and left, and on my way down in the elevator I cried a bit more than a bit, and I didn't dry my tears as I walked past the concierge out to my car. I had told Franziska I wanted to say hello to an old friend, and that was really all it had been.

END

Q5: Tell me some things about this character that I haven't told you. What is he like?

Q6: I'd like you to tell me the story now—the same story I told you, but in your own words.

2NC—Nonconscious Version

The night before Erica's wedding I drove to the hotel to have another talk with Walter. I had lived with Erica, his fiance, for four years, in Mainz, while working on a construction job and at the same time going to night school. Walter had been working on the same construction site and also going to night school. I recall the night school teachers as arrogant, more critical of our accents than of our performance. Most of them couldn't bear the idea that, with our unabashed dialect, we might eventually acquire a university degree, and they forced us to speak in a way that we used to call "night-school German."

Q1a: What is the most important thing I've told you so far?
Q1b: Why?

When I came off shift—sometimes at the same time as Walter— the first thing was always a shower, then fresh clothes and a general sprucing up. Still, we had lime under our fingernails, traces of cement in our eyelashes. We studied math, history, Latin, and when we passed our exams, our teachers behaved as if it were some sort of canonization. After we'd gone on to university there were still— for a while—traces of lime in our hair, of cement behind our ears, sometimes in our nostrils, in spite of Erica's careful inspection of me, after which she would shake her head and whisper in my ear, "You'll never get rid of it, that proletarian background of yours." I won a scholarship and eventually obtained a degree, a B.Comm., with a correct accent, quite good manners, a job in Koblenz, and the prospect of being granted leave of absence to work toward my master's degree.

Either Erica had left me or I her: it was before or after I got my B.Comm. She reproached me for having become too stuck up for her, and I reproached her for having remained too vulgar; over the years her vulgarity had lost its naturalness, it had become deliberate, especially when she came out with details about her job in a lingerie shop, or teased me by looking for traces of cement behind my ears long after I had given up my construction job. To this day, although I haven't set foot on a construction site for eight years (not even my own—we're building a house, Franziska and I), I sometimes carefully inspect my eyelashes and eyebrows in the mirror. This prompts a gentle headshake from Franziska: Not knowing the reason for my concern, she ascribes this behavior to an excess of vanity.

Q2a: What is the most important thing I've told you so far?
Q2b: Why?

In Mainz, Walter had often joined us for supper in our cramming days: on the table a package of margarine, ripped open, potato salad or chips from the store, mayonnaise in a cardboard container; sometimes two fried eggs prepared on the hotplate that never worked properly (Erica was scared of that hotplate: a thread of egg white had once given her an electric shock); also a loaf of bread from which we cut thick slabs—and my fear of grease spots on books and notebooks lying on the table between mayonnaise and margarine. I was constantly confusing Ovid with Horace, and grease spots did appear on the books and on newspapers. As a child I used to be disgusted when I had to take home pickled or kippered herrings wrapped in newspaper. My father would turn to my mother and say with a note of mockery, "What makes him so fastidious, I wonder? He doesn't get it from me, and certainly not from your family."

It was nearly ten when I reached the hotel. On the eighth floor I walked along the corridor looking for Walter's room. In those seven years I had heard from Erica only once, a postcard from Marbella on which she had written, "Boring, boring, boring—and not even any grease spots!".

Before I saw Walter I saw his dark suit on a hanger outside the clothes closet, black shoes underneath, a silver-gray tie on the crossbar of the hanger. I glanced through the open bathroom door

at a wet cigarette in a puddle of bathwater: The shreds of tobacco
dyed the puddle yellow. I saw the glass of whiskey and soda on the
plastic stool, and Walter behind clouds of foam.

"Come right in!" he said. "I imagine you've come to warn me."
He wiped the foam from his face and neck and laughed at me. "Only
don't forget our difference in rank: after all, I do have my Ph.D.,
and you don't—I wonder whether, if it came to a duel, you'd be
qualified to challenge me—and don't kid yourself that you can talk
me out of marrying her! There's just one thing you should know,
just one: in Mainz there was never anything between us, never."

Q3a: What are the directions this could be going? (If subject
     responds with only one or two directions, prompt, "Are
     there any other possibilities?")
Q3b: Which way do you think it will go?
Q3c: Why?

I closed the bathroom door, sat down on his bed, and looked at
the dark suit: that was how, the night before our wedding, my own
suit had hung outside a hotel clothes closet in Koblenz, and my tie
had also been silver-gray.

Walter came out of the bathroom, rubbed himself down in his
bathrobe, put on his pajamas, threw the bathrobe onto the floor,
and, with a laugh, ran the silver-gray tie through his hand. "Believe
me," he said, "I only met her again a year ago, quite by chance,
and—well, now we're getting married. Will you be there tomorrow?"

I shook my head and asked, "In church too?"

"Yes, in church too, because of her parents, who love a good cry
at weddings. The civil ceremony alone isn't enough for the tear
ducts—and she's still vulgar, but already we're using a butter dish."

"Cut it out," I said, taking the glass of whiskey he held out to me.

"I'm sorry," he said, "I really am. Let's have no old-timers' reminiscences, no explanations, no confessions—and no warnings. Just
imagine," said Walter, "she doesn't want us to start building a
house, and I've always looked for a wife who didn't want that. Now
I've found her, at last—she hates building and construction."

"Give her my regards," I said. "I suppose it's quite final, isn't it?"

"Final," he said, "in fact, irrevocable if only because of those
parental tears. We can't do that to them, we can't deprive them of
that."

"As for tears," I said, "they could also shed those if it didn't come
off."

"But those wouldn't be the kind of tears they're after, they want the genuine kind, the real kind, with organ music and candles and all that—and they want the barely audible 'I do.' No. And the honeymoon—where d'you think we're going?"

"Venice?"

"Right—gondolas and color photos. Go ahead and cry a bit on your way down in the elevator."

Q4a: What are the directions this could be going? (If subject responds with only one or two directions, prompt, "Are there any other possibilities?")

Q4b: Which way do you think it will go?

Q4c: Why?

I finished my whiskey, shook his hand, and left, and on my way down in the elevator I cried a bit more than a bit, and I didn't dry my tears as I walked past the concierge out to my car. I had told Franziska I wanted to say hello to an old friend, and that was really all it had been.

END

Q5: Tell me some things about this character that I haven't told you. What is he like?

Q6: I'd like you to tell me the story now—the same story I told you, but in your own words.

APPENDIX B: STUDY 1 GENERIC AND
DETAILED PROPOSITIONS FOR RETELLING
RECALL

Story 1—"Truth and Consequences"

Generic propositions:

1. Girl is described (blond, red-mouthed, lame, etc.)
2. (Charles watched) girl swimming (and/or) hanging out with boys.
3. (Charles heard) girl swearing.

4. Charles was on vacation (with mother).
5. Charles was going to be a priest (and/or) enter seminary in the fall.
6. Girl and Charles meet.
7. Charles tells girl he's going to be a priest.
8. Girl's disability (and/or) swearing in context of conversation.
9. Girl and Charles talk about what girl does.
10. Girl and Charles talk about Charles wanting to be a priest.
11. Charles has uncertainty about being a priest.
12. Charles' mother approaches (reference to mother).

Detail propositions:

1. Charles was sitting with mother (on porch).
2. Mother asks what boys see in girl.
3. Mother was upstairs (swallowing a pill).
4. Girl tells Charles he should join friends (swimming).
5. One of the girl's legs is shorter (longer) than other.
6. Charles tells girl he hadn't noticed leg.
7. Girl wants to be married.
8. Charles' mother always wanted him to be a priest.
9. Charles' father died.
10. Charles went to Catholic school.
11. Girl tells Charles he mustn't be a priest.
12. Charles takes girl's hand.

Story 2—"Nostalgia: or Grease Spots"

Generic propositions:

1. Narrator visits Walter (the night before Erica's wedding.
2. Narrator once lived with/had relationship with Erica (Walter's fiance).
3. Narrator and Walter worked (and/or) went to school together.
4. Narrator graduated (went to university).
5. Narrator reminisces about break-up/separation with Erica.

6. Narrator recalls Erica's taunts (and/or) Erica's traits (vulgarity, etc.)
7. Narrator recalls suppers with Walter and Erica (food, grease on books, etc.).
8. Narrator sees/meets Walter (arrives at hotel, finds room, Walter, etc.).
9. Walter (describes) circumstances of meeting Erica.
10. Walter talks about wedding (and/or) pleasing parents.
11. Narrator leaves (and/or) cries on way out.
12. Narrator refers to Franziska (saying hello to old friend).

Detail propositions:

1. Narrator and Walter had accents.
2. Narrator recalls traces of lime and cement.
3. Narrator felt Erica was vulgar.
4. Narrator hasn't seen Walter/or Erica (or worked construction) in 7, 8 years.
5. Narrator (and Franziska are) building a house.
6. Narrator still inspects self for traces of lime and cement.
7. Narrator feared grease spots on books and papers.
8. Narrator finds Walter in bathtub.
9. Walter's suit reminds narrator of own wedding clothes.
10. Walter (tells narrator he) only met Erica a year ago.
11. Walter tells narrator to cry on his way out.
12. Narrator doesn't dry (hide) tears.

APPENDIX C: CODING MANUAL

The following coding manual illustrates the rules and procedures used to code narrative strategies in the two narrative comprehension studies. The examples used in this manual, though applicable to both studies, are taken mainly from Study 2 (salient examples from Study 1 are found in the main text). These provide detailed guidance on ways to resolve those ambiguous cases that inevitably arise in the analysis of narrative strategies. Also included here are Kappa coefficients for interrater agreement, Study 1 and Study 2. This formula, (where P_o = % agreement observed and P_c = % agreement expected by chance), is taken from Jacob Cohen's "A

Coefficient for Nominal Scales," *Educational and Psychological Measurement, 10* (1), 1960.

$$K = \frac{Po - Pc}{1 - P_c}$$

Retelling Accuracy—Generic

In order to establish retelling accuracy, 12 basic propositions, generic in nature, are derived from the nonconscious version of each story. These propositions should follow the main plot points of the story. For example, "Eveline sits by the window (watching the evening invade the avenue)." The parenthetical material refers to salient plot information that may or may not be present—or present in various forms—within a subject's response. (See Appendix E for a complete list of generic propositions for Study 2 and Appendix B for Study 1.)

Code retelling transcripts for absence or presence of each of the 12 propositions. A generic "hit" would require a basic sense of propositional content—for instance, "There's this poor, unhappy girl who, uh, is sitting by the window, and she's pondering, uh, leaving home" would qualify as a generic hit for the aforementioned proposition. A more ambiguous response, such as "She looked around and she looked out at the avenue, and she thought about her father, who used to come to the field and chase them, I think," would also be considered a hit for that proposition because (a) the rater may make the inference that the girl was sitting by, and looking out a window when she looked out at the avenue, and (b) parenthetical material was included in the response. Shorter retellings, in their synoptical form, may require more inference on the part of the rater than longer retellings, as longer retellings tend to explicate more information about the story. However, a response such as, "Basically, the story of 'Eveline' starts off with her reflecting on her childhood. She lives in a city in Ireland. Her family as a child and the neighborhood had all played in a little field not too far away from where she lived" has no reference to setting or moment, no reference to the propositional content or parenthetical material in question. In this case, no inferences may be made, and the proposition would be coded a "miss."

Total the number of proposition hits in the retellings—out of a possible 12—for each subject and obtain a mean and percentage for each condition. At this time, a count of the number of lines for each retelling and a mean for each condition may also be calculated.

Interrater reliability—Study 1: $K = .77$; Study 2: $K = .77$.

Retellings—Order of Telling Versus Reordering

After the retellings have been coded for all propositional material— we placed numerical notations for proposition hits in the margins of the texts—a schematic of retelling orders may be obtained. This secondary analysis is used to determine the number of subjects who retell the story in the order given versus those who reorder the story into a more linear temporal pattern (i.e., past to present). For this analysis, two coding keys are first derived from the list of basic retelling propositions—one for order of telling, the other for temporal reordering. (As this procedure was not used for Study 2, the following examples are taken from Study 1.) In Study 1, Story 2, for example, the coding key for the order of telling category has the proposition sequence [1,2,3,4,5,6,7,8,9,10,11,12], whereas the reordering category has the sequence [2/3,6,7,5/4,1,8,9,10,11,12]. (The slash marks indicate interchangeable proposition orders.) By examining the numerical ordering of their retelling propositions, subjects would then be coded as meeting one or the other criterion. For instance, in Story 2 a retelling order of [1,2,3,4,6,5,6,8,9,10,12] would qualify as an order of telling; an order of [3,2,4,5,9,10,1,8,7,11] would qualify as a reordering. (Consult Appendix B for the propositional equivalents of these sequences.)

Count the number of subjects who tell the story in the order given and those who reorder the story, and total for each condition.

Interrater reliability—Study 1: $K = 1.00$.

Retelling Accuracy—Detail

In addition to the 12 generic propositions, 12 detail propositions are also derived from the nonconscious version of each story. These propositions are more specific or detailed than the generic and are not necessarily critical to the development of the plot; for instance, "outside the window were new/brick houses." (See Appendix E for a complete list of detail propositions for Study 2 and Appendix B for Study 1.) Unlike the generic propositions, a detail hit requires a specific and accurate reference to the given proposition—in this case, inferences are not made.

Code the retelling transcripts for the absence or presence of detail propositions. Total the number of proposition hits—out of a possible 12—for each subject, and obtain a mean and percentage for each condition.

Interrater reliability—Study 1: $K = 1.00$; Study 2: $K = .97$.

Retellings: Given Versus Beyond the Information Given (BIG)

To code given versus beyond the information given in the retellings, first mark off information units in the retelling transcripts. For instance,

> The story of "Eveline"./ A young woman who, uh, she's been living in the same house all of her life./ Uh, she's been living with her father/ who is sort of bossy and domineering./ Uh, she's very fond of her childhood memories./ She sort of lives in her childhood really./

Code each information unit only once, and either as given or beyond the information given. BIG units require references to or explications about information not provided in the text. Using the preceding example, for instance, "She's very fond of her childhood memories" and "She sort of lives in her childhood really" do not appear in the "Eveline" story and thus would be coded BIG.

Given and BIG units are then further broken down into information units about psychology or consciousness of the character; action, plot, or physical events in the story; and trait features of the character. In the preceding example, "The story of 'Eveline'," "a young woman who, uh, she's been living in the same house all of her life," and "she's been living with her father" would all be coded as action (and given). "Who is sort of bossy and domineering" would be coded as trait (also given). "She's very fond of her childhood memories" and "She sort of lives in her childhood really" would be coded as psychological (BIG).

In each case, a preponderance of one category over another, or in more ambiguous cases, a determination of the underlying logic or intention of the response should be used to guide the rater in his or her coding choices. For instance, although the example "She wants to sort of use him as a way of escape" might be considered an action, the response would be coded psychological because the protagonist's desires or intentions are explicated by the subject.

Count the number of psychological, action, and trait units—both given and beyond the information given—and total for each condition.

Interrater reliability—Study 1: $K = .90$; Study 2: $K = .76$.

Mental Verbs (Most Important Thing and Ways This Could Be Going Questions—Entire Response)

To code mental verbs in the most important thing and ways this could be going questions, mark transcripts for the verbs *think*, *know*, and *believe*. Code all tenses and forms of these verbs (e.g., was thinking, knew, used to believe, etc.). Do not code repairs that occur as part of a hesitation or disfluency. Count these only once. However, do count those instances when a subject knowingly repeats him or herself (e.g., "I don't know. I don't know."). Finally, do not code the expression *you know*, which is often used as a pause filler or lexical punctuation.

The mental verbs code may then be further broken down into a character/subject dichotomy—that is, by attributing the mental verb either to the protagonist of the story or to the subject. This dichotomy may best be conceptualized as (a) a within-story response (character), or (b) the subject's comment on or perception of the story, character, or his/her own experience (subject). In order to establish attribution, first refer to the grammatical subject accompanying the individual mental verb. Code those mental verbs that appear with I, you, we, one, someone, or an abstract authorial voice (e.g., the author) as subject. Two examples of the subject code are: "*I think* her mind is pretty much well made up to go," and "It just leads you to see how many pages are left before *you know* what would happen." Similarly, code those mental verbs that appear with he, she, they, and proper names or types of character, and all quoted material as character. Two examples of the character code are: "Because she's about to leave this place that *she* never *believed* she would leave," and "The *mother* says at the beginning, 'I don't *know* what could be attractive about her."

Count the total number of mental verbs and those attributed to subject or character for each subject, and calculate totals for each condition.

Interrater reliability—Study 1: $K = 1.00$; Study 2: $K = 1.00$.

Temporal Versus Static Responses (Most Important Thing—Why Response)

To code temporal versus static responses, determine the overall tenor of the why response, and mark these either temporal or static. Temporal responses are characterized by past or future considerations (coming from or leading to change or development in the character or the story). Static responses are characterized by a sense of being frozen in time, descriptive only of the present. Whereas the example, "Because it seems like it's setting up a pattern in which something is going to happen between these two in the story" is a clear case of a temporal response, a more difficult call might be, "I think this is the plot. I think this is what the author is intending that we should know from this. I mean, it seems to be what is moving the story along." Here, the first part of the response is static, the second part temporal. In the final analysis, however, the response would be coded as temporal, because "moving the story along" seems to be the underlying logic guiding the preceding portion of the response.

Code temporal and static responses for Round 1 and Round 2, and make a total for each round and condition.

Interrater reliability—Study 1: $K = .80$; Story 2: $K = .87$).

Possibilities and Predictions: Hedged Versus Nonhedged (Ways This Could Be Going Question)

Count the number of possibilities given by the subject as ways this could be going by counting only items given before the prompt, "Do you see any other possibilities?" (Some subjects respond to the prompt by generating several wild possibilities, whereas others remain closer to the text. We therefore decided to stick with the preprompt list.)

Code the subject's response to the way you think it will go portion of the question in the following two ways. Code these predictions either hedged (qualified) or nonhedged (flat). The following is a suggested list of hedge words and expressions, often accompanying verbs, that may be used as a guideline for coding hedged responses. The rule is that if a prediction contains any one expression of uncertainty on the following list except "I think," it is hedged, and if it contains "I think" and a second expression of uncertainty, it is also hedged.

> probably; maybe; might; kind of; sort of; somehow; in some way; likely; looks like; sounds like, and other near equivalent expressions.

Whereas salient examples of the hedged/nonhedged categories may be found in the main text, examples of difficult calls are given here: "I think she will say—I don't—and something will resolve itself about these very strong feelings she has." Although this response has a somewhat hesitant and disfluent quality to it, it would be coded as a nonhedged prediction, given that the verb *think* is not further qualified and there are no other expressions of uncertainty. On the other hand, the example, "I would say that probably what the—what's likely to happen at this point is that she's not going to be—she's not going to achieve any kind of release," would be coded as a hedged prediction given the qualifying stance markers *probably* and *what's likely to happen*.

In addition, in cases where subjects fail to make predictions for any reason, the response is coded as hedged.

Code hedged and nonhedged predictions for Round 1 and Round 2, and create totals for each round and for each condition.

Interrater reliability—Study 1: $K = 1.00$; Study 2: $K = .84$.

Given Versus Beyond the Information Given (BIG)—(Ways This Could Be Going Question— Entire Response)

To code given information versus beyond the information given units in the ways this could be going question, mark transcripts for all units of information given in the text and all units that go beyond the information in the text. As in the retellings, these BIG units are references to or explications of information not given in the story. As a rule, do not code predictions—either as given or as BIG—but do code any information that provides a rationale for, or otherwise supports a prediction. Examples of given units are, "I guess the whole story seems to be about a girl leaving home," and "There's a discrepancy between her initial impression of Gouvernail and what he turns out to be." Examples of BIG units are: "She's torn between these two emotions," and "She seems bored and fed up with her life."

Count the number of given and BIG units for Round 1 and Round 2, and create totals for each round and condition.
Interrater reliability—Study 1: $K = .86$; Study 2: $K = .82$.

Psychology, Action, and Trait as Subcategories of Beyond the Information Given (Ways This Could Be Going Question— Entire Response)

Once the number of BIG units for the ways this could be going question have been coded, determine which units are psychological—referring to aspects of the character's mental life (e.g., "I don't think she understands what's going through her"); actions—referring to the characters intention-driven behaviors (e.g., "It seems like she is returning"); and traits (e.g., "This woman's very simplistic").

Code in psychological, action, and trait categories for Round 1 and Round 2, and create totals for each round and condition.

Interrater reliability for psychological versus action versus trait versus causal—Study 1: $K = .93$; Study 2: $K = .91$.

Psychological Versus Writing Style Versus Plot Interpretations (Ways This Could Be Going Question—Why Response)

To code psychology versus writing style versus plot, first determine the overall interpretive stance of the why response. If a subject did not respond to the why question, go back to the previous response, "Which way do you think it will go?" and code for the underlying logic guiding the response. On the other hand, if the subject's response is "I didn't have enough information about X" or "That's what I want X to be like" or "I'm not too connected to X," code X for its category. Code interpretations as one of the three types. Psychological includes references to the mental life, motives, or intentions of the character. Writing style includes references to tone/mood, genre, or authorial intention—that is, any aspect of the writing taken as a text crafted by an author. This also holds for refusals based on a negative reaction to the writing style (e.g., because it's so boring, annoying, etc.). Plot includes references to plot elements, actions, or physical events in the story.

Examples coded as writing style are, "I'm trying to anticipate the way the author is going to work," and "The whole point of a short story is sort of building up a suspense level and the conflict.

The point is not quite knowing how it's going to turn out so you'll keep reading" (authorial intention); "Because it has more of a tragic depressed mood than a very hopeful mood" (tone/mood); and "Because it seems like one of those stories of a young girl who's had to take care of so much—and suddenly a Prince comes along and he's a sailor" (genre). On the other hand, a response such as "If she leaves, there's no story" would be coded as plot, because the plot element "if she leaves" seems to be guiding the subject's logic. Finally, "I think that's because everything has been moving in the direction of her being kind of forced to confront these feelings that she has, and obviously she's trying to deny that throughout the story" would be coded as psychological, in that it is the character's inner life that provides the motive force guiding the response.

Code these interpretations for Round 1 and Round 2, and create a total for each round and condition.

Interrater reliability—Study 1: $K = 1.00$; Study 2: $K = .97$.

Character Question (BIG): Developmental Versus Nondevelopmental

To code developmental versus nondevelopmental responses in the character question, first identify all units that go beyond the information given. Mark these either as developmental or nondevelopmental and code each unit only once. Developmental responses refer to the way a particular trait, psychological state, or situation has developed or where it may be leading. It is similar to the temporal code except that it is exclusively about the growth or development of the character. Nondevelopmental responses are simply statements of things as they are at present, with no reference to how they got that way or where they are going. Examples of a developmental response are, "She's just becoming a woman and seeing what being a woman can do for her," and "It sounds like she's going to develop into a jealous and disapproving person." Nondevelopmental responses are, "She's probably attractive—attractive and plain all at the same time," and "She does what's expected of her."

Count the number of developmental and nondevelopmental units, and total for each condition.

Interrater reliability—Study 1: $K = .81$; Study 2: $K = .77$.

Categorize developmental responses as psychology, action, or trait using the same criteria described for the ways this could be going question. Do the same for nondevelopmental responses.

Interrater reliability—Study 1: $K = .77$; Study 2: $K = .82$.

Gists: Concluding Interpretations (Study 1 Only)

To code concluding interpretations in the gist response, construct a proposition that incorporates a critical summary interpretation of the story. As this procedure was not used in Study 2, the following examples are from Study 1. For instance, "Charles had conflict regarding his choices." Code as hits all subjects who go beyond a plot description of the story to provide the interpretative response. (See examples in the main text.)

Total the number of subjects providing concluding interpretations, and derive a percentage for each condition.

Interrater reliability—Study 1: $K = 1.0$.

Gists: Theme Versus Story (Study 2 Only)

Theme gists have a deontic quality—like little moral lessons. Story gists refer more specifically to elements in the story and are more descriptive than prescriptive. This code is straightforward, and the reader is referred for examples to the main text.

Interrater reliability—Study 2: $K = 1.0$.

APPENDIX D: STORIES USED IN STUDY 2

Story 3: "Eveline" (Joyce, 1986)

3C—Conscious Version

She sat at the window watching the evening invade the avenue. Her head was leaned against the window curtains and in her nostrils was the odor of dusty cretonne. She was tired.

Few people passed. The man out of the last house passed on his way home; she heard his footsteps clacking along the concrete pavement and afterwards crunching on the cinder path before the new red houses. One time there used to be a field there in which they used to play every evening with other people's children. Then a man from Belfast bought the field and build houses in it—not like their little brown houses but bright brick houses with shining roofs. The children of the avenue used to play together in that field—the Devines, the Waters, the Dunns, little Keogh the cripple, she and her brothers and sisters. Ernest, however, never played: he was too grown up. Her father used often to hunt them in out of the field with his blackthorn stick; but usually little Keogh used to keep *nix* and call out when he saw her father coming. Still they seemed to have been rather happy then. Her father was not so bad then; and besides, her mother was alive. That was a long time ago; she and her brothers and sisters were all grown up; her mother was dead. Tizzie Dunn was dead, too, and the Waters had gone back to England. Everything changes. Now she was going to go away like the others, to leave her home.

Home! She looked round the room, reviewing all its familiar objects which she had dusted once a week for so many years, wondering where on earth all the dust came from. Perhaps she would never see again those familiar objects from which she had never dreamed of being divided. And yet during all those years she had never found out the name of the priest whose yellowing photograph hung on the wall above the broken harmonium beside the coloured print of the promises made to Blessed Margaret Mary Alcoque. He had been a school friend of her father. Whenever he showed the photograph to a visitor her father used to pass it with a casual word:

—He is in Melbourne now.

Q1a: What is the most important thing I've told you so far?
Q1b: Why?

She had consented to go away, to leave her home. Was that wise? She tried to weigh each side of the question. In her home anyway she had shelter and food; she had those whom she had known all her life about her. Of course she had to work hard both in the house and at business. What would they say of her in the Stores when they found out that she had run away with a fellow? Say she was a fool, perhaps; and her place would be filled up by advertisement. Miss Gavan would be glad. She had always had an edge on her, especially whenever there were people listening.

—Miss Hill, don't you see these ladies are waiting?
—Look lively, Miss Hill, please.

She would not cry many tears at leaving the Stores.

But in her new home, in a distant unknown country, it would not be like that. Then she would be married—she, Eveline. People would treat her with respect then. She would not be treated as her mother had been. Even now, though she was over nineteen, she sometimes felt herself in danger of her father's violence. She knew it was that that had given her the palpitations. When they were growing up he had never gone for her, like he used to go for Harry and Ernest, because she was a girl; but latterly he had begun to threaten her and say what he would do to her only for her dead mother's sake. And now she had nobody to protect her. Ernest was dead and Harry, who was in the church decorating business, was nearly always down somewhere in the country. Besides, the invariable squabble for money on Saturday nights had begun to weary her unspeakably. She always gave her entire wages—seven shillings—and Harry always sent up what he could but the trouble was to get any money from her father. He said she used to squander the money, that she had no head, that he wasn't going to give her his hardearned money to throw about the streets, and much more, for he was usually fairly bad of a Saturday night. In the end he would give her the money and ask her had she any intention of buying Sunday's dinner. Then she had to rush out as quickly as she could and do her marketing, holding her black leather purse tightly in her hand as she elbowed her way through the crowds and returning home late under her load of provisions. She had hard work to keep the house together and to see that the two young children who had been left to her charge went to school regularly and got their meals regularly. It was hard work—a hard life—but now that she was about to leave it she did not find it a wholly undesirable life.

Q2a: What is the most important thing I have told you so far? (If subject asks, in this section, or in the whole story so far?, answer: In the story so far).

Q2b: Why?

She was about to explore another life with Frank. Frank was very kind, manly, open-hearted. She was to go away with him by the night boat to be his wife and to live with him in Buenos Aires where he had a home waiting for her. How well she remembered the first time she had seen him; he was lodging in a house on the main road where she used to visit. It seemed a few weeks ago. He was standing at the gate, his peaked cap pushed back on his head and his hair tumbled forward over a face of bronze. Then they had come to know each other. He used to meet her outside the Stores every evening and see her home. He took her to see *The Bohemian Girl* and she felt elated as she sat in an unaccustomed part of the theatre with him. He was awfully fond of music and sang a little. People knew that they were courting and, when he sang about the lass that loves a sailor, she always felt pleasantly confused. He used to call her Poppens out of fun. First of all it had been an excitement for her to have a fellow and then she had begun to like him. He had tales of distant countries. He had started as a deck boy at a pound a month on a ship of the Allan Line going out to Canada. He told her the names of the ships he had been on and the names of the different services. He had sailed through the straits of Magellan and he told her stories of the terrible Patagonians. He had fallen on his feet in Buenos Aires, he said, and had come over to the old country just for a holiday. Of course, her father had found out the affair and had forbidden her to have anything to say to him.

—I know these sailor chaps, he said.

One day he had quarrelled with Frank and after that she had to meet her lover secretly.

The evening deepened in the avenue. The white of two letters in her lap grew indistinct. One was to Harry; the other was to her father.

Q3a: What are the directions this could be going? (If subject gives only one or two directions, ask: Are there any other possibilities?)
Q3b: Which way do you think it will go?
Q3c: Why?

Ernest had been her favorite but she liked Harry too. Her father was becoming old lately, she noticed; he would miss her. Sometimes he could be very nice. Not long before, when she had been laid up for a day, he had read her out a ghost story and made toast for her at the fire. Another day, when their mother was alive, they had all gone for a picnic to the Hill of Howth. She remembered her father putting on her mother's bonnet to make the children laugh.

Her time was running out but she continued to sit by the window, leaning her head against the window curtain, inhaling the odor of dusty cretonne. Down far in the avenue she could hear a street organ playing. She knew the air. Strange that it should come that very night to remind her of the promise to her mother, her promise to keep the home together as long as she could. She remembered

the last night of her mother's illness; she was again in the close
dark room at the other side of the hall and outside she heard a
melancholy air of Italy. The organ-player had been ordered to go
away and given sixpence. She remembered her father strutting
back into the sickroom saying:

—Damned Italians! coming over here!

As she mused, the pitiful vision of her mother's life laid its spell
on the very quick of her being—that life of commonplace sacrifices
closing in final craziness. She trembled as she heard again her
mother's voice saying constantly with foolish insistence:

—Derevaun Seraun! Derevaun Seraun!

She stood up in a sudden impulse of terror. Escape! She must
escape! Frank would save her. He would give her life, perhaps love,
too. But she wanted to live. Why should she be unhappy? She had
a right to happiness. Frank would take her in his arms, fold her in
his arms. He would save her.

She stood among the swaying crowd in the station at the North
Wall. He held her hand and she knew that he was speaking to her,
saying something about the passage over and over again.

Q4a: What are the directions this could be going now? (Prompt
       as before if subject gives just one or two possibilities.)
Q4b: Which way do you think it will go?
Q4c: Why?

The station was full of soldiers with brown baggages. Through
the wide doors of the sheds she caught a glimpse of the black mass
of the boat, lying in beside the quay wall, with illumined portholes.
She answered nothing. She felt her cheek pale and cold and, out of
a maze of distress, she prayed to God to direct her, to show her
what was her duty. The boat blew a long mournful whistle into the
mist. If she went, tomorrow she would be on the sea with Frank,
steaming towards Buenos Aires. Their passage had been booked.
Could she still draw back after all he had done for her? Her distress
awoke a nausea in her body and she kept moving her lips in silent
fervent prayer.

A bell clanged upon her heart. She felt him seize her hand:

—Come!

All the seas of the world tumbled about her heart. He was drawing her into them: he would drown her. She gripped with both hands at the iron railing.

—Come!

No! No! No! It was impossible. Her hands clutched the iron railing in frenzy. Amid the seas she sent a cry of anguish!

—Eveline! Evvy!

He rushed beyond the barrier and called her to follow. He was shouted at to go on but he still called to her. She set her white face to him, passive, like a helpless animal. Her eyes gave him no sign of love or farewell or recognition.

END

   Q5: That's the end of the story. What happened in the end?
   Q6: Tell me some things about this character that I haven't told you. What is she like?
   Q7: This is a difficult question, but I'd like you to give it a try—what do you think the author was trying to say?
   Q8: What kind of story is this? You know, it's not a mystery, it's not a folktale—I don't know, what would you call it?

BREAK: At this point, pause for a few moments and get comfortable before the retelling.

   Q9: I'd like for you to tell me the story now—the same story I told you, but in your own words.
   Q10: Now just tell me, what was the gist of this story?
   Q11: [Asked after questions are completed for both stories for the subject]: How would you compare the two stories?

3NC—Nonconscious Version

She sat at the window watching the evening invade the avenue. Her head was leaned against the window curtains and in her nostrils was the odor of dusty cretonne.

Few people passed. The man out of the last house passed on his way home; his footsteps clacked along the concrete pavement and afterwards crunching on the cinder path before the new red houses. One time there used to be a field there in which they used to play every evening with other people's children. Then a man from Belfast bought the field and built houses in it—not like their little brown houses but bright brick houses with shining roofs. The children of the avenue used to play together in that field—the Devines, the Waters, the Dunns, little Keogh the cripple, she and her brothers and sisters. Ernest, however, never played: he was too grown up. Her father used often to hunt them in out of the field with his blackthorn stick; but usually little Keogh used to keep *nix* and call out when he saw her father coming. That was a long time ago; she and her brothers and sisters were all grown up; her mother was dead. Tizzie Dunn was dead, too, and the Waters had gone back to England. Now she was going to go away like the others, to leave her home.

She looked round the room, reviewing all its familiar objects which she had dusted once a week for so many years. Where on earth had all the dust come from. She might never see again those familiar objects. And during all those years she had never found out the name of the priest whose yellowing photograph hung on the wall above the broken harmonium beside the coloured print of the promises made to Blessed Margaret Mary Alcoque. He had been a school friend of her father. Whenever he showed the photograph to a visitor her father used to pass it with a casual word:

—He is in Melbourne now.

Q1a: What is the most important thing I've told you so far?
Q1b: Why?

She was going to go away, to leave her home. She weighed each side of the decision. In her home she had shelter and food; she had those whom she had known all her life about her. Of course she worked hard both in the house and at business. In the Stores, when they found out that she had run away with a fellow they might say she was a fool; and her place would be filled up by advertisement.

Miss Gavan would be glad. She had always had an edge on her, especially whenever there were people listening.

—Miss Hill, don't you see those ladies are waiting?
—Look lively, Miss Hill, please.

In her new home, in a distant unknown country, it would not be like that. Then she would be married. People would treat her with respect. She would not be treated as her mother had been. Though she was over nineteen, there was sometimes the danger of her father's violence. It was that that had given her the palpitations. When they were growing up he had never gone for her, like he used to go for Harry and Ernest, because she was a girl; but latterly he had begun to threaten her and say what he would do to her only for her dead mother's sake. And now she had nobody to protect her. Ernest was dead and Harry, who was in the church decorating business, was nearly always down somewhere in the country. There was the invariable squabble for money on Saturday nights. She always gave her entire wages—seven shillings—and Harry always sent up what he could but the trouble was to get any money from her father. He said she used to squander the money, that she had no head, that he wasn't going to give her his hardearned money to throw about the streets, and much more, for he was usually fairly bad of a Saturday night. In the end he would give her the money and ask her had she any intention of buying Sunday's dinner. Then she had to rush out and do her marketing, holding her black leather purse in her hand as she elbowed her way through the crowds and returning home late with her load of provisions. It was hard work to keep the house together and to see that the two young children who had been left to her charge went to school regularly and got their meals regularly. It was hard work—a hard life—but now she was about to leave it.

Q2a: What is the most important thing I have told you so far?
      (If subject asks, in this section, or in the whole story so far?, answer: In the story so far).
Q2b: Why?

She was about to have another life with Frank. Frank was very kind, manly, open-hearted. She was to go away with him by the night boat to be his wife and to live with him in Buenos Aires where he had a home. The first time she had seen him he was lodging in a house on the main road where she used to visit. He was standing at the gate, his peaked cap pushed back on his head and his hair tumbled forward over a face of bronze. Then they had come to know each other. He used to meet her outside the Stores every evening and see her home. He took her to see *The Bohemian Girl* and she sat in an unaccustomed part of the theatre with him. He was awfully fond of music and sang a little. People knew that they were courting and he sang about the lass that loves a sailor. He used to call her Poppens out of fun. He had tales of distant countries. He had started as a deck boy at a pound a month on a ship of the Allan Line going out to Canada. He told her the names of the ships he had been on and the names of the different services. He had sailed through the straits of Megallan, and he told her stories of the terrible Patagonians. He had fallen on his feet in Buenos Aires, he said, and had come over to the old country just for a holiday. Her father had found out the affair and had forbidden her to have anything to say to him.

—I know these sailor chaps, he said.

One say he had quarrelled with Frank and after that she had to meet her lover secretly.

The evening deepened in the avenue. The white of two letters in her lap grew indistinct. One was to Harry; the other was to her father.

Q3a: What are the directions this could be going? (If subject give only one or two directions, ask: Are there any other possibilities?)

Q3b: Which way do you think it will go?

Q3c: Why?

Her father was becoming old lately; he would miss her. Not long before, when she had been laid up for a day, he had read her out a ghost story and made toast for her at the fire. Another day, when their mother was alive, they had all gone for a picnic to the Hill of Howth. Her father had put on her mother's bonnet to make the children laugh.

Time was running out but she continued to sit by the window, leaning her head against the window curtain, inhaling the odor of dusty cretonne. Down far in the avenue a street organ played. She had promised her mother to keep the home together as long as she could. On that last night of her mother's illness she was in the room at the other side of the hall, and outside she had heard the same air of Italy. The organ-player had been ordered to go away and given sixpence. Her father strutted back into the sickroom saying:

—Damned Italians! coming over here!

She saw her mother's life—that life of sacrifices closing in final craziness. She heard again her mother's voice saying with foolish insistence:

—Derevaun Seraun! Derevaun Seraun!

She stood among the swaying crowd in the station at the North Wall. Frank held her hand and spoke to her, saying something about the passage over and over again.

Q4a: What are the directions this could be going now? (Prompt as before if subject gives just one or two possibilities.)
Q4b: Which way do you think it will go?
Q4c: Why?

The station was full of soldiers with brown baggages. Through the wide doors of the sheds she saw the black mass of the boat, lying in beside the quay wall, with illumined portholes. She answered nothing. The boat blew a long mournful whistle into the mist. If she went, tomorrow she would be on the sea with Frank, steaming towards Buenos Aires. Their passage had been booked.
A bell clanged. He seized her hand:

—Come!

She gripped at the iron railing.

—Come!

No! No! No! It was impossible.

—Eveline! Evvy!

He rushed beyond the barrier and called to her to follow. He was shouted at to go on but he still called to her. She set her face to him. Her eyes gave him no sign of love or farewell or recognition.

END

Q5: That's the end of the story. What happened in the end?

Q6: Tell me some thing about this character that I haven't told you. What is she like?

Q7: This is a difficult question, but I'd like you to try it any-way—what do you think the author was trying to say?

Q8: What kind of story is this? You know, it's not a mystery, it's not a folktale—I don't know, what would you call it?

BREAK: At this point, pause for a few moments and get comfortable before the retelling.

Q9: I'd like for you to tell me the story now—the same story I told you, but in your own words.

Q10: Now just tell me, what was the gist of this story?

Q11: [Asked after questions are completed for both stories for the subject]: How would you compare the two stories?

Story 4: "A Respectable Woman" (Chopin, 1984)

4C—Conscious Version

Mrs. Baroda was a little provoked to learn that her husband ex-pected his friend, Gouvernail, up to spend a week or two on the plantation.

They had entertained a good deal during the winter; much of the time had also been passed in New Orleans in various forms of mild dissipation. She was looking forward to a period of unbroken rest, now, and undisturbed tete-a-tete with her husband, when he in-formed her that Gouvernail was coming up to stay a week or two.

This was a man she had heard much of but never seen. He had been her husband's college friend; was now a journalist, and in no sense a society man or "a man about town," which were, perhaps, some of the reasons she had never met him. But she had uncon-sciously formed an image of him in her mind. She pictured him tall, slim, cynical; with eye-glasses, and his hands in his pockets; and she did not like him. Gouvernail was slim enough, but he wasn't very tall nor very cynical; neither did he wear eye-glasses nor carry his hands in his pockets. And she rather liked him when he first presented himself.

But why she liked him she could not explain satisfactorily to herself when she partly attempted to do so. She could discover in him none of those brilliant and promising traits which Gaston, her husband, had often assured her that he possessed. On the contrary, he sat rather mute and receptive before her chatty eagerness to make him feel at home and in face of Gaston's frank and wordy hospitality. His manner was as courteous toward her as the most exacting woman could require; but he made no direct appeal to her approval or even esteem.

Q1a: What is the most important thing I've told you so far?
Q1b: Why?

Once settled at the plantation he seemed to like to sit upon the wide portico in the shade of one of the big Corinthian pillars, smoking his cigar lazily and listening attentively to Gaston's experience as a sugar planter.

"This is what I call living," he would utter with deep satisfaction, as the air that swept across the sugar field caressed him with its warm and scented velvety touch. It pleased him also to get on familiar terms with the big dogs that came about him, rubbing themselves sociably against his legs. He did not care to fish, and displayed no eagerness to go out and kill grosbecs when Gaston proposed doing so.

Gouvernail's personality puzzled Mrs. Baroda, but she liked him. Indeed, he was a lovable, inoffensive fellow. After a few days, she gave over being puzzled and remained piqued. In this mood, she left her husband and her guest, for the most part, alone together. Then finding that Gouvernail took no manner of exception to her action, she imposed her society upon him, accompanying him in his idle strolls to the mill and walks along the batture. She persistently sought to penetrate the reserve in which he had unconsciously enveloped himself.

Q2a: What is the most important thing I have told you so far? (If subject asks, in this section, or in the whole story so far?, answer: In the story so far).
Q2b: Why?

"When is he going—your friend?" she one day asked her husband. "For my part, he tires me frightfully."

"Not, for a week yet, dear. I can't understand; he gives you no trouble."

"No. I should like him better if he did; if he were more like others, and I had to plan somewhat for his comfort and enjoyment."

Gaston took his wife's pretty face between his hands and looked tenderly and laughingly into her troubled eyes. They were making a bit of toilet sociably together in Mrs. Baroda's dressing-room.

"You are full of surprises, ma belle," he said to her. "Even I can never count upon how you are going to act under given conditions." He kissed her and turned to fasten his cravat before the mirror.

"Here you are," he went on, "taking poor Gouvernail seriously and making a commotion over him, the last thing he would desire or expect."

"Commotion!" she hotly resented. "Nonsense! How can you say such a thing? Commotion, indeed! But, you know, you said he was clever."

"So he is. But the poor fellow is run down by overwork now. That's why I asked him here to take a rest."

"You used to say he was a man of ideas," she retorted, unconciliated. "I expected him to be interesting, at least. I'm going to the city in the morning to have my spring gowns fitted. Let me know when Mr. Gouvernail is gone; I shall be at my Aunt Octavie's."

That night she went and sat alone upon a bench that stood beneath a live oak tree at the edge of the gravel walk.

She had never known her thoughts or her intentions to be so confused. She could gather nothing from them but the feeling of a distinct necessity to quit her home in the morning.

Mrs. Baroda heard footsteps crunching the gravel; but could discern in the darkness only the approaching red point of a lighted cigar. She knew it was Gouvernail, for her husband did not smoke. She hoped to remain unnoticed, but her white gown revealed her to him. He threw away his cigar and seated himself upon the bench beside her; without a suspicion that she might object to his presence.

Q3a: What are the directions this could be going? (If subject gives only one or two directions, ask: Are there any other possibilities?)

Q3b: Which way do you think it will go?

Q3c: Why?

"Your husband told me to bring this to you, Mrs. Baroda," he said, handing her a filmy, white scarf with which she sometimes enveloped her head and shoulders. She accepted the scarf from him with a murmur of thanks, and let it lie in her lap.

He made some commonplace observation upon the baneful effect of the night air at that season. Then as his gaze reached out into the darkness, he murmured, half to himself:

" 'Night of south winds—night of the large few stars!

Still nodding night—' "

She made no reply to this apostrophe to the night, which indeed, was not addressed to her.

Gouvernail was in no sense a diffident man, for he was not a self-conscious one. His periods of reserve were not constitutional, but the result of moods. Sitting there beside Mrs. Baroda, his silence melted for the time.

He talked freely and intimately in a low, hesitating drawl that was not unpleasant to hear. He talked of the old college days when he and Gaston had been a good deal to each other; of the days of keen and blind ambitions and large intentions. Now there was left with him, at least, a philosophic acquiescence to the existing order—only a desire to be permitted to exist, with now and then a little whiff of genuine life, such as he was breathing now.

Her mind only vaguely grasped what he was saying. Her physical being was for the moment predominant. She was not thinking of his words, only drinking in the tones of his voice. She wanted to reach out her hand in the darkness and touch him with the sensitive tips of her fingers upon the face or the lips. She wanted to draw close to him and whisper against his cheek—she did not care what—as she might have done if she had not been a respectable woman.

The stronger the impulse grew to bring herself near him, the further, in fact, did she draw away from him. As soon as she could do so without an appearance of too great rudeness, she rose and left him there alone.

Before she reached the house, Gouvernail had lighted a fresh cigar and ended his apostrophe to the night.

Q4a: What are the directions this could be going now? (Prompt as before if subject gives just one or two possibilities.)

Q4b: Which way do you think it will go?

Q4c: Why?

Mrs. Baroda was greatly tempted that night to tell her husband—who was also her friend—of this folly that had seized her. But she did not yield to the temptation. Besides being a respectable woman she was a very sensible one; and she knew there are some battles in life which a human being must fight alone.

When Gaston arose in the morning, his wife had already departed. She had taken an early morning train to the city. She did not return till Gouvernail was gone from under her roof.

There was some talk of having him back during the summer that followed. That is, Gaston greatly desired it; but this desire yielded to his wife's strenuous opposition.

However, before the year ended, she proposed, wholly from herself, to have Gouvernail visit them again. Her husband was surprised and delighted with the suggestion coming from her.

"I am glad, chere amie, to know that you have finally overcome your dislike for him; truly he did not deserve it."

"Oh," she told him, laughingly, after pressing a long, tender kiss upon his lips, "I have overcome everything! you will see. This time I shall be very nice to him."

END

Q5: That's the end of the story. What happened in the end?

Q6: Tell me some things about this character that I haven't told you. What is she like?

Q7: This is a difficult question, but I'd like you to try it anyway—what do you think the author was trying to say?

Q8: What kind of story is this? You know, it's not a mystery, it's not a folktale—I don't know, what would you call it?

BREAK: At this point, pause for a few minutes and get comfortable before the retelling.

Q9: I'd like for you to tell me the story now—the same story I told you, but in your own words.

Q10: Now just tell me, what was the gist of this story?

Q11: [Asked after questions have been completed for both stories for the subject]: How would you compare the two
stories?

4NC—Nonconscious Version

Mrs. Baroda learned that her husband expected his friend, Gouvernail, up to spend a week or two on the plantation.

They had entertained a good deal during the winter; much of the
time had also been passed in New Orleans in various forms of mild
dissipation. She was expecting a period of unbroken rest, now, and
undisturbed tete-a-tete with her husband, when he informed her
that Gouvernail was coming up to stay a week or two.

This was a man she had heard much of but never seen. He had
been her husband's college friend; was now a journalist, and in no
sense a society man or "a man about town," which were, perhaps,
some of the reasons she had never met him. She pictured him
tall, slim, cynical; with eye-glasses, and his hands in his pockets.
Gouvernail was slim enough, but he wasn't very tall nor very cynical; neither did he wear eye-glasses nor carry his hands in his
pockets.

She saw in him none of those brilliant and promising traits which
Gaston, her husband, had often assured her that he possessed. On
the contrary, he sat rather mute and receptive before her attempts
to make him feel at home and in face of Gaston's frank and wordy
hospitality. His manner was as courteous toward her as the most
exacting woman could require; but he made no direct appeal to her
approval or even esteem.

Q1a: What is the most important thing I've told you so far?
Q1b: Why?

Once settled at the plantation he seemed to like to sit upon the
wide portico in the shade of one of the big Corinthian pillars,
smoking his cigar lazily and listening attentively to Gaston's experience as a sugar planter.

"This is what I call living," he would utter with deep satisfaction,
as the air that swept across the sugar field caressed him with its
warm and scented velvety touch. It pleased him also to get on
familiar terms with the big dogs that came about him, rubbing
themselves sociably against his legs. He did not care to fish, and
displayed no eagerness to go out and kill grosbecs when Gaston
proposed doing so.

He was a lovable, inoffensive fellow. After a few days, she left her husband and her guest, for the most part, alone together. When Gouvernail took no manner of exception to her action, she began accompanying him in his idle strolls to the mill and walks along the batture.

Q2a: What is the most important thing I have told you so far? (If subject asks, in this section, or in the while story so far?, answer: In the story so far).

Q2b: Why?

"When is he going—your friend?" she one day asked her husband.

"Not for a week yet, dear. I can't understand; he gives you no trouble."

"No. It would be better if he did; if he were more like others, and I had to see to his comfort and enjoyment."

Gaston took his wife's pretty face between his hands and looked tenderly and laughingly into her eyes. They were making a bit of toilet sociably together in Mrs. Baroda's dressing-room.

"You are full of surprises, ma belle," he said to her. "Even I can never count upon how you are going to act under given conditions." He kissed her and turned to fasten his cravat before the mirror.

"Here you are," he went on, "taking poor Gouvernail seriously and making a commotion over him, the last thing he would desire or expect."

"Commotion!" she replied. "Nonsense! But, you know, you said he was clever."

"So he is. But the poor fellow is run down by overwork now. That's why I asked him here to take a rest."

"You used to say he was a man of ideas," she went on. "Interesting, at least. I'm going to the city in the morning to have my spring gowns fitted. Let me know when Mr. Gouvernail is gone; I shall be at my Aunt Octavie's."

That night she went and sat upon a bench that stood beneath a live oak tree at the edge of the gravel walk.

Mrs. Baroda heard footsteps crunching the gravel; but could discern in the darkness only the approaching red point of a lighted cigar. It was Gouvernail, for her husband did not smoke. Her white gown revealed her to him. He threw away his cigar and seated himself upon the bench beside her; without a suspicion that she might object to his presence.

Q3a: What are the directions this could be going? (If subject
gives only one or two directions, ask: Are there any other
possibilities?)

Q3b: Which way do you think it will go?

Q3c: Why?

"Your husband told me to bring this to you, Mrs. Baroda," he
said, handing her a filmy, white scarf with which she sometimes
enveloped her head and shoulders. She accepted the scarf from him
with a murmur of thanks, and let it lie in her lap.

He made some commonplace observation upon the baneful effect
of the night air at that season. Then as his gaze reached out into
the darkness, he murmured, half to himself:

" 'Night of south winds–night of the large few stars!

Still nodding night—' "

She made no reply to this apostrophe to the night, which indeed,
was not addressed to her.

Gouvernail was in no sense a diffident man, for he was not a self-
conscious one. His periods of reserve were not constitutional, but
the result of moods. Sitting there beside Mrs. Baroda, his silence
melted for the time.

He talked freely and intimately in a low, hesitating drawl. He
talked of the old college days when he and Gaston had been a good
deal to each other; of the days of keen and blind ambitions and
large intentions. Now there was left with him, at least, a philosophic
acquiescence to the existing order—only a desire to be permitted
to exist, with now and then a little whiff of genuine life, such as he
was breathing now.

She only vaguely grasped what he was saying. She listened to
the tones of his voice.

As soon as she could do so, she rose and left him there alone.

Before she reached the house, Gouvernail had lighted a fresh
cigar and ended his apostrophe to the night.

Q4a: What are the directions this could be going now? (Prompt
as before if subject gives just one or two possibilities.)

Q4b: Which way do you think it will go?

Q4c: Why?

When Gaston arose in the morning, his wife had already departed. She had taken an early morning train to the city. She did
not return till Gouvernail was gone from under her roof.

There was some talk of having him back during the summer that followed. That is, Gaston greatly desired it; but this desire yielded to his wife's opposition.

However, before the year ended, she proposed, wholly from herself, to have Gouvernail visit them again. Her husband was surprised and delighted with the suggestion coming from her.

"I am glad, chere amie, to know that you have finally overcome your dislike for him; truly he did not deserve it."

"Oh," she told him, after pressing a kiss upon his lips, "I have overcome everything! You will see. This time I shall be very nice to him."

END

    Q5: That's the end of the story. What happened in the end?

    Q6: Tell me some things about this character that I haven't told you. What is she like?

    Q7: This is a difficult question, but I'd like you to give it a try anyway—what do you think the author was trying to say?

    Q8: What kind of story is this? You know, it's not a mystery, it's not a folklore—I don't know, what would you call it?

BREAK: At this point, pause for a few minutes and get comfortable before the retelling.

    Q9: I'd like for you to tell me the story now—the same story I told you, but in your own words.

    Q10: Now just tell me, what was the gist of this story?

    Q11: [Asked after questions for both stories have been completed with the subject]: How would you compare the two stories?

APPENDIX E: STUDY 2 GENERIC AND
DETAILED PROPOSITIONS FOR
RETELLING RECALL

Story 3—"Eveline"

Generic propositions:

    1. Eveline sits by the window (watching the evening invade the avenue).

2. Eveline [thinks about] her childhood (references to her family).

3. Eveline's brothers and sisters are all grown up now/her mother is dead.

4. Eveline is going to go away, to leave her home.

5. Eveline looks around the room (reviewing all the familiar objects).

6. Eveline [thinks about] her hard life (working, raising the children).

7. Eveline [thinks about] her father (his violence, drunkenness, squabbles over money).

8. Eveline [thinks about] the new life she will have with Frank.

9. Eveline [thinks about] meeting Frank (their courtship, Frank's past, her father's disapproval).

10. Eveline [remembers] her mother's life/the promises she made to her.

11. Eveline and Frank are at the quay (Frank calls to Eveline, beckons her to come).

12. Eveline does not leave with Frank (her eyes give him no sign of love or farewell or recognition).

Detail propositions:

1. Outside the window were new/brick houses.

2. Children on the avenue used to play together in the field.

3. Eveline never found out the name of the priest in the photograph.

4. Eveline was nineteen.

5. One of Eveline's brothers was dead.

6. Eveline was going to live in Buenos Aires (Argentina).

7. Frank told Eveline stories of the ships he was on.

8. Eveline's father disapproved of the affair.

9. Eveline wrote letters to the people she was leaving.

10. Once when she was younger, Eveline's father put on her mother's bonnet.

11. Eveline saw the boat (black mass) at the station.

12. Eveline gripped the iron railing.

Story 4—"A Respectable Woman"

Generic propositions:

1. (Mrs. Baroda learns) her husband's friend is coming to visit.
2. Gouvernail is different from the way Mrs. Baroda pictures him (cynical, glasses, etc.).
3. Mrs. Baroda tries to see to Gouvernail's comfort and enjoyment (to get to know him).
4. Gouvernail is quiet and courteous/loveable and inoffensive (characteristics).
5. Gouvernail settled in at the plantation (sitting, smoking, listening to Gaston).
6. Mrs. Baroda complains to her husband about Gouvernail.
7. (One night) Gouvernail approaches/meets Mrs. Baroda in the garden.
8. Gouvernail begins to talk about himself (his youth, ambitions, etc.).
9. Mrs. Baroda leaves Gouvernail alone in the garden.
10. (The next morning) Mrs. Baroda goes to town (not returning until Gouvernail is gone).
11. Mrs. Baroda at first opposes the idea of Gouvernail returning.
12. (Before the year's end) Mrs. Baroda wants Gouvernail to visit the plantation.

Detail propositions:

1. Mrs. Baroda wants to be alone with her husband.
2. Mrs. Baroda has never seen or met Gouvernail.
3. Gouvernail was Gaston's college friend.
4. Gouvernail didn't like to fish or hunt.
5. Mrs. Baroda began accompanying Gouvernail on his walks.
6. Mrs. Baroda asks her husband why Gouvernail is not like other guests.
7. Mrs. Baroda is going to stay with her aunt.
8. Mrs. Baroda recognizes Gouvernail by his lighted cigar.
9. Gouvernail brings Mrs. Baroda a scarf.
10. Gouvernail murmurs an apostrophe/poem to the night.

11. Gouvernail is gone when Mrs. Baroda returns.
12. Mr. Baroda is surprised/delighted at his wife's suggestion.

ACKNOWLEDGMENT

This research was supported by NICHHD grant number HD20807 to Jerome Bruner.

REFERENCES

Bartlett, F. (1932). *Remembering*. Cambridge, MA: Cambridge University Press.
Böll, H. (1986). Nostalgia: or Grease Spots. In H. Böll (Ed.), *The stories of Heinrich Böll*. New York: Alfred A. Knopf.
Bruner, J. (1986). *Actual minds, possible worlds*. Cambridge, MA: Harvard University Press.
Chopin, K. (1984). A respectable woman. In K. Chopin (Ed.), *The awakening and selected stories*. New York: Viking Penguin.
Feldman, C. (in press). Oral metalanguage. In D. Olson & N. Torrance (Eds.), *Literacy and orality* (working title). Cambridge: Cambridge University Press.
Gill, B. (1961). Truth and consequences. In R. B. Goodman (Ed.), *75 short masterpieces: Stories from the world's literature*. New York: Bantam.
Joyce, J. (1986). Eveline. In J. Joyce (Ed.), *Dubliners*. New York: Penguin.
Mandler, J. (1984). *Stories, scripts, and scenes: Aspects of schema theory*. Hillsdale, NJ: Lawrence Erlbaum Associates.
Morton, A. (1980). *Frames of mind: Constraints on the common sense conception of the mental*. Oxford: Clarendon Press.
Nelson, K. (1986). *Event knowledge: Structure and function in development*. Hillsdale, NJ: Lawrence Erlbaum Associates.
Propp, V. (1986). *The morphology of the folktalk*. Austin, TX: University of Texas Press.
Trebasso, T., & Sperry, L. (1985). Causal relatedness and the importance of story events. *Journal of Memory and Language, 24*(5), 595–611.

2

Some Things That Narratives Tell Us About the Mind

Wallace Chafe
University of California at Santa Barbara

In a variety of ways, narratives provide evidence for the nature of the mind. I try to justify that statement with a rather wide-ranging discussion of how and why narratives can be an important vehicle for mental research. This is neither a review of the literature nor a report on a particular study, but a presentation of some personal views that come from a long-standing and continuing interest in what narratives can do for linguistics, anthropology, and psychology. I see narratives as overt manifestations of the mind in action: as windows to both the content of the mind and its ongoing operations.

I am bold enough here to try to present a partial theory of the mind's content and operations, based on narrative data. I believe that linguists are in as good a position as anyone to understand something about how the mind works. Psychologists, who might be thought to have first claim to this territory, have forfeited some of their rights to it by their self-imposed handicaps during most of this century, handicaps from which the well-publicized contributions of cognitive science have hardly managed to free them entirely. I say this less as criticism of others than as justification of my own boldness in dealing with matters that go well beyond language itself, which is my proper turf.

THE MIND AS A CREATIVE MODEL-BUILDER

I think of the mind as a device that allows the human organism to deal with its surroundings in ways that are more complex and effective than those available to any other creature. It does this above all through its ability to imagine; that is to say, to create elaborate representations of the world around it, to represent within itself its own view of what the world surrounding the organism is like.

This view of the mind as an organ for building models of the world is quite different from the view, I hope by now largely rejected, that it functions to mediate between a stimulus and a response. But it is also different from the currently more popular infomation-processing view. The primary function of the mind is not to take in information from the world and submit it to various kinds of processing through some complex system of filters. Rather, its constant activity is to create its own representations of the world.

But that is a difficult thing to do, and the mind needs help. In its model-building activity it is guided and constrained by two quite different influences. One is the information that reaches it from the outside world—from sensory input. The mind builds models of the world, not of course in isolation from it, but taking account of what the senses convey about that world. The senses can be limited and deceptive, but they do provide elaborate information concerning the world that surrounds the organism in which the mind resides. It is interesting, however, that the mind can go on creating representations of the world even in the absence of "real" sensory input; constructing, as it were, its own input, as in dreams. Dreams may be the strongest evidence we have that the mind goes on busily constructing its own representations, regardless of what may be coming in from the outside. The main thing that dreams lack is coherence. When left to its own devices, the mind creates a kaleidoscope of loosely strung together experiences. Sensory input during our waking hours may force these experiences to hang together in terms of spatio-temporal constancies that are present in, and imposed by, the outside world itself.

The mind is at the same time guided and constrained by schemas: prepackaged expectations and ways of interpreting that are already available to it. To some extent these schemas will have been created by each individual mind. To a large extent, however, they will have been supplied by the society of minds of which that individual mind is a member. Some of them may even be innate. The mind is constantly confronted with new experiences. In purely physical terms, sensory input is always new. The mind, however, never acts as if everything is new. Quite the contrary. It applies the models it already has to almost everything it encounters. Creativity in modeling the world is difficult, and calls for a significant expenditure of cognitive energy. Whether from cognitive laziness or from simple lack of ability, people avoid originality in modeling whenever they can.

Prepackaged models of the world are supplied for us above all by our cultures; they are what a culture is all about. Religions, ideologies, folklores, systems of education—all provide us with ready-made models we can use for dealing with new experiences. We may superimpose some idiosyncratic interpretations of our own, so that each of us has our own schematic mix. Only rarely, however, do we create brand new models to explain a particular input, or simply for the joy of doing so. Good artists and good scientists may do this more than other people, or at least it is an expected part of their professions.

This is then one thing, and perhaps the most important thing, that narratives can give us evidence for: the fact that the mind does not record the world, but rather creates it according to its own mix of cultural and individual expectations. Some years ago we were able to observe this creative process systematically by presenting many people with a film and asking them later to narrate their recall of the experience. Having been confronted initially with the same physical sights and sounds, people created many different experiences for themselves. I cite here four examples, two from American viewers and two from Greek viewers, all quoted from Tannen (1980). All four have to do with the manner in which a man was picking pears. One American viewer saw him as gentle in his handling of the pears:

> . . . A—nd uh— . . . tsk he was picking pears. . . . Just rather slowly, and he did it . . . so that you could hear the sound of the pears being . . . torn from the . . . tree, and he put them in an apron that he had, . . . the whole idea he picked pears came down the ladder, . . . put them . . . one by one . . . into this basket. . . . He . . . y you got . . . the feeling that he pretty much liked his pears, . . because he was so . . gentle with them. (Tannen, 1980, p. 61)

Another saw him at fault because he was too slow a picker:

> He's very deliberate . . . plucking the . . the um . . . the pears off the tree, and . . . you know you hear this . . . s—sharp little crunch as . .

as he pulls each one off, and he's doing it . . very slowly, and putting
them in [breath] his apron. [breath] . . . tsk And then . . climbing very
carefully . . down the . . . the ladder, and placing them in baskets,
and he'd never make it as a fruitpicker. . . . [laugh] He would starve.
(Tannen, 1980, p. 62)

One of the Greek viewers saw his pear-picking in terms of a romanti-
cally viewed participation in a harvest:

A—nd mm tsk it insisted tha—t that which he did he lived. . . . That
n—in other words—— . . . the fact tha—t he was cultivating the ea—
rth, that he was gathering the—se . . . the harvest, . . . was for him
something special. . . . It was worth somethi—ng . . . tsk he lived that
which he did, he liked it. (Tannen, 1980, p. 63)

Another Greek viewer interpreted his actions more negatively:

. . . His movements basically—gath . . . gathering the fruits don't
show a person . . . who loves them very much he pulls them very . .
I don't know. . . . I didn't like generally the way he was pulling them.
(Tannen, 1980, p. 63)

I believe it is crucially important for people to realize that such
discrepant modeling of physically identical inputs goes on constantly around us. I believe it happens much more than we are
generally aware, for there is little evidence of it unless it is revealed
in an overt way, as through a narrative. If people understood and
made allowances for these rampant differences in each other's model-building, most of the world's most grievous problems would be
a large step closer to being solved.

THE EXPECTED AND THE UNEXPECTED

Schemas, as I suggested, can be thought of as structures of expectations. We expect the world to be a certain way, and as long as
we can make it conform to our expectations, perhaps with some
pushing and shoving and the ignoring of much that surrounds us,
then our model-building proceeds smoothly. But the world is very
complex and the schemas available to any one individual are very
limited. No set of schemas can come close to accounting for everything the mind is confronted with. What happens when we face an
input that conflicts with our established expectations? We react,

it seems, with excitement, anger, and aggression. This emotional arousal brought on by an unexpected input has the adaptive value of putting us in a state where we are better able to deal with it. We do not take the unexpected sitting down, but enter a state where we are prepared to do something about it. An unexpected input is a threat to our accustomed modeling of the world, and our primary reaction is to reject it by getting rid of its source. Excitement, anger, and aggression are essential to this rejection process. From this reaction comes the satisfaction people find in xenophobia, and the everyday satisfaction people feel in complaining about things that are unfamiliar.

Because we are in this sense wired up to cope with inputs that conflict with our expectations, the absence of such inputs over any extended period creates in us an intolerable state of boredom. Ironically, we are not content with inputs that conform to our expectations, but prefer experiences that contain the unexpected, that arouse us to reject their source. Rejecting the unfamiliar is what we do best. From this follows the fact that we are satisfied only with narratives whose point is some kind of conflict with expectations. It has often been noted that narratives that entirely fit expectations are not really narratives at all: "John went to a restaurant. He asked the waitress for coq au vin. He paid the check and left" (Schank & Abelson, 1977, p. 38).

It has been said that the worst fear of narrators is to have their audience ask "So what?" when they are finished (Labov, 1972, p. 366). The primary way to avoid that is to construct the narratives around something that is difficult to account for. Narratives that present a conflict with expectations provide excitement by exercising the mind's innate capacity to react to and deal with inputs of such a kind.

The following narrative, volunteered during a conversation, illustrates this point. I refer to it as the hiking narrative. I introduce it now because of its clear invocation of unexpectedness, but I use it subsequently to illustrate some other points. The punctuation marks at the ends of the lines indicate various terminal intonation contours: the comma a rising pitch, the period a falling one, and the colon a level one. The dots show pauses: two dots a very brief pause and three dots a pause of half a second or longer. The dash indicates a lengthening of the syllable, as in "a—nd" in line 2. The lines in brackets were said by someone other than the principal speaker. Tuolomne Meadows is an area in the high country of Yosemite National Park. This conversation took place on July 24, several years ago:

1. . . I was on the bus today,
2. . . . a—nd there was this woman saying:
3. . . her so—n works for the ranger service or whatever.
4. . . . and . . . there was this sno—w,
5. . . . chest high at Tuolomne Meadows.
[6. . . . Really?]
7. . . . That's what she said,
[8.   Really.]
9. . . Now I don't know:
10. maybe she's . . she was just s—crewy.
[11. . . Well maybe it's just . . up above Tuolomne Meadows or
    something.]
12. Yeah.
13. . . . Cause they said that . . you know . . that usually by
    Fourth of July:
14. . . it's totally clear.
[15. Yeah,]
[16. . . and David said it was really nice up there.]
[17. . . the weather was great.]
18. Mm.
[19. . . /you know,/]
20. . . Cause it's beautiful up there,
21. but it is . . . pretty high,
[22.   Mhm,
23. . . . The last time . . I was there,
24. . . I was only there once;
25. . . Tuo . . Tuolomne once.
26. . . . and um . . . a bunch of us were hiking;
27. . . . and I guess we'd hiked all day:
28. . . I don't know:
29. . . we were almost to the top:
30. . . to this lake:
31. . . where we gonna go:
32. it was
33. . . . Altitude was pretty:
34. . . I mean the air was pretty thin;
35. . . I mean you could feel it.

36. . . . And there was these two women,
37. . . hiking up ahead of us.
38. . . . And you sort of got,
30. to a rise,
40. and then the lake,
41. was kind of right there,
42. where we were gonna . . . camp.
43. . . . And the two of them,
44. . . got to the rise,
45. . . and the next minute,
46. . . . they just . . fell over;
47. . . totally.
48. . . I mean I guess . . the s—top was just too much,
49. . . .and they . . both of them just totally passed out.
50. . . I mean
[51. You're kidding.]
52.   No.
53. It was amazing;
54. I mean we didn't know what to do with them;
55. I mean they both came to life.
56. . . You know,
57. . . very quickly but;
58. . . . I guess,
59. . . the hike,
60. and then . . all of a sudden stopping,
61. and the oxygen thing,
62. must have really confused them but.
[63.   Hm,
64. . . . So we had them over for bread,
[65.   mhm,]
66. later {laugh},
67. we . . figured we could lose them in the middle of the night,
[68.   {laugh}   yeah,]
[69. Gee,]
70. . . It was really odd;
71. . . . because . . . I felt kind of . . . s—pacy,
72. but I didn't . . . feel . . close to passing out,

The first piece of unexpectedness occurred in lines 4 and 5:

4. ... and ... there was sno—w,
5. ... chest high at Tuolomne Meadows.

unexpected if one knew that this conversation was taking place near the end of July. The following lines expressed a series of reactions to this unexpectedness:

[6. ... Really?]
7. ... That's what she said,
[8. Really.]
9. .. Now I don't know:
10. maybe she's .. she was just s—crewy.
[11. .. Well maybe it's just .. up above Tuolomne Meadows or something.]
12. Yeah.

The principal speaker then went on to say explicitly what the normal expectation was:

13. ... Cause they said that .. you know .. that usually by Fourth of July:
14. .. it's totally clear.

an expectation that was reinforced by another speaker:

[15. Yeah,]
[16. .. and David said it was really nice up there.]
[17. .. the weather was great.]

At which point the principal speaker's mention of the unusual elevation served both as a way of explaining the snow, and as a cue for the narrative that followed:

20. ... Cause it's beautiful up there,
21. but it is .. pretty high,

During the narrative that followed, another consequence of the high elevation served to foreshadow the eventual climax:

34. . . I mean the air was pretty thin;
35. . . I mean you could feel it.

The climax was finally realized in the lines:

46. . . . they just . . fell over;
47. . . totally.
48. . . I mean I guess . . the s—top was just too much,
49. . . and they . . both of them just totally passed out.

an unexpected event, even under those circumstances. Again there was a reaction from the audience, and a reinforcement by the narrator:

[51. You're kidding.]
52.   No.
53. It was amazing;

Then came an attempt at an explanation:

58. . . . I guess,
59. . . the hike,
60. and then . . all of a sudden stopping,
61. and the oxygen thing,
62. must have really confused them but.

and a fear that the unexpected event might be repeated:

67. we . . figured we could lose them in the middle of the night,

closing with a reiteration of its oddity, placed in the context of the narrator's own more normal experience:

70. . . It was really odd;
71. . . . because . . I felt kind of . . . s—pacy,
72. but I didn't . . . feel . . close to passing out,

The entire narrative, then, was built on unexpectedness, frequently remarked on by both the narrator and audience. That was what made it worth telling, just as real experience saves us from boredom when it provides events that challenge the prepackaged schemas in our minds.

UNITS OF THOUGHT AND LANGUAGE

So far we have looked at certain things that narratives in their entireties can suggest to us about the mind. We have seen in them evidence for a creative rather than a recording mind, and we have seen that one of the mind's chief functions is to deal with events that are contrary to expectations. I now shift to a very different perspective, one in which we look at how narratives are produced in real time. In the remainder of this chapter I suggest a few of the things we can learn from narratives regarding the changing states that the mind passes through as it recalls and verbalizes experiences (see Chafe, 1977, 1980, 1987). As we proceed, I make frequent reference to the foregoing hiking narrative, quoting from it as appropriate.

To begin with, it seems now well established that spoken narratives (in fact, all examples of spoken language) tend to be produced in spurts of vocalization called *intonation units*. These units are characterized above all by a terminal intonation contour; that is, each of them ends with one of a set of pitch contours that signal the end of a minimal coherent stretch of speech. They also exhibit at least one intonation peak (a point of highest pitch and stress), and they are typically separated from each other by hesitations, anything from a slight break in timing to a pause of several seconds. The hiking narrative was written with each intonation unit in a separate line.

These intonation units represent a physical segmentation of the stream of speech. It makes sense to think of each of them also as a verbalization of just that cluster of information that is active at a particular time. Such a cluster might be called an *idea unit*. From the evidence of intonation units, the amount of information that can be active at any one time—the amount contained in an idea unit—is that which can be expressed in about five words of English. Because intonation units have a mean length of about 2 seconds (including pauses), we can also infer that one idea unit is replaced by another at about 2-second intervals. This, at least, is the pace of thought while it is being expressed in language. It would be interesting to know whether silent thought, as in daydreaming, follows a similar pace. It may or may not be true that such unverbalized thought can proceed more rapidly, because it is possible that some of the 2 seconds occupied by an intonation unit is taken up with the act of producing language itself.

STATES OF ACTIVATION

Narratives provide evidence that information can be in any one of three *states of activation.* I refer to information as being either active, semiactive, or inactive. A comparison with vision is instructive. Active information is like the part of a scene that is in foveal vision, that is being processed with maximum acuity, that is in the focus of consciousness. The comparison with vision is probably more than just a metaphor, vision being the aspect of the brain's activity that is most representative of consciousness as a whole. To carry the comparison further, just as part of the visual scene is registered peripherally rather than focally, there is other information that is in a semiactive state, in peripheral rather than focal consciousness. Finally, there is a much larger amount of information that is inactive, like the part of a scene that is outside the field of vision. This view of information as being either active, semiactive, or inactive is an alternative to the more traditional view that it resides in a particular storage area such as short-term or long-term memory.

Idea units themselves have parts. It is easiest to dwell on one kind of component of an idea unit: a *referent,* the idea of a person or thing. In the course of a narrative, any particular referent may be verbalized in a variety of different ways. For example, one of the referents in the hiking narrative was verbalized as "these two women" in 36, as "the two of them" in 43, and as "they" in 46.

In lines 35–37 of the hiking story the narrator said:

35. . . . I mean you could feel it.
36. . . . And there was these two women,
37. . . . hiking up ahead of us.

Within the mind of the speaker, the referent in question was presumably either inactive or semiactive prior to line 36. It must then have become fully activated during the interval between 35 and 36, most likely during the initial pause of 36. The speaker's principal intention in uttering 36 was to introduce this referent into the minds of the addressees, where it became an active concept for them as soon as it was introduced. There was a lag between the mental processes of the speaker and those of the addressees with respect to the precise time at which this referent was activated. Whereas it became active for the speaker during the initial pause of 36, it became active for the addressees only as a result of hearing the words *these two women.*

Such a referent has often been said to provide "new" information, but whether the speaker judges it to be a brand new referent for the addressees, as here, or whether it is judged to be an already known, though inactive referent turns out to be unimportant. The important thing is the speaker's judgment that it is being changed for the addressees from the inactive to the active state. Hence, rather than new, I call such a referent *previously inactive* (or, more accurately, judged by the speaker to have been previously inactive in the mind of the addressee).

The next few lines had a different topic:

38. . . . And you sort of got,
39. to a rise,
40. and then the lake,
41. was kind of right there,
42. where we were gonna . . . camp.

During the period of time occupied by these lines, the referent in question failed to be refreshed and must have lapsed into the semi-active state for the hearer, who must also have judged that it became semi-active for her addressees. In the next line, however, it was returned to the active state:

43. . . . And the two of them,

When we consider the linguistic consequences of these processes of activation, deactivation, and reactivation, it is important to realize that the changes that took place during the initial pauses of 36 and 43 were somewhat different:

36. . . . And there was these two women,
43. . . . And the two of them,

The pause in 36 saw the activation of a referent that was (judged by the speaker to have been) previously inactive (for the address-ees). The pause in 43 saw the activation of a referent that was (judged by the speaker to have been) previously semiactive (for the addressees). Language treats these two kinds of events differently, both syntactically and lexically.

Syntactically, the referent in 36 is introduced with the construction *there* plus a form of the verb *be:* "there was X." In 43 the same referent occurs as the subject of a clause, a clause that is completed in the separate intonation unit 44:

43. . . . And the two of them,
44. . . got to the rise,

Lexically, in 36, the use of the indefinite demonstrative *these* as well as of the full noun phrase *two women* both signal the activation of something that had been previously inactive for the addressees. In 43, on the other hand, the use of the definite article *the* as well as the pronoun *them* signals the identifiability of these women, in accord with what the speaker assumed to have been their already semi-active status for the addressees. Thus the clause:

36. . . . And there was these two women,

appropriately signals the activation of a previously inactive referent, whereas the phrase:

43. . . . And the two of them,

functioning as the subject of the following predicate, appropriately signals the activation of a previously semiactive referent.

In 46 the same referent reappears under yet a third set of conditions:

46. . . . they just . . fell over;

Having been reactivated in 43, this referent remained at this point still active in the mind of the speaker, and she assumed that it was still active in the minds of the addressees as well. Such already active referents are typically verbalized, as here, with pronouns, and they are pronounced with low pitch and weak stress; in other words, with minimal prominence. These properties of the word *they* appropriately signal the already active status of the referent at this point. Such a referent has often been said to supply old or given information, but (assumed by the speaker to be) already active (in the mind of the addressee) is a more accurate character-ization.

Examples like this show the importance for language of a speak-er's model-building with respect to processes occurring in the mind of an addressee. Language could not function as it does if a speaker were not constantly creating his or her own version of the address-ee's mental processes. But there are other, more purely cognitive implications as well.

LIMITS ON ACTIVATION

Although the possibility needs further study, it would appear from a variety of observations made so far that each new idea unit can contain no more than one previously inactive concept (using *concept* as a cover term for referents and other components of idea units such as the ideas of states and events). That is, a speaker is normally constrained to verbalize only one new concept at a time, if *new* is taken to mean previously inactive.

To fully appreciate this constraint it is necessary to understand that a unitary concept can be expressed in a sequence of words, and that some words are irrelevant to the constraint. Take the following sequence as an example:

20. . . Cause it's beautiful up there,
21. but it is . . pretty high,

The previously inactive concept in 20 was verbalized as "is beauti-ful," an expression that I take to verbalize a single concept. Also present in this intonation unit were (a) the dummy pronominal subject *it*, with no referent at all; (b) the adverbial phrase *up there*, whose referent (the area above Tuolomne Meadows) was already active at this point; and (c) the conjunction *cause*, which is irrele-vant to the constraint we are discussing. In 21, the previously inactive concept was verbalized as "is high." Also present were (a) the dummy subject *it*; (b) the intensifying adverb *pretty*; and (c) the connective *but*.

Honesty requires me to point out cases likely to be taken as counterexamples to the one-new-concept-at-a-time constraint. Such cases are well illustrated in the hiking narrative by the line:

34. . . I mean the air was pretty thin;

I mean functions as an epistemic particle, and *pretty* again as an intensifier, both being irrelevant to the constraint. But we are left with "the air was thin." The question is whether *the air* and *be thin* are not two separate concepts, thus showing two previously inactive concepts within the same idea unit. The one-new-concept-at-a-time constraint, on the other hand, would require us to interpret "the air was thin" as having the same conceptual unity that appears in phrases like *it was raining*. This unitary interpretation, which I believe has intuitive plausibility, is supported by the presence in this intonation unit of only one peak of intonational prominence (on the word *thin*). The pronunciation of this line does not, in fact, suggest that the air and the thinness are being separately focused on, as they would be if the speaker had said something like, "Let me tell you about the air. It was pretty thin."

If we allow interpretations of this sort in some admittedly problematic cases, then the one-new-concept-at-a-time constraint holds up well in the spoken language data I have examined. It is potentially as important as, and more relevant to, the present discussion than the "seven plus or minus two" constraint on short-term memory (Miller, 1956). It means, apparently, that a speaker (and very likely a thinker) is unable to change more than one item from the inactive to the active state during the creation of any single idea unit, and thus is a crucial aspect of the flow of thought.

THE MIND'S NEED FOR ORIENTATION

Narratives also give evidence that the mind actually requires certain kinds of information in order to operate successfully. There appears to be a need for orientation in terms of the organism's location in space, in time, in a social context, and with relation to ongoing events. There also appears to be at least a secondary need for orientation with respect to weather. In Chafe (1980, pp. 40–47) I pointed out that narratives confirm an important wisdom in the folk belief that, on recovering from a spell of unconsciousness, a person's first question is "Where am I?", a request for orientation in space. We can imagine the same person following that question with another asking for an orientation in time: "What time is it?" or the like. A question regarding the social context might come next: "Who are you?" or "Who are these people?" The context of events might be established with a question like "What's going on?" "What's it like outside?" would also not be out of place.

It is well known that narratives typically begin with the provision of a setting, one or more intonation units that provide the kinds of orientation just described. A narrative typically starts out with a statement of the particular place, time, characters, and background activity against which the events of the narrative proper then unfold. This setting may serve the mental needs of both the speaker and the hearer. On the one hand, a narrator may find it useful for his or her own needs to establish this kind of information. On the other hand, a narrator may also realize that the audience has such a need, which must be satisfied before the narrative can proceed.

The first two lines of the hiking narrative:

1. . . I was on the bus today,
2. . . . a—nd there was this woman saying:

provide information on a location ("on the bus"), a time ("today"), a person ("this woman"), and an activity ("saying"). As the conversation went on, another orientation shortly became necessary:

23. . . . The last time . . . I was there,
24. . . I was only there once;
25. . . Tuo . . Tuolomne once.
26. . . . and um . . . a bunch of us were hiking;

Lines 23 and 24 provide a temporal setting. Line 25 then specifies a location, and 26 mentions some people and a background activity in which they were engaged. Climatic conditions may not always play as crucial a role as they do in this example:

33. . . . Altitude was pretty:
34. . . I mean the air was pretty thin;
35. . . I mean you could feel it.

Some important new protagonists and their own background activity were added next:

36. . . . And there was these two women,
37. . . hiking up ahead of us.

The mind's need for orientation in space, time, characters, events, and weather can be viewed as a necessity for establishing a chunk of semiactive material that provides a background against which the events of the narrative are, one after another, given active attention. But this chunk of semiactive material may include more than just the setting; it may also include some of the major referents and events that constitute the narrative's plot. At any particular time during the production of a narrative, there is a chunk of semiactive information that is considerably larger in scope than any piece of information that is fully active. Furthermore, a chunk of semiactive information remains in that state for a significantly longer period of time than any piece of information remains in the active state.

At certain points in a narrative, however, a speaker will replace one major chunk of semiactive information with another. Now, whereas a narrator may move easily from one idea unit to the next as long as these idea units can be activated within the same semiactive chunk, narratives provide evidence that it is cognitively more costly to change scenes—to exchange one chunk of semiactivated information for another. Evidence for this cognitive difficulty comes from the extra time and verbal fumbling that may accompany such a change.

The pear stories provide many examples of the pausing and fumbling that take place when there is a change of location, time, characters, and/or events. In the following excerpt, the lengths of pauses longer than one tenth of a second are indicated in parentheses (taken from Chafe, 1985, p. 83):

59. . . And he pulls the (.8) tsk goat by the guy who's up in the tree,
60. (.9) and disappears.
61. (.9) A—nd (2.9) the next people . . who come by,
62. (.9) and there's a little boy on a bicycle:
63. . . who comes by from the other direction,

At the beginning of 61, if we regard the word "a—nd" as a pause filler, there is a total of 4.35 seconds of hesitating before the words *the next people.* Even that phrase turns out to be a kind of mistake, because there was really only one person who came by, as is finally clarified in 62. Thus the entire intonation unit 61 is really a disfluency that is eventually set straight in 62 and 63.

The most obvious change in the content at this point is the introduction of a new and important character, one who is to become the protagonist of the story from now on. But there is also a change of location, realized in the film by a change of scene and in the narrative by the words *from the other direction*. There is a major shift in the event structure as well. The narrator had just finished with some minor events involving a goat, and is now about to embark on a series of events leading up to a theft of pears, one of the pivotal incidents in the film. It is clear that between 60 and 62 the speaker replaced one major cluster of semiactive information with another, and quite evidently this replacement was both a time-consuming and a somewhat confusing cognitive operation.

The boundary between one chunk of semiactive material and another may be manifested in other ways, as is well illustrated by the following sequence in the hiking narrative:

20. . . Cause it's beautiful up there,
21. but it is . . pretty high,
[22. Mhm,]
23. . . . . The last time . . I was there,

Lines 20 and 21 show a decrescendo, with the level of volume decreasing to pianissimo by the end of 21. One hears, in fact, that the speaker has exhausted the content of a chunk of semiactive information. Line 21, in other words, sounds like the end of a paragraph. There is experimental evidence that people are able to recognize paragraph boundaries (that is, major changes in orientation) from prosodic information alone (Lehiste, 1979), on the basis of such clues as declining volume and tempo. Such a boundary at the end of 21 seems to have been recognized by another party to this conversation, who inserted the back channel sound *mhm* at just this point. The narrator then entered a new chunk of semiactive information in 23 with a marked increase in volume and tempo. Here she reestablished the location and established a new time, as well as new characters and events. Just as 21 sounds like the end of an old paragraph, 23 sounds like the beginning of a new one.

CONCLUSION

I suggested a variety of ways in which the study of narratives can help us understand the workings of the mind. Most important of all, I think, is the observation that different people may supply very different narratives of a physically identical input. We can take this as evidence that the mind is not a device that makes a faithful recording of what goes on in the world around it, but that it is rather designed to create its own models of that world. Second, although the mind possesses schemas that help it in this model-building activity, it is at the same time especially well equipped to react to inputs that conflict with its schematic expectations. Without such inputs it enters a state of boredom; with them it enters a state of excitement that prepares it to reject the sources of disturbance. Hence, the only successful narratives are those that provide a conflict with expectations.

I pointed out that narratives exhibit a segmentation into intonation units that can be interpreted as the verbal expressions of idea units. In any particular idea unit, its referents and other components may be assumed by the speaker to have been already active, previously semiactive, or previously inactive in the mind of the audience. These different properties of referents have a clear effect on the way they are verbalized—lexically, syntactically, and intonationally. There is, furthermore, an interesting constraint on the generation of idea units. An idea unit cannot contain more than one previously inactive concept, a constraint that suggests that the mind is able to activate only one new concept at a time.

Finally, narratives give evidence that the mind has a need for orientation in terms of space, time, social context, and ongoing events. Hence the frequent provision of settings, not only at the beginnings of narratives, but at whatever points the orientation may change. When such changes take place, and when there is a replacement of one major chunk of semiactive information with another, speakers exhibit a hesitating and a fumbling that suggest cognitive difficulty. Such change points are also manifested in changes in volume and tempo as the speaker exhausts the content of one semiactive chunk and enters into another.

These are surely not the only things that narratives can tell us about the mind and its activities, but I hope that they have at least been suggestive of ways in which narratives can serve as important sources of insight into the mental processes of those who produce them.

REFERENCES

Chafe, W. (1977). The recall and verbalization of past experience. In R. W. Cole (Ed.), *Current issues in linguistic theory* (pp. 215–246). Bloomington, IN: Indiana University Press.

Chafe, W. (1980). The deployment of consciousness in the production of a narrative. In W. Chafe (Ed.), *The pear stories: Cognitive, cultural, and linguistic aspects of narrative production* (pp. 9–50). Norwood, NJ: Ablex.

Chafe, W. (1985). Some reasons for hesitating. In D. Tannen & M. Saville-Troike (Eds.), *Perspectives on silence* (pp. 77–89). Norwood, NJ: Ablex.

Chafe, W. (1987). Cognitive constraints on information flow. In R. Tomlin (Ed.), *Coherence and grounding in discourse* (pp. 21–51). Amsterdam: John Benjamins.

Labov, W. (1972). *Language in the inner city.* Philadelphia: University of Pennsylvania Press.

Lehiste, I. (1979). Sentence boundaries and paragraph boundaries—perceptual evidence. In P. R. Clyne, W. F. Hanks, & C. L. Hofbauer (Eds.), *The elements: A parasession on linguistic units and levels* (pp. 99–109). Chicago: Chicago Linguistic Society.

Miller, G. A. (1956). The magical number seven, plus or minus two: Some limits on our capacity for processing information. *Psychological Review, 63,* 81–97.

Schank, R., & Abelson, R. (1977). *Scripts, plans, goals, and understanding.* Hillsdale, NJ: Lawrence Erlbaum Associates.

Tannen, D. (1980). A comparative analysis of oral narrative strategies: Athenian Greek and American English. In W. Chafe (Ed.), *The pear stories: Cognitive, cultural, and linguistic aspects of narrative production* (pp. 51–87). Norwood, NJ: Ablex.

3

Thinking About Narrative

David R. Olson
Ontario Institute for Studies in Education

In conjoining narrative and thought we take a bold initiative. In the classical tradition, dominant in our literate society, narrative is taken as the antithesis of thought. Narrative is a natural, unreflective, uncritical form of discourse that is the opposite of more reflective forms of discourse such as history or philosophy. At the hands of the classical Greeks, for example, the oral narrative tradition was attacked and set aside as poetic and fanciful. In its place Plato erected logical argument and prosaic discourse, which were taken to be the linguistic forms appropriate for systematic, reflective thought. These latter have continued to dominate our conceptions of thinking to this day.

One finds changes analogous to those which occurred in classical Greece in the history of Western Europe. Kittay and Godzich (1987) discussed the emergence of prose discourse in 12th-century France. Prior to that time, important discourse was versified. They pointed out how, during that period, verse came to be seen as a form of adornment that lacked the directness of prose. They then discussed what is distinctive about prose, suggesting with Boaz (1925) that the special feature of prose is that it is written to be read, rather than listened to. Earlier, Hamilton (1978) wrote about the two harmonies, now both written forms, that 17th-century writers and speakers had to choose between, namely, verse and prose. We now think of Alexander Pope's *Essay on Criticism*, written in 1711, as decidedly odd in that it developed a prosaic theme, namely, an analysis of poetry, but it did so through the use of verse. Within a century, however, verse had become aesthetic, whereas the burden of rationality fell, progressively, on written prose.

John Dewey (1933), in his characteristically illuminating book *How We think*, advanced an account of thinking and indicated the form of thinking that is worthy of attention by the schools. He referred to it as *reflective thinking* and characterized it in terms of problems, hypotheses, observations, inferences, and conclusions, the epistemological concepts we identify with systematic, scientific thought. In theories advanced under the name of *cognitive science*, thinking is identified with inference and rules of inference; in such discourse there is no reference to narrative or to narrative thought. This was true as long as literacy was identified with rationality.

In the past two decades the oral tradition, and in particular, oral narratives have come to be seen as a form of discourse not inferior to that characteristic of a literate tradition but rather as embodying a distinctive form of language and thought. Havelock (1976, 1982) can be given much of the credit for showing that the Homeric Greeks, who passed on their traditions through oral means, primarily the oral epic poems the *Iliad* and the *Odyssey*, were an advanced civilization with specialized use of language related to a distinctive mode of thought. Although radically different from the literate tradition with which we are more familiar, the oral tradition, too, embodies systematic means for the evolution and transmission of culture.

More recently, Bruner (1985) contrasted two distinctive modes of thought, *narrative* and *paradigmatic*, which characterize individuals quite independently of literacy or of a literate tradition. Some individuals have access to both modes of thought whereas others, for example, historians as opposed to philosophers, may specialize in one or the other. My concern is with the relations between modes of discourse and forms of thought and, in particular, the ways that literacy may interact with those modes of discourse and, consequently, with forms of thought.

Writers such as Havelock and Bruner have helped to revive the notion that our identification of thought with the analytic, logical prose preferred by the classical Greeks was shortsighted. Rationality is too important to be identified with a single technology. How then do forms of discourse relate to modes of thought?

Narrative structures provide a format into which experienced events can be cast in the attempt to make them comprehensible, memorable, and shareable. Such structures are perhaps the most common, if not universal, means of structuring series of events. They are no less common and important in a literate tradition than they are in an oral tradition, even if they may take a somewhat different form in the two cases.

The differences between oral and literate narratives arise from the fact that narratives are not a simple reflection of the events themselves. They are a construction, a linguistic artifice. The properties of narratives are imposed on events to make them comprehensible and memorable. Thus, the seeing of events as a narrative involves the creative and inventive activity of the storyteller. Both oral and written narratives appear to share some properties including notions of beginnings, middle, ends, the separation of the event structure from the narrative structure, and the particular stance of the narrator to the story (see Brewer, 1985; Bruner, 1985; Propp, 1968). The skillful use of these forms constitutes an important form of thought. Narratives, oral or written, represent events in comprehensible form and thereby make those events into objects of consciousness, reflection, and analysis.

There is nothing natural about narrative; it is a linguistic form analogous to rhyme. Narrative form, when applied to experienced or imagined events, creates a story. These stories are constructed and interpretive in nature, memorable, functional, and entertaining. Good narratives are all four. They serve their archival functions only if they are remembered; they serve their interpretive functions only if the forms are generalizable and applicable. Narratives, then, can be seen not only as devices for storing information for re-use but also as forms of thought—devices for interpreting experience and informing action. How do oral and written narratives serve these functions?

Havelock (1982) examined the forms of the oral Homeric narratives to determine how they serve their intellectual and cultural purposes. The Homeric Greeks' use of language and their form of thought derived from the need to preserve a record of their traditions in a period of wholly oral communication. In the absence of writing, information could be preserved only in the memories of living human beings. To be memorable, Havelock (1982) argued, "the epic 'syntax' . . . is not only essentially narrative in character, . . . it] reports all information in the form of concrete and particular events which happen in sequence, not as propositions which depend on each other in logical connection" (p. 226). Further, "The gods of Homer and Hesiod [are] a necessary ingredient in the vocabulary of oral description and orally preserved record" (p. 227). The oral Homeric tradition involved "a panorama of happenings not a statement of principles" (p. 223). These properties of oral narrative derive from the fact that, as mentioned, if they are to serve social functions, they must be memorable.

How does literacy alter this picture? Narrative creates stories that can be retold and to some extent become the objects of further stories. Such talk would be indicated in the metalanguage available for talking about those oral stories. Just what the form of that metadiscourse is, remains a matter of some discussion, my impression being that the metalanguage for oral stories will focus on the content rather than the form; the form is what is preserved in writing and hence attracts a new, or at least elaborated metalanguage.

Writing serves to fix a text; the text then becomes the content for *commentary*. Texts fixed by writing, at least in an appropriate cultural context, become the subject of interpretation, analysis, reflection, and criticism. Writing is usually judged important because of its mnemonic and archival uses: I suggest that it is important for the commentary it generates.

Writers such as Havelock (1982) and Ong (1982) pointed out that when writing began to serve the memory function, mind could be redeployed to carry out more analytic activities such as examining contradictions and deriving logical implications. It is the visible artifact which, as they saw, was to release the mind from its burden on memory and free it up for analytic, logical thought. Just how quickly this transformation took place is a matter of some dispute. Writers such as Morrison (1987) and Saenger (1982) argued that the transformation was not complete until the 10th or 12th century. Nonetheless, literacy, particularly literacy in an alphabetic script, appears to have contributed to the development of a specialized, analytic form of discourse and a corresponding mode of thought.

Although these theories are correct in pointing to the distinctive properties of writing as a representational medium for culture and cognition—its permanence through time and across space, its invariance, its explicitness—they uniformly overlook the problem that literacy created. Whereas writing solved the problem of information storage, it created what I call the meaning or interpretation problem. Although writing preserves the very words of a text, it does not preserve the meaning. The text has to be interpreted. It is the progressive solutions to the interpretation problem that have been so important to the conceptual shifts that are associated with literacy.

The problem of interpretation arises when there is a perceived gap between the text and its interpretation. In an oral tradition, the jongleur or reciter/performer (see Kittay & Godzich, 1987), is both preserver, transmitter, and interpreter of the text. Interpretation in such an oral tradition is not essentially different from asking what a speaker means in conversational discourse. With writing, the text, author and interpreter roles come apart. It is here, I suggest, that the interpretation problem becomes critical.

Consider an example drawn from Stock's (1983) discussion of interpretation. In the Christian Bible, we read that Jesus took some bread and, eating it, said "This is my body." His followers found that utterance completely comprehensible and memorable and used it as a model for the ritual of the Mass. But when the narrative including that utterance was written down, it became an object that could be read by diverse readers who saw the utterance in different ways; the text became the object of interpretation. Just exactly what did the utterance mean: Did it literally mean that the bread became flesh? Did it mean it was similar to flesh? Did it mean the bread was a reminder of the body? Or all of these? Such considerations led to the theory of interpretation attributed to Cassian in the 4th century:

> The letter shows us what God and our fathers did;
> The allegory shows us where our faith is hid;
> The moral meaning gives us rules of daily life;
> The analogy shows us where we end our strife.
>
> (Ozment, 1980, p. 66)

These interpretive assumptions prevailed until the Reformation. Luther reduced the traditional four senses of Scripture to two. His technical vocabulary and the categories of theology shifted considerably from 1509 to 1521, but they settled into the notion of *one historical meaning*, which he came to contrast with the interpretations, that is, the traditions, of the church. For Luther, the scripture said what it meant. It required not interpretation but reading. A firm line was drawn between what was in the text and what were taken to be interpolations, accretions, and distortions that were added to the text. This line demarked the text as the objectively given, which could then be distinguished from the subjectively interpreted, what the text says relative to what the reader brings to the text. We now know that the problem of distinguishing between what is given by a text and what is contributed by the reader is not a simple, perhaps even soluble, one. The point is that people dealing with these texts took it to be a clear and useful distinction.

These historical remarks illustrate how the fixing of a text through writing (although there are other ways to fix a text) makes that text the object of interpretation and reinterpretation. These interpretive activities require the development of concepts, marked in a metalanguage, for talking and thinking about language and meaning.

Texts can also serve as models for the world and for human action. Stock (1986) described the formation, in the Middle Ages, of what he called "textual communities" in which groups of people, organized around a text and an interpreter, saw themselves, not only as believers, but as living lives according to a script. That script could be used as a standard against which to judge their lives as good or evil. In such a case, it is not merely that stories could be created to represent events in one's life, but rather that one could try to live one's life in terms of the written text.

A final legacy of texts is that texts, including narrative ones, come to be seen as existing in nature quite separate from the storytelling practices of the culture. The world comes to be seen as being composed of texts. Mink (1978) discussed the notion of "universal history," the view that "the past actually is an untold story and that there is a right way to tell it" (p. 143). The historian is seen as simply telling the story rather than inventing the story. Mink argued that this is a mistake; the historian invents the story; narrative provides a form for interpreting and reinterpreting the past. Yet the notion that there is an untold story present in the events themselves comes from the assumption that the world has the properties of a fixed text, written once for all time.

TEXTS AS OBJECTS OF THOUGHT:
FROM DISCOURSE TO METADISCOURSE

We have seen how narrative serves as a formula or framework into which events can be cast to make them comprehensible, memorable, and communicable. That is the primary way in which narrative serves thought. All cultures, it appears, construct narratives, pass them on, and interpret them. But these narratives take a somewhat different form when they are to serve as cultural archival resources. In an oral culture, they get transformed into versified narratives— "a panorama of happenings not a platform of principles" (Havelock, 1982, p. 223), whereas in a literate culture they get transformed into narrative prose. To the cultures familiar with these forms of discourse, whether verse or prose, the familiar form of discourse seems to be "a natural, naked way of speaking" as Sprat, historian of the Royal Society wrote (1966/1677, p. 56). But they involve distinct forms of thought, notwithstanding their transparency.

But I take the argument one step further. These forms of discourse involve, indeed require, different forms of metalanguage. Leech (1983), pointed out that every language involves a metalanguage. Different forms of discourse, however, require distinctive metalanguages. The metalanguage specialized for talk about prosaic discourse is a metalanguage about texts, their meanings, their authors' meanings, and their readers' interpretations. Notions of synonomy, paraphrase, sameness of meaning, and possible interpretations become central. As mentioned earlier, written text preserves form, not meaning, and the meaning must be reconstructed by the reader. As part of an oral tradition, a reader may be instructed as to how to read a text; the written text then simply becomes a mnemonic for what was taught orally. For a reader who is not taught how to read or interpret a text, or if, like Luther, a reader comes to doubt the validity of the teaching, the meaning of the text must be constructed from the text itself. This is what allows issues of interpretation to become paramount and a metalanguage specialized for issues of meaning to evolve.

The concepts that are developed for commentary on prosaic text are useful for the sort of reflective thinking we call critical thinking. In the remainder of this chapter I discuss briefly the history of these metalinguistic concepts and then turn to some studies of children's acquisition of this set of concepts and their implications for thinking.

THE DEVELOPMENT OF METADISCOURSE CONCEPTS

The issue of what is given, that is fixed in the world, arose first in connection with what is in a text. In ordinary experience, everything is changing—buds turn into flowers, which turn into seed pods, which turn into new plants, which produce more buds, and so on. There is little room for giveness here. A text, on the other hand, may be consulted repeatedly and through time yielding the same reading every time. But of course they are read, that is, interpreted differently by different readers at each time. Recall our discussion of Jesus' statement, "This is my body." A text is taken as invariant across readings, or we may say, invariant across interpretations. A text provides a prototypical notion of the given.

But if texts provide a given, where do all of those other ideas that a reader arrives at come from? Historically there were two solutions. They too were in the text, (the Medieval view), or they were contributed by the reader (the modern view). The contributions made by the reader gave a new sense to the role of the mind of the reader in understanding texts and understanding the world. Thus Francis Bacon, a spokesman for the 17th-century attitude to texts and to nature, could say: "God forbid that we should give out a dream of the imagination for a pattern in the world" (1620/1965, p. 323). For Bacon, as for Luther, some structure was in the world and some was in the imagination of the reader or viewer. The important point for Reformation theology was to discern what was in Scripture from what was the creation or contribution of the reader, just as in early modern science the important point was to discern what was given in nature from what was a "dream of the imagination." This was the root of the text/interpretation distinction and the beginning of the observation/inference distinction. It is also, of course, the basis of the objective/subjective distinction that was to be so central in the writings of Immanuel Kant.

CHILDREN'S ACQUISITION OF METADISCOURSE CONCEPTS

If these concepts, marked in a metalanguage, are not only devices for textual and scientific analysis but also important concepts for thinking, then we should see that children's understandings of themselves, texts, and the world develop as they sort out these conceptual distinctions. Indeed, they should develop in parallel.

In our research my colleague Nancy Torrance and I have attempted to examine children's understanding of the relations between a written text, its meaning, and its interpretations. The text/interpretation distinction is important to critical reading, reflective writing, and to literate discourse generally.

Although our understanding of the development of the say/mean distinction is far from complete, it seems clear that when children are 6 or 7 years of age they begin to acknowledge that a single utterance may generate more than one interpretation. Thus, we have observed that if, in a story context, 7- or 8-year-old children encounter a referentially ambiguous sentence such as "Bring me my red shoes," they come to acknowledge that it could refer to either of two pairs of red shoes, even if it is clear from the context that the speaker intended it to refer to only one of those pairs. They, therefore, come to acknowledge that a failure in understanding could be the result of misinterpretation rather than, for example, not listening or bad luck (Olson, 1977; Robinson, Goelman, & Olson, 1983).

At an earlier age, children believe that if the speaker intended to say "Bring the new red shoes" when she said "Bring the red shoes," (a) she told which red shoes to bring, (b) she said "the new red shoes," and (c) any failure on the part of the listener must be a failure to listen or remember. Indeed, when asked for the exact words the speaker said, children at this age continue to report what she meant to say rather than what she actually said. We infer from such findings that they have a limited understanding of the expression/intention relation (Torrance & Olson, 1987).

Other researchers reported similar effects with young children. Robinson and Robinson (1977) and Robinson, Goelman, and Olson (1983) attributed the difficulty to children's failure to distinguish the message from the speaker's intentions. Beal and Flavell (1984), Bonitatibus and Flavell (1985), and Bonitatibus (1988) related it to a failure in metacognition, roughly, a lack of awareness of what children know, and Flavell (1986, 1988) attributed it to the difficulty children have in assigning two representations to the same event. All agreed that preschool children fail to recognize that a single utterance may be interpreted in more than one way. Moreover, such children appear to assume an identity between the meaning of the utterance and the meaning of the speaker. Hence, in attempting to report what was said, they report what the speaker meant.

Other studies indicate some of the variables that affect this conflation. Hedelin and Hjelmquist (1986) reported that if preschool children are told to repeat a message to another person, they will make direct quotations and reject offered paraphrases. Similarly, if they do not know the speaker's intention, they are more likely to notice an ambiguity of what was said than if they do know that intention (Beal & Flavell, 1984). Because most text is readily comprehensible, most understanding tends to be dominated (quite appropriately) by the putative meaning rather than its form. Only when these two are put into conflict is it clear that children do not hold the utterance or wording as invariant and independent of its interpretations.

The course of development of children's notions of a text and its interpretation is not known, although important work has been done on their knowledge of genre (see Applebee, 1978; Britton, 1970; Stein & Trabasso, 1981). Indeed, what a text and its interpretation are is a complex question. Texts can be read without interpretation; that is what we usually refer to as *decoding*. A traditional assumption is that there is a fixed order—first reading (a fixed text) and then interpreting it. Traditional (and unsatisfactory) theories of reading also assume a fixed order of instruction—first decoding, then understanding. Yet modern theories of literary criticism (Bleich, 1978; Fish, 1980) deny that there is any real distinction; all reading involves interpretation. Modern cognitive psychology makes the same point about reading (Goelman, Oberg, & Smith, 1984; Spiro, Bruce, & Brewer, 1980); reading is largely a matter of making sense or interpreting. It is tempting, therefore, to simply identify reading, understanding, comprehending, and interpreting.

One way to reconcile these different views is to distinguish the cognitive activities involved in reading and interpreting oral and written language from the child's conceptions of those processes. The former, the cognitive processes, may, indeed, be relatively similar for reading and interpreting. The concepts, however, are responsible for children's awareness and understanding of those processes, an understanding that may be relevant to such metalinguistic judgments as that of ambiguity, interpretation, and misinterpretation. Children's understanding of the relation between a text and its interpretation progresses through three stages. These stages map more or less directly onto the notion of invariance of text. We may distinguish three levels of invariance of text corresponding to three levels of interpretation.

1. At first level, children take a text to be invariant if it generates the same interpretation; this is text as intentional structure. Interpretation is simply grasping that intentional structure.

2. At the next level, children take a text to be invariant if it expresses the same meaning. This is text as literal meaning. Interpretation is comprehension or understanding of the meaning of text; the text is assumed to have one meaning, one interpretation.

3. At the third level, children, although we suspect it is primarily adults who take this stance, take a text to be what is invariant across the interpretations or construals it allows. This is text as semantic structure. Interpretation is a matter of exploring and grasping those possible meanings.

At the first level, texts, meanings, and interpretations are synonymous; a story told in different words would be the same text (thus straining normal usage). The youngest children's responses to our say/mean task exemplify this stance. At the second level, children become extremely literal-minded; meaning is in the text and any interpretations arrived at are assumed to be present in the text. Anything else would be regarded as misinterpretation. Only at the third level would children perform essentially as literate adults recognizing the possibility of ambiguity and multiple interpretations of fixed texts.

Where, then, do children get these notions? They get them from talking about the texts they encounter. The concepts involved are used by parents and teachers in reading and interpreting texts. They are called into play every time a parent or teacher asks a question such as "What does he mean?" "Why did he say that?" "What did her mother think she meant?" and the like.

In some recent studies, Janet Astington and I (Olson & Astington, 1989) explored older students' knowledge of metalinguistic and metadiscourse notions, notions that are used for talking about expressions, intentions, and interpretations. These notions are embodied in a group of speech act and mental state terms including *state, claim, deny, concede* on one hand and *assume, infer, hypothesize, remember* on the other.

To this end we constructed a multiple-choice test describing events and utterances of children and adults that concluded by one speaker claiming, denying, conceding, or the like some point made by the other speaker. Children were required to select the most important speech act or mental state word in that context.

The general finding is, not unexpectedly, that competence on the task increases significantly with age. Considering all subjects, the majority of the 12-year-olds performed at, or not much above, chance level, whereas most senior high school students were correct for most items.

For such verbs as *concede* and *interpret* the percentage of students answering correctly went from about 25% for 12-year-olds to about 95% for university students. For some items, such as that involving *remember*, the difficulty primarily depended on the difficulty of the distracting alternatives. For other items, such as that involving the term *hypothesize*, children incorrectly selected that verb because the subject matter was science. But overall, the findings confirm our hypothesis that these concepts are primarily schooled or literate concepts useful for talking about prosaic texts. Hence, they are more familiar to some children than to others, and they are used in some domains than in others.

But these concepts are useful not only for thinking about texts. They are equally important for thinking about nature and about the self. Distinctions between what is given and what is created or imagined, what is in a text and what is an interpretation, what is observed in nature and what is inferred by the mind, although they are not absolute categories, are critical constituents of modern thought. In this way a form of discourse contributes to the formation of a mode of thought.

ACKNOWLEDGMENT

I am grateful to Denese Coulbeck for editorial and bibliographic assistance.

REFERENCES

Applebee, A. (1978). *The child's conception of story: Ages two to seventeen.* Chicago: The University of Chicago Press.

Bacon, F. (1965). The great instauration. M. S. Warhart (Ed.), *Francis Bacon: A selection of his works.* Toronto: Macmillan of Canada. (Originally published in 1620)

Beal, C., & Flavell, J. (1984). Development of the ability to distinguish communicative intention and literal message meaning. *Child Development 55*(3), 920–928.

Bleich, D. (1978). *Subjective criticism.* Baltimore, MD: Johns Hopkins University Press.

Boaz, E. (1925). Stylistic aspects of primitive literature. *Journal of American Folklore, 38,* 329–339).

Bonitatibus, G. (in press). What is said and what is meant in referential communication. In J. W. Astington, P. L. Harris, & D. R. Olson (Eds.), *Developing theories of mind* (pp. 326–340). Cambridge, England: Cambridge University Press.

Bonitatibus, G., & Flavell, J. (1985). Effect of presenting a message in written form on young children's ability to evaluate its communicative adequacy. *Developmental Psychology, 21*(3), 455—461.

Brewer, W. (1985). The story schema: Universal and culture-specific properties. In D. Olson, N. Torrance, & A. Hildyard (Eds.), *Literacy, language, and learning: The nature and consequences of reading and writing* (pp. 167–194). Cambridge, England: Cambridge University Press.

Britton, J. (1970). *Language and learning.* London: Allen Lane/The Penguin Press.

Bruner, J. (1985). *Actual minds, possible worlds.* Cambridge, MA: Harvard University Press.

Dewey, J. (1933). *How we think.* New York: D.C. Heath.

Fish, S. (1980). *Is there a text in this class? The authority of interpretive communities.* Cambridge, MA: Harvard University Press.

Flavell, J. (1986). The development of children's knowledge about the appearance reality distinction. *American Psychologist, 41,* 418–425.

Flavell, J. (1988). The development of children's knowledge about the mind: From cognitive connections to mental representations. In J. W. Astington, P. L. Harris, & D. R. Olson (Eds.), *Developing theories of mind* (pp. 244–267). Cambridge, England: Cambridge University Press.

Goelman, H., Oberg, A., & Smith, F. (Eds.). (1984). *Awakening to literacy.* London, England: Heinemann.

Hamilton, K. (1978). *The two harmonies: Poetry and prose in the 17th century.* Westport, CT: Greenwood Press.

Havelock, E. (1976). *Origins of western literacy.* Toronto: OISE Press.

Havelock, E. (1982). *The literate revolution in Greece and its cultural consequences.* Princeton, NJ: Princeton University Press.

Hedelin, L., & Hjelmquist, E. (1986). *Preschool mastery of the form/content distinction in communicative tasks* (Mimeo). Department of Psychology, Göteborg, Sweden.

Kittay, J., & Godzich, W. (1987). *The emergence of prose: An essay in prosaics.* Minneapolis, MN: University of Minnesota Press.

Leech, G. N. (1983). *Principles of pragmatics.* London: Longmans.

Mink, L. (1978). Narrative form as a cognitive instrument. In R. Canary & H. Kozicki (Eds.), *The writing of history: Literary form and historical understanding* (pp. 129–149). Madison, WI: University of Wisconsin Press.

Morrison, K. (1987). Stabilizing the text: The institutionalization of knowledge in historical and philosophical forms of argument. *The Canadian Journal of Sociology, 12*(3), 242–274.

Olson, D. (1977). From utterance to text: The bias of language in speech and writing. *Harvard Educational Review, 47*(3), 257–281.

Olson, D., & Astington, J. (in press). Talking about text: How literacy contributes to thought. *Journal of Pragmatics.*

Ong, W. (1982). *Orality and literacy: The technologizing of the word.* London: Methuen.

Ozment (1980). *The age of reform 1250–1550: An intellectual and religious history of late Medieval and Reformation Europe.* New Haven, CT: Yale University Press.

Propp, V. (1968). *Morphology of the folktale.* Austin, TX: University of Texas Press.

Robinson, E., Goelman, H., & Olson, D. (1983). Children's understanding of the relation between expressions (what was said) and intentions (what was meant). *British Journal of Development Psychology, 1,* 75–86.

Robinson, E., & Robinson, W. (1977). Children's explanations of communication failure and the inadequacy of the misunderstood message. *Developmental Psychology, 13*(2), 151–161.

Saenger, D. (1982). Silent reading: Its impact on late medieval script and society. *Viator, 13,* 367–414.

Spiro, R., Bruce, B., & Brewer, W. (Eds.). (1980). *Theoretical issues in reading comprehension: Perspectives from cognitive psychology, linguistics, artificial intelligence, and education.* Hillsdale, NJ: Lawrence Erlbaum Associates.

Sprat, T. (1966). *History of the Royal Society of London for the improving of natural knowledge* (J. I. Cope & H. W. Jones, Eds.). St. Louis: Washington University Press. (Originally published in 1667)

Stein, N. L., & Trabasso, T. (1981). What's in a story: Critical issues in story comprehension. In R. Glaser (Ed.), *Advances in the psychology of instruction* (pp. 213–267). Hillsdale, NJ: Lawrence Erlbaum Associates.

Stock, B. (1983). *The implications of literacy.* Princeton, NJ: Princeton University Press.

Stock, B. (1986). Texts, readers, and enacted narratives. *Visible Language, 20*(3), 294–301.

Torrance, N., & Olson, D. (1987). Development of the metalanguage and the acquisition of literacy: A progress report. *Interchange, 18*(1/2), 136–146.

4

The Joint Construction of Stories by Preschool Children and an Experimenter

A. D. Pellegrini
Lee Galda
University of Georgia

Developmental and educational psychologists have a long history of using the adult–child interactional context as a crucible for studying children's development and learning (Bronfenbrenner, 1979). Relations between parents' interaction patterns (e.g., parents' language teaching styles) and measures of children's development were described in early studies in this area (e.g., Hess & Shipman, 1965). More recently, researchers have recognized that children and adults influence each other during interaction (e.g., Bell, 1979). This transactional orientation had replaced the earlier unidirectional model (i.e., parent affecting child) because it seems to more accurately describe the interpersonal dynamics of adult–child interaction.

In an effort to further describe the dynamics of adult–child interaction, a group of researchers (e.g., Rommetveit, 1979; Wertsch, 1976, 1985) has noted that adults and children frequently do not share the same definition of an interactional situation; that is, intersubjectivity between interlocuters does not exist. Adult definitions of situations are usually specifically stated in the instructions given to children; for example, "Tell a story about this picture." Children's definitions of the same specified situation often differ, despite the adult instructions; for example, children may interpret instructions to tell stories as instructions to describe the picture (Pellegrini,

113

Galda, & Rubin, 1984). This lack of intersubjectivity between an adult and children became clear to us in our analyses of experimental protocols wherein a well-trained experimenter asked preschoolers to tell stories about different props (Pellegrini & Galda, 1988). In listening to the taped sessions, it became very clear that the experimenter used different elicitation techniques with different children, and the use of elicitation strategies seemed to change within individual sessions.

The first objective of the present study was to describe the different verbal interaction styles used by this experimenter in establishing intersubjectivity with young children in experimental storytelling contexts. Our analyses were guided by Wertsch's (1985) discussion of the negotiation of intersubjectivity between an adult and a child in the zone of proximal development. Wertsch (1979) suggested that adult–child interactions progress through four distinct levels in the negotiation of intersubjectivity, or a common situation definition. These levels reflect the extent to which adults transfer responsibility for task completion from themselves to the children. Initially, the adult takes most of the responsibility for task completion; adults use low-demand, high-direction strategies. As intersubjectivity is established, children assume more responsibility for task completion; adults use higher demand and less directive strategies. To examine the patterns by which experimenter–child intersubjectivity was established, we categorized the experimenter's functional uses of language with factor analysis. We expected the specified four factors to reflect the movement away from adult task responsibility to child task responsibility. In short, our analyses tested the generalizability of Wertsch's four-level model. Further, we also analyzed the probability of this four-level model progressing in its specified sequence (Bakeman & Gottman, 1986). Whereas the factor analyses provide macro-level category definitions, the sequential analyses provide microgenetic information.

We chose to examine the functional language of one specific experimenter interacting with many different children in two different storytelling contexts for a number of reasons. First, examination of an adult's functional uses of language with children is an interesting way of understanding the ways in which children move toward independent functioning (Wertsch, 1985). Second, the examination of a specific experimenter's language was interesting to us so that we could describe the process by which an objective experimenter and children came to jointly define a task according to the prespecified definition. We assumed, following Wertsch (1985), that children and adults do not initially share a common task definition. For example, when a child is asked "Tell me a story about these things," he or she may describe or label the stimulus materials. The experimenter, then, tries to establish mutual definition by joint interaction; for example, "Yes, these are pill bottles. Tell me a story that has pill bottles in it." These analyses, then, should provide interesting insight into the interpersonal dynamics of the experimenter–child relationship.

Such descriptions of the establishment of experimenter–subject intersubjectively are also important because the amount of experimenter guidance provided is an important indicator of children's task competence (Brown, Bransford, Ferrera, & Campione, 1983; Pellegrini, Brody, & Sigel, 1985). Adults, generally, provide more guidance and support, or scaffolding, to use Bruner's (1975) term, with less competent children than with more competent children.

The second objective of the study was to examine variation in the functional language factors due to children's age, gender, task ability, and tast context. The effect of child variables (age, gender, and storytelling ability) on adult–child interaction is part of our transactional orientation, which states that interlocutors affect each other. Previous work (e.g., Wertsch, 1985) examined the effects of one child variable, age, on the establishment of intersubjectivity and found that adults assume less task responsibility as a function of children's age. However, children's ability in a task, for example, the ability to produce a story, also should also affect adult language. Indeed, the storytelling ability effect should be similar to the age effect in that the adult should assume more responsibility with less able and/or younger children.

The other child variable, gender, is interesting to the extent that it interacts with the different experimental storytelling contexts. In the present study, our two experimental contexts were having children tell stories about blocks and styrofoam shapes and doctor props. These props tend to be male and female preferred, respectively, by preschoolers (Rubin, Fein, & Vandenberg, 1983). As a result, boys should exhibit more competence in the functionally ambiguous blocks context than in the functionally explicit doctor props context, and girls should exhibit more competence in the explicit context than in the ambiguous context. As such, adults should assume less task responsibility for children in their preferred contexts.

Context comparisons are also interesting in their own right. Previous research has shown that preschool children have a more difficult time constructing story-like play episodes with functionally ambiguous props, like blocks, than with functionally explicit props, like doctors kits (Pellegrini, 1985). As such, we would expect less intersubjectivity in the ambiguous than in the explicit context.

Our story production tasks extend the previous, and very limited, literature on the social construction of narratives. Previous work has examined the interaction between adults and children in retelling, not producing, a story (McNamee, 1979). We are less concerned with the mental processes that typify retelling tasks (i.e., remembering and reproducing stories) than with the processes by which new narratives are constructed. Our approach should provide insight into the development of children's narrative competence.

The third objective of the study was concerned with the instructional aspect of the zone of proximal development. We were interested in the adult strategies that most effectively enabled children to generate independent stories. Following the notion of the zone of proximal development, we were concerned with the transfer of task responsibility from adult to child (Vygotsky, 1978). A measure of children's independent functioning in the present study was the number of consecutive story events they were able to produce without adult intervention. The zone of proximal development predicts that adults adjust their interaction style as a function of children's competence in a task. For this reason, we examined the adult interaction variables that were the best predictors of high-ability and low-ability children's sustained event production. Ability was defined in terms of children's storytelling (i.e., length of stories told). The model predicts that more demanding, less supportive strategies (e.g., evaluations) will be used with the more able children and less demanding, more supportive strategies (e.g., story slots) will be used with less able children (Pellegrini et al., 1985). Our analyzes, however, identify not only the most effective predictors of children's independent storytelling, but also describe the sequence in which these strategies were used. That is, we first conduct a series of stepwise multiple regression analyses to identify significant predictors; then we conduct sequential lag analyses (Bakeman & Gottman, 1986) using the significant predictors to determine the sequence in which these predictors were used.

The sequential analyses are important for both theoretical and applied perspectives. From a theoretical point of view these analyses help us to better understand the stream of behavior in adult–child interaction. For example, do certain adults (such as experimenters) treat interaction sessions as pedagogical events by initially using high-demand strategies (so children can exhibit their levels of competence) and then moving to low-demand strategies if children do not understand the high-demand strategies? On the other hand, adults may treat interaction sessions as informal dialogue sessions and, consequently, use a series of low-demand strategies.

Sequential analyses are also interesting from an applied, educational perspective. Knowing that certain interaction strategies effectively predict children's performance and the sequence in which they occur is necessary for effective pedagogy. For example, knowing that high- and low-demand strategies are effective predictors of children's task competence is important (Pellegrini et al., 1985), but it does not inform us of the most effective order.

In summary, the general intent of this study was to describe the ways in which preschool children and an experimenter jointly constructed stories. These data should help us more clearly understand the dynamics of adult–child interaction.

METHOD

Subjects

The children all attended a university preschool and were participants in a larger, ongoing study. Children were randomly selected from each of their age-graded classrooms. The 43 boys and 43 girls ranged in age from 26–68 months. The mean age, in months, for each of the three age groups was: 37.35 $(SD = 4.94)$, 48.95 $(SD = 2.60)$, 60.16 $(SD = 4.29)$. The experimenter was a female graduate student.

Procedures

Individual children were escorted to an experimental playroom in the school. Children were observed in two separate, counterbalanced, storytelling conditions. In the functionally ambiguous, male-preferred storytelling condition children were presented with the following props: wooden and colorful plastic blocks of various sizes, numerous styrofoam shapes, and pipe cleaners. In the functionally explicit, female-preferred condition, children were presented with the following props: doctors' kits, dolls, smocks, blankets, and pill bottles. In each context the experimenter instructed children to "Tell a story about these toys." The experimenter was told that we were interested in children's ability to tell stories about the props and was instructed to provide minimal and uniform help so as to enable them to tell stories.

Measures

All interaction between children and the experimenter was video-taped and transcribed, following procedures outlined by Ochs (1979). The unit of analysis was the adult utterance, defined as a linguistic unit separated by spaces of 1 second (Garvey, 1984). Adult utterances were classified according to an inductive functional system that would account for all utterances. That is, each utterance was classified according to the function it served in the discourse. These functions are listed following:

Alternate use: Asks how prop can be used in a way other than its intended function; for example, "How else could you use that?"

Ask for extension: Asks to provide more information; for example, "Can you say more about that?"

Clarifies: Generally, tries to supplement information in a pre-ceeding utterance; for example, "It's not the one I wanted most."

Clarifies props: Gives more information about props; for example, "That's to listen to your heart."

Clarification question: Attempts to get child to clarify previous prop-relevant utterance; for example, "What do you mean by that?"

Description: A declarative that describes props or actions; for example, "It's red."

Describes actions: Describes children's actions; for example, "You're moving it."

Describes props: Described a play prop; for example, "It's red."

Descriptive question: Attempts to elicit a description of a prop or action; for example, "What's it look like?"

Direct attention: An imperative that directs children's attention to the task at hand; for example, "Now, let's continue to build."

Drama marker: Where the experimenter reacted, non-proposi-tionally, to the child's story as if she were a participant in the story or play theme; for example, "Uh oh."

Evaluation: The experimenter evaluated a story or story compo-nent; for example, "That's very strange."

Filler: Nonpropositional contingently respondent utterances; for example, "Hmm."

Mark: Begin: Frame that marks beginning of story; for example, "Once upon a time."

Mark: End: Frame that marks ending; for example, "All done."

Label: Label an experimental prop; for example, "That's a stethoscope."

Label question: Tries to elicit a label; for example, "What's that called?"

Playset: Establishes a playful/fantasy script; for example, "Can you play with these things?"

Reinforcement: Contingently responds to an utterance with an agreement or compliment; for example, "Good."

Relate to previous experience: Tries to establish a relation between the experimental situation and child's previous history; for example, "Haven't you seen anything like this before?"

Repeat: Repeats previous utterance.

Reprimand: Censures or admonishes a child; for example, "Don't throw blocks."

Role Clarification: Clarifies the role of a character in a story or fantasy episode; for example, "He's a different monster."

Role Clarification Question: Asks for the clarification of a character in a story or a fantasy, for example, "Who's the mother?"

Takes role: Takes a fantasy role.

Rules: Uses rules for participating in the session; for example, "We're not allowed to stand on tables here."

Additive slot: Repeats a child's story/fantasy utterance and ends the utterance with an additive conjunction; for example, "The robbers ran and———."

Casual slot: Repeats a child's story/fantasy utterance and ends the utterance with a casual conjunction; for example, "The five demons were mean because———."

Event slot: Asks the child what happens now or next in a story or fantasy episode; for example, "What happens now?"

Temporal slot: Repeats a child's fantasy/story utterance and ends the utterance with a temporal conjunction; for example, "The bridge fell and then———."

Story elicitor–general: Generally asks child to tell a story; for example, "Can you tell me a story now?"

Story elicitor–specific: Asks children to tell story about a specific prop or aspect of it; for example, "Tell me a story about that round block."

Asks to verbalize: Asks child to verbalize; for example, "Tell me what you are doing there."

Supplies verbalization: Provides verbalization that she tried to elicit in previous utterance; for example, "It looks like a truck to me."

In addition to the functional uses of language just mentioned, the number of adult and child utterances and turns was coded. Adult and child utterances were included to determine the extent to which each contributed to the discourse. Turns are an indicator of joint participation.

The stories children told were categorized according to the number of events in each story (Pellegrini, 1985). In the case where more than one story was told, children received separate event scores for each story. Based on the mean number of events in all of our stories, children were classified (using a median-split procedure) as high- or low-ability storytellers. In addition, the number of sustained child story events was coded. That is, the number of consecutive story events, without the interruption of adult language, was coded. This is a measure of independent storytelling.

Reliability of the functional language and story categories was established by raters independently coding the transcripts of 20 sessions. Observers were given extensive training and practice using the functional and story coding schemes. Reliability was .81 Kappa for the functional system and .94 Kappa for the story events.

Results

The results are presented according to the objectives of the study. First, the experimenter's language was subjected to factor analysis, using a varimax rotation; a four-factor solution was specified. The four-factor solution was based on Wertsch's (1979, 1985) description of the four processes adults used with children to establish intersubjectivity. The factor pattern is displayed in Table 4.1; the four factors accounted for 12% of the variance in the interactions.

Factor 1 is an adult lead (high loadings from adult utterances, supply verbalizations, asking to verbalize), playful (high loadings from playset, role take) factor. The second factor can be described

TABLE 4.1
Varimax Four-Factor Solution to Experimenter's Language

	Factor 1	2	3	4
Alternate use	.36	−.13	−.10	.41
Asks extension	−.14	.35	−.13	.06
Asks question	.00	.12	.04	.08
Clarify	−.00	.08	−.25	.54
Clarify prop	.28	.03	.07	−.24
Clarify question	−.01	.01	.59	.06
Describe	−.03	.00	.50	−.07
Describe action	.02	.20	−.09	−.00
Describe prop	.36	.17	.43	.11
Describe question	.17	−.19	.22	.01
Direct attention	.40	−.01	−.03	−.02
Drama	.21	.56	.00	.06
Evaluate	.15	.21	−.20	.13
Filler	.20	.50	−.01	−.01
Label	.08	.14	.53	.03
Label question	.00	.06	.61	−.10
Mark: Begin	.08	−.28	.41	.08
Mark: End	.20	−.13	.31	.12
Playset	.48	.02	−.10	.15
Reinforce	.05	.58	.07	.12
Relate experience	−.21	.20	.24	−.25
Repeat	−.11	.67	.29	.15
Reprimand	−.18	−.02	.19	.46
Role-clarify	.23	.16	.08	.57
Role-clarify question	−.08	.13	.02	.69
Role-take	.58	.25	.20	.26
Rule	.29	.36	.10	.14
Slot: add	−.07	.14	.39	.14
Slot: caus	.05	−.22	.03	.13
Slot: event	.38	.03	.34	.12
Slot: temp	−.30	.34	.24	.07
Story elicit general	−.13	.13	.34	−.14
Story elicit spec	.22	.02	.49	.48
Ask verbal	.66	.03	.01	−.13
Supply verbal	.73	.24	.04	.12
Turns	.04	.83	.27	.08
Adult utterance	.52	.61	.40	−.13
Child utterance	−.23	.30	.00	.54

as a low-level joint interaction factor to the extent that it was typified by high loadings from turns (indicating joint interaction) and low-level adult utterances (e.g., filler and reinforcements). The third factor is an adult lead (high loadings from adult utterances) story elicitation factor (high loadings from general and specific story elicitors, additive and event slots, and story frame markers).

The fourth, and last, factor is a child-centered (high loadings from children's utterances) play-story factor (high loadings from role-taking and specific story elicitors). It seems as though factors 1, 2, 3, and 4 reflect levels in the establishing of intersubjectivity as described by Wertsch (1985).

Next we tested the probability of factors 1 through 4 occurring in their specified sequence. In this analysis we first identified the language function that best typified each factor (i.e., highest factor loading). The functions for factors 1 through 4 were: (a) ask to verbalize, (b) reinforce, (c) label question, and (d) role-take, respectively. Next, we calculated the transitional probabilities of these utterances following each other in a two-state model at lag 1 (i.e. 1 to 2, 2 to 3, 3 to 4). Our sequential analyses followed procedures outlined by Bakeman and Gottman (1986). In this model, transitional probabilities between states are converted to z scores. If z scores exceeded 1.96, the difference between the observed and expected transitional probabilities reached statistical significance ($p < .05$). The probabilities, all of which were statistically significant, were: 1–2 : .57; 2–3 : .13; 3–4 : .08.

The second series of analyses were age (3:3-, 4-, and 5-year-olds) × gender (2) × ability (2 : high, low) × story context (2 : explicit, ambiguous) repeated measures analyses of variance (ANOVA); age, gender, and ability were between-subjects variables and story context was the within-subjects variable. The separate dependent measures were the individual factor scores for factors 1 through 4. Post hoc analyses utilized Students'-Newman Keuls procedure at the .05 level.

For factor 1, significant age × ability [$F (2,155) = 5.76, p < .004$, and gender × ability, $F (1,155) = 8.62) p < .003$] interactions were observed. The age × ability interaction revealed a significant difference within the 3-year-olds, where low-ability children ($M = .68$) elicited more playful adult leads than high-ability children ($M = -.20$). The gender × group interaction suggests that low-high differences were only for the girls, with lows ($M = .27$) eliciting more than highs ($M = -.29$). For factor 2, a significant main effect for ability was observed, $F (1,155) = 67.57, p < .0001$, with the high group ($M = .54$) eliciting more factor 2 utterances than the low group ($M = -.55$).

Two significant interactions were observed for factor 3: age × gender × ability [$F (2,155) = 5.49, p < .005$] and age × gender × ability × context [$F (2,155) = 4.95, p < .008$], as well as a main effect for context [$F (1,155) = 20,80, p < .0001$. The four-way interaction is described because it mediated the other effects. High-ability 3-year-old girls in the explicit context (M = 1.88) elicited more adult-led story elicitation than all boys except the 5-year-olds in the ambiguous context (M = .66).

The factor 4 ANOVA revealed two significant three-way interactions: age × ability × context [F (2,155) = 4.44, p < .01], and gender × ability × context [F 1,155) = 7.12, p < .008]. The only significant comparison in the age × ability × context interaction was that 3-year-old high-ability children in the blocks context (M = 123) elicited more child-centered, play-story utterances than 4-year-old low-ability children in the explicit context (M = −.38). The gender × ability × context interaction revealed that high-ability boys in the explicit context *(M* = .34) elicited more child-centered, play-story utterances than low-ability boys in the explicit context (M = −.26) and low-ability girls in the ambiguous context *(M* = −.25).

The third series of analyses began with stepwise multiple regressions. The criterion variable was the longest number of consecutive story events children generated without adult intervention. Predictor variables were individual measures of the experimenter's language. Because we assume that the adult language used varied by children's ability, separate regression equations were calculated for high and low groups. These results are summarized in Table 4.2.

Generally, the results suggest that for high-ability children, turns, evaluations, drama, and fillers were related to sustained story production. For low-ability children, clarification questions,

TABLE 4.2
Stepwise Regressions for Adult Behavior
and Sustained Child Story Events × Group

	df	F	R^2	Beta	p
	High Group—Uninterrupted Story				
Turns	*1,78*	*24.49*	*.24*	*.17*	*.0001*
Evaluations	*2,78*	*31.75*	*.46*	*1.59*	*.0001*
Drama	*3,78*	*25.87*	*.51*	*.79*	*.0001*
Filler	*4,78*	*23.87*	*.50*	*.62*	*.0001*
	Low Group—Uninterrupted Story				
Clarification question	1,78	5.06	.09	1.03	.02
Describe	2,78	5.33	.17	3.04	.007
Clarify	3,78	5.49	.24	2.74	.002
Utterance	4,78	5.38	.30	-.02	.001
Slot event	5,78	5.74	.36	.23	.0003

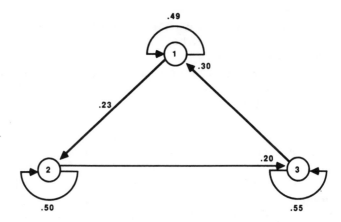

FIG. 4.1.   Significant* state** transitions for high-ability children.

adult utterances, slot-event, descriptions, and clarifications were related to children's uninterrupted stories.

The next series of analyses were sequential-lag analyses (Bakeman & Gottman, 1986). The intent of these analyses was to describe the probability of occurrence of the effective predictors of children's independent storytelling (as identified by the regression analyses). Like the regression analyses, separate calculations were made for high- and low-ability children. The language functions examined for the high-ability group included: evaluations, drama, and fillers. For the low-ability group we examined clarification questions, descriptions, clarifications, and slot events. In Fig. 4.1 and 4.2 the significant transitional probabilities for high- and low-ability groups, respectively, are displayed.

The analysis for the high-ability group suggests that the experimenter tended to repeat each of the functions. Further, the evaluation function was followed by the drama function, which was followed by fillers. For low-ability children we did not observe such repetitions. The only significant transition with the low-ability group was from descriptions to descriptive questions.

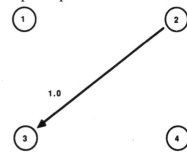

FIG. 4.2.   Significant* state** transitions   for   low-ability children.

DISCUSSION

In this chapter we describe the way in which an adult experimenter and a group of preschool children undertook the social task of constructing stories. A crucial part of this process, we argue, was the way in which the adult and children established intersubjectivity; that is, how the children's definitions of tasks came to match the adult's definition. The descriptive work of Wertsch (1979, 1985) and his colleagues suggested that adults and children went through a four-step process in establishing intersubjectivity.

To test this hypothesis we induced a category system that described the experimenter's functional uses of language with children. Those functions were factor analyzed and subjected to sequential lag analyses. The results supported Wertsch's four-level hypothesis to the extent that we identified four factors that documented a progression from adult to child task responsibility. More specifically, our Factor 1 was composed of functions that had the adult assuming responsibility for a substantial portion of the task (e.g., asking children to verbalize and supplying verbalization) and treating the task as a play task (high loadings from play set and role-take), not a storytelling task. Factor 1 shows that the adult was overtly guiding the children (by asking them to verbalize) at a play, not a storytelling, task. The following example illustrates this point.

Experiment (E): OK. Hilda what do we have here? Can you tell me a story about these things?

Hilda (H): Building with blocks. (But not talking or looking at E).

E: Can you tell me what you're doing?

H: (Shakes her head no without looking at E).

E: You're building a tower aren't you.

H: Yes.

E: Let's play that you're a builder and I'm your helper.

This child's reluctance to participate in the experimenter-defined task of telling a story about the props led the experimenter to assume more task responsibility by actually talking for the child and by redefining the task according to what she thought was the child's definition of the task. This may have been done to help the child feel comfortable in a relatively novel situation.

Factor 2 is characterized by low-level joint participation. More specifically, both interlocuters were participating, but the adult was using fillers and reinforcement after the children's utterances. This pattern is similar to Keenan and Klein's (1975) description of young children's discourse among themselves. In this pattern, interlocuters use fillers and other non-propositional utterances to maintain conversational coherence. Use of such nonpropositional utterances seems to serve at least two discourse functions. First, they serve as contingent responses to children's utterances and, as such, should increase the likelihood of children's subsequent verbalizations and participation. Second, the adult's use of these utterances informs the child that she wants the discourse to continue because she is meeting her conversational duty of responding to the child's utterance. Factor 2 indicates more intersubjectivity than Factor 1 to the extent that both interlocuters are participating in the discourse, not only the adult.

Factor 3 is characterized by the experimenter encouraging children to tell stories. This represents movement toward adult task definition. They moved from playful, adult-led discourse (Factor 1), to low-level joint discourse (Factor 2), to the adult encouraging children to engage in her version of the tasks. Because this version seems different to the child (as evidenced by Factors 1 and 2), the adult is assuming task responsibility. For example:

E: Jake, we have lots of doctor tools here. I want you to tell me a story about them. Can you make up a story about them? Jake (J): A story?

E: Yeah. Here's a stethescope. Tell me a story about a doctor and a stethescope.

J: I can't.

E: Sure you can. Just try. The doctor could be listening to this little girl's heart and say, "Well, how's your heart today?"

J: The doctor saw this sick girl and said "How's your heart?"

E: Good. The doctor said how's yours and————.

With this factor, both interlocuters recognize the task demands of telling a story but the experimenter structures the interaction such that she tells or helps the child tell the story.

The fourth factor completes the intersubjectivity process to the extent that the child seems to be taking more responsibility and the experimenter taking less responsibility for telling stories. For example:

E: Bridget, here are some doctor tools. You can do lots of things with them—play with them and tell stories about them. I want you to tell me a story about them. OK?

Bridget (B): Once upon a time this girl got a shot. She cried and cried.

E: She got a shot and cried! Tell me more of the story about the shot.

B: Yup. But her Momma said "It'll only hurt for a minute." Then she stopped crying.

The results of the factor and sequential analyses empirically support the notion that children begin experimental tasks with very different definitions of the situations than those of the experimenter. The experimenter seemed to accommodate initially to the children's points of view by playing with them and reinforcing their conversational contributions. In short, the experimenter and the children established intersubjectivity by initially interacting around the task as defined by the children. The adult, through her guidance, enabled children to engage in the task as she defined it.

There are obvious limitations to these analyses. The use of a single experimenter may limit the generalizability of our results. This, however, is only one indicator of generalizability; another is replication (Lykken, 1968). In light of our analyses replicating Wertsch (1979, 1985), we feel that they are generalizable.

We were also interested in the extent to which each of these factors varied as a function of child variables (i.e., age, gender, and storytelling ability) and story contextual variables (functionally ambiguous, male-preferred, and explicit, female-preferred, props). The analysis of Factor 1 suggests that the experimenter used most of these strategies with low-ability, 3-year-old children, especially girls. Thus, the least intersubjectivity existed between the experimenter and the low-ability, youngest girls. Factor 2 results indicate that more intersubjectivity exists between the experimenter and the high-ability children than between her and the low-ability children. Thus, these two ANOVA's suggested that the experimenter took more responsibility for helping younger, less able children understand the task demands as she defined them. The results for Factors 3 and 4 support this conclusion to the extent that they (as indicators of greater intersubjectivity than Factors 1 and 2) were most frequently used with older and more able children.

These ability and age effects, however, were mediated by context and gender effects. For example, in Factor 3, the experimenter used most of these types of utterances with older boys in the male-preferred and girls in the female-preferred contexts. As such, children and the experimenter more easily established intersubjectivity in gender-preferred contexts. From a young age, children seem to realize that they are expected to exhibit competence with sex-role-appropriate props and not with sex-role-inappropriate props (Huston, 1983).

The next series of analyses are concerned with an applied dimension of our data: identification of the adult strategies that are the best predictors of children's independent storytelling. Our theoretical orientation, following Vygotsky (1978) and other (e.g., Pellegrini, 1985; Wertsch, 1985), suggests that instruction should occur in the child's zone of proximal development. This model posits that adults adjust their teaching style as a function of children's competence in a task. Adults assume more responsibility for task completion with the less competent than with the more competent children. Results from this (i.e., the factor analyses) and other studies (e.g., Pellegrini et al., 1985) support this claim. We initially identified the adult strategies, through stepwise multiple regression analyses, that were the best predictors of children's independent storytelling. We obtained very different predictors for high- and low-ability children. Facilitative interaction with the high-ability children was characterized by joint interaction (i.e., turns) and the experimenter making high cognitive demand (i.e., evaluations). For the low-ability children, however, the facilitative experimenter strategies included clarifying and describing the storytelling props and providing event slots for the children to fill. In short, our data are consistent with the tenets of the zone of proximal development. From an instructional perspective, these results are useful in suggesting that different strategies should be used with different children. The notion that specific strategies are more effective teaching tools than others (e.g., high-demand questions being superior to low-demand questions) is inadequate because it does not take children's status into account; that is, it is unidirection.

In order to more accurately describe facilitative teaching strategies, specific sequences of language functions with different types of children must be identified (e.g., Siegel, 1979). With high-ability children, the experimenter repeated herself frequently. This pattern may have been a strategy to help the children understand the task demands. Further, the experimenter moved from a high-demand strategy (i.e., evaluation) to a low-demand strategy (i.e., demand). It may be that she used the high-demand strategy so that the children could exhibit their highest level of competence. Lower level strategies may have been used next as a contingent response (i.e., use of filler) or if children did not respond appropriately to the high-demand strategy. For example, the adult may have used a drama strategy to reinvolve the child in story-like interaction, dramatic play. Dramatic play interaction, because of its similarity to storytelling (Galda, 1984), may have been an intermediate point on the reestablishing of intersubjectivity.

The sequential analysis for the low-ability children was clearcut: Descriptions led to clarification questions. This sequence is interesting in light of the sequence used with the high-ability children. With the latter group, repetition was used to help children understand the task demands. With the low-ability group, the experimenter defined the situation, through description, and explicitly asked children to clarify. By asking the low-ability children clarification questions, she was making an explicit check on their task understanding. Repetition, on the other hand, is not an explicit check because it does not demand a child's response. Again, the more able children assume more task responsibility than the less able children.

In conclusion, our results suggest that adults and children initially define experimental tasks very differently. Mutual definition is socially negotiated according to children's competence in specific contexts.

ACKNOWLEDGMENTS

Pellegrini's efforts on this chapter were supported by the Institute for Behavioral Research (University of Georgia) and a grant from the A. L. Mailman Foundation. We acknowledge Supoat Charenkavanich for his help with data analysis.

REFERENCES

Bakeman, R., & Gottman, J. (1986). *Observing interaction: An introduction to sequential analysis.* New York: Cambridge University Press.

Bell, R. (1979). Parent, child, and reciprocal influences. *American Psychologist, 10,* 821–826.

Bronfenbrenner, U. (1979). *The ecology of human development.* Cambridge, MA: Harvard.

Brown, A., Bransford, J., Ferrera, R., & Campione, J. (1983). Learning, remembering, and understanding. In J. Flavell & E. Markman (Eds.), *Handbook of child psychology* (Vol. 3, pp. 77–166). New York: Wiley.

Bruner, J. (1975). From communication to language. A psychological perspective. *Cognition, 3,* 255–287.

Galda, L. (1984). Narrative competence: Play, story telling, and comprehensions. In A. Pellegrini & T. Yawkey (Eds.), The development of oral and written language in social context (pp. 105–119). Norwood, NJ: Ablex.

Garvey, C. (1984). *Children's talk.* Cambridge, MA: Harvard.

Hess, R., & Shipman, V. (1965). Early experience and the socialization of cognitive modes in children. *Child Development, 36,* 869–886.

Huston, A. (1983). Sex-typing. In E. Hetherington (Ed.), *Handbook of child psychology: Socialization, personality, and social development* (Vol. 4, pp. 387–468). New York: Wiley.

Keenan, E., & Klein, E. (1975). Coherency in children's discourse. *Journal of Psycholinguistic Research, 4,* 365–380.

Lykken, D. (1968). Statistical significance in psychological research. *Psychological Bulletin, 70,* 151–159.

McNamee, G. (1979). The social interaction origins of narrative skills. *The Quarterly Newsletter of the Laboratory of Comparative Human Cognition, 1,* 63–68.

Ochs, E. (1979). Transcription as theory. In E. Ochs & B. Schieffelin (Eds.), *Developmental pragmatics* (pp. 43–72). New York: Academic.

Pellegrini, A. (1985). The narrative organization of children's play. *Educational Psychology, 5,* 17–25.

Pellegrini, A., Brody, G., & Siegel, I. (1985). Parents' bookreading habits with their child. *Journal of Educational Psychology, 77,* 332–340.

Pellegrini, A., & Galda, L. (1988). The effects of age and context on children's use of narrative language. *Research in the teaching of english, 22,* 183–195.

Pellegrini, A., Galda, L., & Rubin, D. (1984). Context in text: The development of oral and written language in two genres. *Child Development, 55,* 1549–1555.

Rommetveit, R. (1979). On the architecture of intersubjectivity. In R. Rommetveit & R. Blakar (Eds.), *Studies of language, thought, and verbal communication.* London: Academic.

Rubin, K., Fein, G., & Vandenberg, B. (1983). Play. In E. M. Hetherington (Ed.), *Handbook of child psychology, socialization, personality and social development* (Vol. 4, pp. 693–779). New York: Wiley.

Sigel, I. (1979). On becoming a thinker: A psychoeducational model. *Educational Psychologist, 14,* 70–78.

Vygotsky, L. (1978). *Mind in society.* Cambridge, MA: Harvard.

Wertsch, J. (1979). From social interaction to higher psychological processes. A clarification and application of Vygotsky's theory. *Human Development, 22,* 1–22.

Wertsch, J. (Ed.). (1985). *Culture, communication, and cognition: Vygotskian perspectives.* New York: Cambridge University Press.

5

Canonicality and Consciousness in Child Narrative

Joan Lucariello
New School for Social Research

Two essential characteristics of narratives, or stories, are pentadic imbalance and the consciousness or subjectivity of the protagonists. A central question in the study of narrative thought is how children come to think narratively. What lies behind their understanding of dramatic imbalances and character subjectivity? Before attempting an answer to this question, a brief discussion of these story features is necessary.

Kenneth Burke, in his classic *Grammar of Motives* (1969), noted that, at a minimum, narrative requires an actor, an action, a goal or intention, a scene, and an instrument. These provide the skeleton of Burke's "Pentad." The drama or trouble or crisis inherent in narrative emerges from an imbalance among elements in the Pentad. These imbalances are what make for gripping stories. For example, actions fail to achieve goals (e.g., the love of Romeo and Juliet does not bring them and their feuding families together), or scenes and agents are out of kilter (e.g., the bright, fair, open, little Eppy arriving at the old, isolated, dreary home of the stingy recluse Silas Marner in George Eliot's novel by the same name), or actions are performed by unlikely agents (e.g., the convict, and not the interested wealthy old lady, sponsors the advancement of Pip in Dickens' *Great Expectations*). The notion of imbalance may also be talked about as a breach of a canonical state. Not only has narrative or story been thought to arise from such breaches (Bruner, 1986; Burke, 1969), but so too cultural crises or social dramas (Turner, 1980). In such cases there is a "breaching" of cultural legitimacy. Good story hinges on a breach or departure from expectation or conventionality.

A second critical feature of narratives, noted by Greimas and Courtes (1976), is the subjectivity of the protagonists. Narrator subjectivity may be included here as well. In the narratives of classic myth and folklore, there is a convention of marking stance as if the narrator were virtually divine: omniscient, omnipresent, and directly in touch with the ontology of the story and the consciousness of its protagonists. In more recent narrative fiction, the narrator's stance has been more explicitly marked, and in addition to the protagonists in the story having points of view or perspectives, in modernist and postmodernist fiction the narrator does as well, if only the stance of epistemic uncertainty. Many modern theorists agree that no description of narrative is complete without reference to stance, that stories are relativized with respect to the perspective of the narrator (see Chatman, 1978). This means that any developed narrative must have (as Greimas & Courtes, 1976, put it) a double landscape: one of the world of action depicted in the story, the other of the world of consciousness in the minds both of the protagonists and narrator.

Given these features of narrative, the issues of narrative thinking may be addressed: How may narrative thinking be characterized, and how may it develop? Narrative thinking involves, in part, the comprehension or understanding of imbalances as such. Such comprehension presupposes knowledge of canonical states, in that imbalances consist in violating knowledge of the canonical relations that may exist among pentadic elements. Accordingly, the child needs to garner experience with conventional happenings, and represent knowledge of such experience to understand when other happenings, even those depicted in a story, vary starkly, bespeaking of breach or imbalance.

Young children appear to have knowledge of the canonical relations among agents, actions, goals, scenes, and instruments. Preschoolers show a clear understanding of commonplace, familiar events (see Nelson, 1986). These events include birthday parties, making cookies, going to the grocery store, snack at school, and the school day in general. Bruner and Lucariello (1989) found evidence for such knowledge at an even more tender age. In examining the presleep monologues of a child (Emmy) between her second and third birthdays, they came across many monologic passages detailing and elaborating the routine events comprising this child's daily life. Indeed, Emmy appeared to be expending a great deal of effort to "get it together" in terms of understanding the regular activities in which she participated. Among the events she strove to understand were what happens in the morning upon awakening, including visits from friends before going out, what happens at the babysitter's and (later) nursery school, what happens when she's put to bed, and what happens on various outings, such as the store and library. This knowledge of the relations among agent, action, goal, instrument, and scene in ordinary events may be requisite for the development of narrative thought, which hinges on the noncanonical event.

But what of the second key feature of narrative under discussion here, that of the elaboration of action in terms of a landscape of consciousness? What provokes a child into such an elaboration? What moves the child from the mere exposition or rendering of the occurrence of actions to an introduction of character subjectivity or mind in relation to action? It may be the case that pentadic imbalance itself serves as a trigger for this elaboration. Pentadic imbalance is a likely candidate as a narrative-trigger, because it almost of necessity requires explanation, and such explanations often appeal to the consciousness of actors. For instance, in response to the action of a priest murdering a youth, the listener is impelled to provide a motive. The hearer/reader may spontaneously generate an interpretation that takes into account the mind-set of the actors (e.g., the youth *knew* that the priest was a fraud). In contrast, for the non-narrative cases of pentadic balance (e.g., the priest heard Confession) no elaboration of action is called for. Pentadic balance is easily handled by the laws of action and convention alone, whereas imbalance sets one to thinking about the contents of mind, such as intentions.

It seems highly likely, therefore, that there is an interaction between features of narrative. Pentadic imbalance may elicit the attribution of consciousness to story characters or actors, whereas balance has little or no such provocative power, and, in fact, may depress such attributions.

Some key notions about narrative thought are explored in the present research. One is the premise that breach or noncanonicality is rooted in the knowledge of canonical relations among pentadic elements. The second is that breach has the effect of thrusting the perceiver into the landscape of consciousness, whereby story action is linked to the minds of the protagonists.

The study of these premises bears important implications for
research on child narrative in general. A major focus in the literature on children and stories has been the study of the child's knowledge about stories (Applebee, 1978; Mandler, 1983). So, for example, there have been attempts to describe the basic characteristics
of the constituent structure of stories (e.g., a formal node or device
that marks the narrative as a story—"once upon a time"), and
to compare children's story comprehension and production along
these dimensions. The folk tale, stemming from the oral tradition,
is the prototype story on which such research is based. In this
chapter, however, knowledge other than story knowledge per se is
seen as key to the development of narrative thinking in children. It
is the child's understanding of life events, canons of the commonplace, that is thought to enable the appreciation of dramatic imbalance. Moreover, whereas these prior approaches to child story
knowledge have a structural orientation, the approach in this chapter is functionally based, emphasizing the contexts or occasions
eliciting narrative thought (e.g., breach).

An additional implication for research on child narrative comes
from the proposal that child knowledge is essential to narrative
thinking. The importance of a cognitive variable in the development of such thought is emphasized, whereas recently attention
has been directed primarily to the role of social-interactive variables (e.g., McNamee, 1988; Paley, 1981).

With regard to the experimental design, two kinds of transformations (breach and nonbreach) were derived from stories used in the
investigation. Breach is best depicted by transforming a highly
ritualized event. Accordingly, stories about a birthday party served
as the canonical base from which breach transformations involving
character action and character state were constructed. Nonbreach
is best depicted by making changes in a more loosely structured
event. In this case, stories about an after-school visit from cousins
served as the canonical base. Further canonical or nonbreach story
versions were derived by making corresponding changes in character action and character state. Both events, the birthday party and
the visit, were thought to be well known; that is, highly familiar to
young children.

Kindergarten children heard these stories and then were asked
to add information about the actions and events in them. The
design focuses on story comprehension, in terms of the perception of
imbalance, and on story production or narrative extension, in terms
of the contribution of a level of consciousness.

Because the notion of pentadic imbalance presumably has meaning only in terms of the ritually based birthday stories that are transformed in the direction of breach, it was thought that these stories would accomplish the most by way of generating narrative thought. That is, the addition of information to stories, and particularly the addition of information related to character consciousness, was hypothesized to be more associated with these stories.

METHOD

Stimuli

The organization or arrangement of the 12 stimuli stories are noted in Table 5.1. There were 3 additional birthday stories, along with three corresponding visit stories, for a total of nine in each group. These additional stories involved other types of transformations that are not treated here.

Canonical or balanced versions of the birthday and visit stories (1a, 1c, 2a, 2c) were thought to depict events well known to young children. These stories were also structurally similar to one another. This was true in terms of their length (the approximate number of words), their syntactic structure (the overall number of sentences, and the number of simple and complex sentences), and their narrative characteristics (the number of characters and actions depicted). They differed in that transformations in the birthday party story were thought to represent breach transformations,

TABLE 5.1
Story Stimuli by Pentadic Arrangement and Story/Transformation
Type (Number of Subjects in Parentheses)

Pentadic Arrangement	Birthday Breach*	Visit Nonbreach*
Agent–action balance	1a (6)	2a (8)
Agent–action transformation*	1b (8)	2b (8)
Agent–scene balance	1c (7)	2c (6)
Agent–scene transformation*	1d (9)	2d (9)
Combined transformations*	1e (7)	2e (7)
Agent–scene transformation		
Agent–action transformation		
Mixed:	1f (8)	2f (6)
Agent–scene balance		
Agent–action transformation*		
Total subjects	45	44

whereas transformations in the visit story were thought to represent nonbreach transformations.

The structural similarity of stories within type was also con-
trolled. Within birthday and visit story types, stories were identical
except for the transformations of canonical material with noncanonical in the birthday stories, and canonical material with other
canonical in the visit stories.

Following are the 12 experimental stories and their corresponding questions. Story 1a represents the core birthday story from
which transformations were spun. Similarly, Story 2a represents
the core visit story from which transformations were spun.

Story 1a—Agent-Action Balance (Birthday)

Mary woke up on her birthday.
There was going to be a party.
Lots of friends came to the party and they all brought presents.
Mary's mother put the birthday cake on the table.
Everyone sang "Happy Birthday" and Mary blew out the candles.
Mary's father took pictures with a camera.
Everybody played games and went home.

Story 1b—Agent-Action Transformation

Blew out the candles changed to *threw water on the candles.*

QUESTIONS (1a,1b):
1. How come Mary (blew out/threw water on) the candles?
2. What did the other kids do when Mary (blew out/threw water
   on) the candles?
3. What did Mary's parents do when Mary (blew out/threw water
   on) the candles?

Story 1c—Agent-Scene Balance

Mary was very happy inserted after *There was going to be a party.*

Story 1d—Agent-Scene Transformation

Mary was very unhappy inserted after *There was going to be a
party.*

QUESTIONS (1c,1d):

1. How come Mary was (happy/unhappy)?

Story 1e—Combined Transformations:
Agent-Scene and Agent-Action

Mary was very unhappy inserted; *blew out the candles* changed to *threw water on the candles.*

QUESTIONS (1e):

1. How come Mary was unhappy?
2. How come Mary threw water on the candles?
3. What did the other kids do when Mary threw water on the candles?
4. What did Mary's parents do when Mary threw water on the candles?

Story 1f—Mixed: Agent-Scene Balance;
Agent-Action Transformation

Mary was very happy inserted; *blew out the candles* changed to *threw water on the candles.*

QUESTIONS (1f):

1. How come Mary was happy?
2. How come Mary threw water on the candles?
3. What did the other kids do when Mary threw water on the candles?
4. What did Mary's parents do when Mary threw water on the candles?

Story 2a—Agent-Action Balance (Visit)

Johnny came home from school one day.

There was going to be a visit from his cousins.

His cousins came over and brought lots of toys.

Johnny's mother cut carrots on the table.

Everyone did their homework and Johnny painted some pictures.

Johnny's father fixed a lamp with a screwdriver.

Everybody ate dinner and Johnny's cousins left.

Story 2b—Agent-Action Transformation

Painted some pictures changed to *hung some pictures.*

QUESTIONS (2a,2b):

1. How come Johnny (painted/hung) some pictures?
2. What did Johnny's cousins do when Johnny (painted/hung) some pictures?
3. What did Johnny's parents do when Johnny (painted/hung) some pictures?

Story 2c—Agent-Scene Balance

Johnny was very happy inserted after *There was going to be a visit from his cousins.*

Story 2d—Agent-Scene Transformation

Johnny was very unhappy inserted after *There was going to be a visit from his cousins.*

QUESTIONS (2c,2d):

1. How come Johnny was (happy/unhappy)?

Story 2e—Combined Transformations: Agent-Scene and Agent-Action

Johnny was very unhappy inserted; *painted some pictures* changed to *hung some pictures.*

QUESTIONS (2e):

1. How come Johnny was unhappy?
2. How come Johnny hung some pictures?
3. What did Johnny's cousins do when Johnny hung some pictures?

4. What did Johnny's parents do when Johnny hung some pictures?

Story 2f—Mixed: Agent-Scene Balance; Agent-Action Transformation

Johnny was very happy inserted; *painted some pictures* changed to *hung some pictures*.

QUESTIONS (2f):
1. How come Johnny was happy?
2. How come Johnny hung some pictures?
3. What did Johnny's cousins do when Johnny hung some pictures?
4. What did Johnny's parents do when Johnny hung some pictures?

Procedure

Story orders were constructed for the administration of the total 18 experimental stories. Each birthday story was paired with each visit story (e.g., 1a with 2a, 2b, 2c, 2d, 2e, 2f, 2g, 2h, 2i), with the order of the pairing counterbalanced. This led to 81 pairings. These pairings were randomly assigned to subjects.

Kindergarten children served as subjects. All stories were on tape. Each child heard one birthday and one visit story (as indicated by the pairing arrangement). Children were told that they were going to hear some stories on tape, and that afterward the interviewer would talk to them about the stories. Children heard one story and received the questions for that story before the second story was presented.

Children were encouraged to answer the story questions. They were told that there was no right or wrong answer, and that anything they said would be fine. If a child explicitly stated that he or she could not answer a question due to an inability to remember the story text, the child was told that they could make up the answer. If a child did not respond to a question after one or two probes, such as "Can you think of (repeat question)?," the next question was asked. Questions for each story were always asked in the same order.

Coding

Child responses to story questions were coded into three major response type categories: story builders, nonadditions, and nonresponses. Nonresponses represent those occasions when children provide no information in response to story questions. Story builders add thematically relevant information to the story. This information represents instances of narrative thinking on the child's part. Nonadditions either add no information to the story at all or add information that does not elaborate on the character or action in question. The story builder and nonaddition categories were comprised of several subcategories of responding:

Story Builders

Basic Narrative Contributions. These contributions add information, are centrally related to the characters and actions in question, and are often associated with the dramatic pentadic categories.

1. Action (physical)—(e.g., What did Johnny's parents do when Johnny painted some pictures?—"Maybe they hanged 'em up on the refrigerator with tape"; What did Mary's parents do when Mary threw water on the candles?—"Stayed back a little").

2. Agent—(e.g., How come Johnny painted some pictures?— "He wasn't old enough to do homework yet so he painted some pictures instead"; How come Mary threw water on the candles?— "She couldn't blow 'em out").

3. Scene—(e.g., How come Johnny painted some pictures?— "Cause he had nothing to do with his cousins").

4. Dialogue—(e.g., What did Johnny's cousins do when Johnny hung some pictures?—"Asked him when he draw them").

Consciousness Contributions. These contributions add a subjective or internal dimension to the story. This dimension provides the cognitive and/or affective perspective of the characters.

1. Affectively laden—these might include actions (e.g., What did Mary's parents do when Mary threw water on the candles?—"I think punished her"), or dialogic activities (e.g., What did Johnny's parents do when Johnny hung some pictures?—"Told him that they were very nice"; What did the other kids do when Mary threw water on the candles?—"They just laughed"), or the direct reporting of a

mental or internal state (e.g., What did Johnny's cousins do when Johnny hung some pictures?—"Liked 'em"; What did Mary's parents do when Mary threw water on the candles?—"Get mad at her").

2. Intentions or Goals—(e.g., How come Mary threw water on the candles?—"To get them out"; How come Johnny hung some pictures?—"Because he wanted his cousins to think the house looks nice").

3. Cognitive—(e.g., How come Mary was unhappy?—"She didn't know it was her birthday").

Nonadditions

Textual answers. These answers rely in different ways on the material presented in the story text. They generally do not add information to the story.

1. Literal—rely on material that appears in the story text (e.g., How come Mary blew out the candles?—"Cause it was her birthday"; What did Johnny's cousins do when Johnny painted some pictures?—"Did homework").

2. Transformations/violations—change the story material in some way. These responses can actually violate the information presented in the story (e.g., How come Mary was unhappy?—"Her Dad wasn't home"), or transform story material (e.g., What did Johnny's parents do when Johnny painted some pictures?— "Mommy cooks dinner" instead of the literal "mother cut carrots").

3. Scrambles—inappropriate use of story information in answering a question. These scrambles were primarily temporally inappropriate, in that events presented as occurring later in story time are employed to address issues arising earlier in story time (e.g., How come Johnny was unhappy?—"He couldn't reach to hang up the pictures"; How come Mary was unhappy?—"Cause not enough people came and she wanted more").

Peripheral Answers. These answers add only incidental information to the story.

1. Nonconstructions—add thematically unrelated material to characters, actions, or events in question (e.g., How come Mary was unhappy?—"Maybe she lost something"; What did Johnny's

parents do when Johnny hung some pictures?—"The father went to get food from the store").

2. Generalizations—provide general information, applicable to anyone or any situation (e.g., How come Johnny painted some pictures?—"He felt like it" or "He wanted to"; How come Mary was happy?—"Well because on birthdays people can be happy because they get a lot of presents and they're happy when they get what they want").

Nonresponses

In these cases of nonresponses, the child said nothing at all or made statements such as "I don't know" or "I can't think of anything" in response to story questions.

RESULTS

The following represents a report of the data from the 12 stimuli stories analyzed. The number of subjects comprising each story condition is presented in Table 5.1.

For each of the 12 stories, the percentage of each of the three response types was determined. This was accomplished by dividing the total number of each response type by the total number of all responses, and multiplying the resulting figures by 100. For stories with multiple questions (1a, 1b, 1e, 1f, 2a, 2b, 2e, 2f), the percentage of each response type per question was determined by the aforementioned method, and these percentages were then summed and divided by the number of questions (three or four) to obtain a story mean for each response type. Next, means for each of these three response types were determined for the following four groupings of the stories: birthday balanced stories (1a, 1c), birthday breach transformed stories (1b, 1d, 1e, 1f), visit balanced stories (2a, 2c), and visit nonbreach transformed stories (2b, 2d, 2e, 2f). These data are presented in Table 5.2.

The first thing to note about these data is that, for the most part, children did provide responses to the story questions. Nonresponses accounted for a range of between 5% and 25% of the responses to story questions. Nonadditions represented the most common response type, accounting for a range of 43% to 83% of the responses to story questions. Several factors may account for this. The child may interpret the experimental task as a memory test, in which the aim is verbatim or accurate recall of story text material in

TABLE 5.2
Response Types for Story Groupings

Story	Story Builders	Nonadditions	Nonresponses
Birthday			
X̄ balanced stories	11.2	83.4	5.5
(1a,1c)			
X̄ breach transformed stories	42.6	43.2	14.3
(1b,1d,1e,1f)			
Visit			
X̄ balanced stories	12.5	83.4	4.2
(2a,2c)			
X̄ nonbreach transformed stories	25.9	49.2	25.0
(2b,2d,2e,2f)			

response to questions. A second possible factor may be the child's inability to generate new information in response to story questions. Narrative thinking may be just emerging in children of this age. Moreover, the actual design incorporated many story conditions that were not thought to elicit narrative thought. Story builder responses represent an important focus of the present analysis. As can be seen in Table 5.2, they account for a range of 11% to 43% of the responses to story questions across these four groupings of stories. To get a more refined look at this response type, they are tabled separately by pentadic arrangement and story/transformation type (birthday/breach versus visit/nonbreach) in Table 5.3.

The subcategory of story builder responses, consciousness contributions, constitutes another important aspect of the data analysis. To obtain the percentage of consciousness contribution responses per story, the total number of such responses was divided by the total number of all responses (story builders–basic narrative and consciousness contributions, nonadditions, and nonresponses), multiplied by 100. For stories with multiple questions, the same procedure as just described was used to obtain a story mean. These data are presented in Table 5.4.

The hypotheses guiding this experimental work lead to the expectation of certain patterns in these data. Noncanonicality or imbalance is thought to trigger narrative thinking. It is the birthday stories bearing breaches or imbalances that are considered to represent noncanonical relations among pentadic elements, whereas the visit stories are presumably valueless in terms of such representation. Accordingly, stories 1b, 1d, 1e, and 1f ought to yield more narrative thinking, evidenced by story builder responses, than their counterpart, nonbreach transformation stories (2b, 2d, 2e, and 2f).

TABLE 5.3
Percentage of Story Builder Responses for Each Story
by Pentadic Arrangement and Story/Transformation Type
(Story Number in Parentheses)

Pentadic Arrangement	Birthday Breach*	Visit Nonbreach*
Agent–action balance	(1a) 22.3	(2a) 25.0
Agent–scene balance	(1c) 0	(2c) 0
Agent–action transformation*	(1b) 64.7	(2b) 41.7
Agent–scene transformation*	(1d) 22.0	(2d) 11.0
Combined transformations*	(1e) 42.9	(2e) 21.5
Agent–scene transformation		
Agent–action transformation		
Mixed	(1f) 40.6	(2f) 29.2
Agent–scene balance		
Agent–action transformation*		
Mean balanced stories (a,c)	11.2	12.5
Mean transformed stories (b,d,e,f)	42.6	25.9

The results presented in Tables 5.3 and 5.4 confirm this prediction. Similarly, stories involving balance (1a, 1c, 2a, and 2c) are expected to yield little in the way of narrative thinking on the reasoning that canonicality or balance does not elicit narrative thought, and in fact, may dampen such thinking. Moreover, because birthday stories 1a and 1c and visit stories 2a and 2c are taken to depict canonicality, the level of story builder responses across these story types

TABLE 5.4
Percentage of Consciousness Contribution Responses for Each Story
by Pentadic Arrangement and Story/Transformation Type
(Story Number in Parentheses)

Pentadic Arrangement	Birthday Breach*	Visit Nonbreach*
Agent–action balance	(1a) 5.7	(2a) 8.3
Agent–scene balance	(1c) 0	(2c) 0
Agent–action transformation*	(1b) 48.5	(2b) 29.2
Agent–scene transformation*	(1d) 22.0	(2d) 0
Combined transformations*	(1e) 25.0	(2e) 10.7
Agent–scene transformation		
Agent–action transformation		
Mixed	(1f) 25.0	(2f) 16.7
Agent–scene balance		
Agent–action transformation*		
Mean balanced stories (a,c)	2.9	4.2
Mean transformed stories (b,d,e,f)	30.1	14.2

should be comparable. Here again, these predictions are confirmed by the results (see Tables 5.3 and 5.4).

The finding that the balanced versions of each of these story types (1a, 1c, 2a, and 2c) yield similar responding is very important. Within this experimental design, instead of depicting breach and nonbreach transformations by altering a single story, different stories were used. Accordingly, it is critical that these different stories, birthday and visit, are generally comparable to the child's eye in terms of their familiarity and status as canonical events. The similarity in responding across them (1a–2a; 1c–2c) indicates that they may indeed be generally equivalent to the child.

To test the statistical significance of the aforementioned patterns, chi-square analyses were performed. The number of different children providing story builder responses was determined for each of the 12 stories. For stories with multiple questions, this was determined by considering responses across questions.

For the breach versus canonical comparison, the number of children showing story builder responses was summed across the breach birthday stories 1b, 1d, 1e, and 1f (22 of 32), and across the related, nonbreach transformation visit stories 2b, 2d, 2e, and 2f (13 of 30). A chi-square analysis on these numbers yielded a significant result [x^2 (2) = 5.17, $p <$ .05]. The same analysis was conducted considering only the number of children providing consciousness contributions to these stories with a similar result [x^2 (2) = 5.23, $p <$ .05]. These findings indicate that imbalance or breach does indeed trigger narrative thinking.

A comparison of the remaining stories 1a and 1c versus 2a and 2c should not yield a significant difference, because in this case all stories represent a canonical or balanced relation among pentadic elements. The total number of children exhibiting narrative thinking was 3 of 13 for stories 1a and 1c, and 3 of 14 for stories 2a and 2c. A chi-square analysis revealed no significant difference in story building responses across birthday balanced and visit balanced stories. This was true also for the secondary analysis involving consciousness contributions only. These data indicate that canonicality has no special status in generating narrative thinking, as evidenced by story builders.

Another way to analyze these data is to conduct a within-story type analysis and compare the number of children for the birthday stories providing story builder responses for the presumably canonical ones (1a,1c), and the presumably noncanonical ones (1b,1d). The expectation is for greater narrative thinking in the noncanonical story conditions. Three of 13 and 10 of 17 children contributed story builder responses in the canonical and non-canonical conditions, respectively. These figures differ significantly [x^2 (2) = 5.43, $p < .02$], confirming the predicted pattern. The same comparisons with the visit stories would not be expected to yield a significant difference. These stories are not thought to represent a canonical–noncanonical comparison, but rather the comparison of two canonical conditions. The number of children showing story builder responses for stories 2a and 2c is 3 of 14, and for 2b and 2d is 5 of 17. These figures, as predicted, did not differ significantly [x^2 (2) = .84].

Some provocative examples of narrative thinking by these young children are provided to lend support and color to these conclusions. Presented here are story builder responses.

As to why Mary was unhappy:

1. "She might not have wanted her birthday to be on that day . . . cause she probably um thought it was gonna be on the next day and then when she woke up she remembered it was gonna be on that day and she didn't know what to wear."

How come Mary threw water on the candles:

2. "She didn't wanna blow the candles out . . . I think she was um, um sad, um because um I think she didn't wanna have the birthday" (no mention of Mary's state in this story text).
3. "She couldn't blow them out . . . cause they were magic candles."

The following are some responses given to the question about what the other kids did when Mary threw water on the candles:

4. "Did they think it was boring . . . cause they never saw anybody throw water on the candles?"
5. "Didn't wanna eat the cake . . . cause it's wet."

Finally, below are some responses pertaining to the questions on parental behavior when Mary threw water on the candles:

6. "They both went on each, one side of her, and uh, maybe they stayed back a little. . . . They didn't wanna get wet."
7. "They helped her. . . . So she would get them right on the candles."
8. "They might have spanked her."

The present data provide support for the idea that breach or a noncanonical relation among the pentadic elements of agent, action, scene, instrument, and goal leads to narrative thinking. Additionally, the present data offer some preliminary and interesting refinements about the nature of breach. For example, not all breaches appear to be equivalent. In terms of the present research, two kinds of breach were explored: agent–action and agent–scene. The agent–action breach was a greater catalyst for narrative thinking, as measured by story builder responses, than the agent–scene breach. This was determined by the use of the Fisher Exact Probability test, comparing the number of children showing story builder responses in stories 1b (eight of eight) and 1d (two of seven), $p <$ .005. Although with Story 1b the child has more opportunity to display narrative thought by virtue of this story having three associated questions, in comparison to the one question of Story 1d, other factors as well may account for this difference. For example, action, in comparison to character (internal) state, may be the more salient dimension for children, and accordingly violations in action may be more easily detected. Also, there may be a greater degree of difficulty in addressing imbalances that involve character internal state than external physical action.

An additional aspect of breach or imbalance that receives some preliminary treatment here is the dynamic interaction among multiple breaches. For example, Story 1b involved throwing water on the candles only, whereas Story 1f involved Mary's being happy and throwing water, and Story 1e involved Mary's being unhappy and throwing water. The percentage of children providing consciousness contribution responses across these stories respectively is: 100% (8 of 8), 75% (6 of 8), and 57% (4 of 7). In stories 1b and 1f no clue, in terms of character state, is provided to account for the character's action. State is either not specified at all, or if specified is not explanatory (e.g., Mary is happy). This may have the effect of highlighting the action imbalance, and accordingly the highest levels of narrative responding are achieved on these stories. However, in Story 1e, where Mary is unhappy and threw water on the candles, the imbalance in character state is in harmony with or resonates to the imbalance in character action. The perception of imbalance may be depressed in such cases. Moreover, the story itself in terms of character state may provide a reason for the action imbalance, creating no need for narrative extension. That is, the reason why Mary threw water on the candles is because she is unhappy. Accordingly, the lowest level of narrative responding across these three stories was found for Story 1e. Because complex and sophisticated stories may incorporate numerous imbalances that interact with one another in the text, the process of how children handle multiple breaches represents another key element of narrative thought.

SOME CONCLUSIONS

The data from the present investigation point to the important influence of the child's conceptual system in the development of narrative thought. The child's understanding of canonical events enables the appreciation of dramatic imbalance or crisis. In the preschool and early school-aged years, the child has formed representations of a range of routine events, and this knowledge stands as one domain of canonicality. Whenever there is canonicality, there is the potential for narrative thought, which has, at heart, trouble, consisting in violations of the canon. So breach has a basis in child knowledge. Moreover breach apparently serves as a narrative trigger. Upon encountering noncanonicality, the child is thrust into the landscape of consciousness, whereby story action is linked to the minds of the protagonists. In the face of breach, the child has no recourse in the arena of action, but is compelled to move into the subjective plane.

Additional research on these issues seems in order. Distinguishing different kinds of breach along with their effects might be quite revelatory of child thought. For example, if action breaches are more salient than state (internal) breaches, why is this the case? Also, the workings of multiple breaches, a characteristic of complex stories, deserves further investigation. Moreover, in keeping with the "functional" approach to narrative emphasized in this chapter, it would be interesting to note if violations of canon, as they occur in real life activity, lead to spontaneous story production by children. In showing that breach pushes the perceiver toward the attribution of consciousness to story characters, this research indicates one possible occasion for narrative thought. The issues of why and when we tell stories, and how stories may vary depending on things such as the purposes of the teller and listener and the situational context, constitute some of the functional aspects of narratives. As Herrnstein Smith (1980) noted, for a theory of narrative to be complete such issues must be incorporated. These areas then represent some directions for future research along functional lines.

ACKNOWLEDGMENTS

This investigation was supported by the National Institute of Mental Health, National Research Service Award 1 F32 MH09296 to Joan Lucariello. Portions of this chapter were presented at the meeting of the Society for Research in Child Development, April 1987, Baltimore, and the Fourth International Conference on Event Perception and Action, August 1987, Trieste, Italy. Many thanks to the official reviewer of this chapter, Lucia French, who made important suggestions toward revision of this manuscript. Additional thanks go to Jerome Bruner, Katherine Nelson, Joe Glick, and Amy Kyratzis, who made incisive contributions throughout the course of this work. Requests for reprints should be sent to: Joan Lucariello, Graduate Faculty—Psychology, New School for Social Research, 65 Fifth Ave., New York, New York 10003.

REFERENCES

Applebee, A. (1978). *The child's concept of story: Ages two to seventeen.* Chicago: University of Chicago Press.

Bruner, J. (1986). *Actual minds, possible worlds.* Cambridge, MA: Harvard University Press.

Bruner, J., & Lucariello, J. (1989). Monologue as Narrative Recreation of the World. In K. Nelson (Ed.), *Narratives from the crib* (pp. 73–97). Cambridge: Harvard University Press.

Burke, K. (1969). *A grammar of motives.* Berkeley: University of California Press.

Chatman, S. (1978). *Story and discourse.* Ithaca: Cornell University Press.

Greimas, A., & Courtes, J. (1976). The cognitive dimension of narrative discourse. *New Literary History, 7,* 433–447.

Herrnstein Smith, B. (1980). Narrative versions, narrative theories. In W. J. T. Mitchell (Ed.), *On narrative* (pp. 209–232). Chicago: University of Chicago Press.

Mandler, J. (1983). Representation. In J. H. Flavell & E. M. Markman (Eds.), *Handbook of child psychology: Vol. 3. Cognitive development* (4th ed., pp. 420–494). New York: Wiley.

McNamee, G. (1988). The social origins of narrative skills. In M. Hickmann (Ed.), *Social and functional approaches to language and thought* (pp. 287–304). New York: Academic Press.

Nelson, K. (Ed.). (1986). *Event knowledge: Structure and function in development.* Hillsdale, NJ: Lawrence Erlbaum Associates.

Paley, V. (1981). *Wally's stories.* Cambridge, MA: Harvard University Press.

Turner, V. (1980). Social dramas and stories about them. In W. J. T. Mitchell (Ed.), *On narrative* (pp. 137–164). Chicago: University of Chicago Press.

6

Narrative and the Child's Theory of Mind

Janet W. Astington
Ontario Institute for Studies in Education

Here is the farm. Here is the stable. The horse lives here with one little foal. Here is the cowshed. The cow lives here with two little calves. Here is the barn. The cat lives here with three little kittens. Here is the pigsty. The pig lives here with four little pigs. Here is the duckpond. The duck lives here with five little ducklings. Here is the orchard. The hen lives here with six little chicks. Here is the field. The sheep live here with all the little lambs. Here is the farmer with all his animals

—Gagg (1958)

At 2 years of age this was my daughter's favorite story. Bedtime after bedtime I listed off the farmer's animals as we turned the page to look at each picture. Fourteen years later I scarcely needed to find the book to write the text out. It's a straightforward descriptive catalog, with pleasing repetition and systematic variation at each turn of the page.

By 4 years of age my daughter's tastes had changed. Her favorite book was now *The Fairy Tale Treasury* (Briggs & Haviland, 1974); for example, from "The Emperor's New Clothes":

The emperor thought he would like to see it while it was still on the loom. So, accompanied by a number of selected courtiers, among whom were the two faithful officials who had already seen the imaginary stuff, he went to visit the crafty impostors, who were working away as hard as ever they could at the empty loom. "It is magnificent!" said both the officials. "Only see, Your Majesty, what a design! What colours!" And they pointed to the empty loom, for they thought no doubt the others could see the stuff. "What!" thought the emperor; "I see nothing at all! This is terrible! Am I a fool? Am I not fit to be emperor? Why, nothing worse could happen to me!" "Oh, it is beautiful!" said the emperor. "It has my highest approval!" and he nodded his satisfaction as he gazed at the empty loom. Nothing would induce him to say that he could not see anything. (pp. 176–177)

What happened in those 2 years? When we read the stories in *The Fairy Tale Treasury* we had entered a new world. I cannot say we had entered the fictional world. The farm book was a fiction, but it did not seem like a real story. What was the difference?

THE DUAL LANDSCAPE OF NARRATIVE

The answer to my question came while I was reading Jerome Bruner's (1986) description of narrative thought in *Actual Minds, Possible Worlds*. Bruner contrasted two modes of thought, paradigmatic and narrative. Put somewhat baldly, the contrast is a version of the well-known contrast between the sciences and the arts, but Bruner's treatment is detailed and subtle. Paradigmatic, or logico-scientific, thought is concerned with physical reality. It deals with issues of truth, with observation, analysis, and proof. Its concern is to build theories, to explain physical phenomena in terms of general content-free laws, and so its interest is in abstraction, verification, argument, and conclusion. Its language is akin to logic and mathematics. Narrative thought, on the other hand, is concerned with psychic, not physical, reality. It deals with issues of human experience, with beliefs and doubts, intentions and emotions. Its language is that of drama and story.

The striking characteristic of a good story, Bruner suggested, is that it simultaneously recounts reality, that is, events and actions in the real world, and the participants' perception of that reality—their beliefs, hopes, and fears. There are two landscapes, as it were:

One is the landscape of action, where the constituents are the arguments of action: agent, intention or goal, situation, instrument, something corresponding to a "story grammar." The other landscape is the landscape of consciousness: what those involved in the action know, think, or feel, or do not know, think, or feel. (Bruner, 1986, p. 14)

For instance, in one landscape the weavers are busily working away; the emperor and his courtiers are watching them. In the other landscape the weavers are only pretending to weave; the watchers each know they themselves see nothing, but each thinks the others see something wonderful . . . and so on. Both of these landscapes are represented in the story. However, the latter is already a representation; it is the fictional characters' representations of the fictional reality. Thus, the storyteller has to represent those representations, and the listener has to understand this landscape as the representation of a representation. To appreciate the story the listener has to comprehend both these landscapes simultaneously, the landscape of reality and the landscape of consciousness. This is the heart of understanding narrative, and this is what the 4-year-old, but not the 2-year-old, can achieve.

We can represent the features of this second landscape, the landscape of consciousness, as attitudes to propositions; for example:

$$believe(x)$$
$$desire(y)$$
$$intend(z)$$

The emperor believes his courtiers see beautiful cloth.
The emperor desires his courtiers not discover that he can't see it.
The emperor intends not to tell the courtiers he sees nothing.

The youngest children themselves have such propositional attitudes; they have beliefs, desires, and intentions. The crucial change that occurs between 2 and 4 years of age is the development of an awareness of these mental states in themselves and in others, that is, the development of an ability to represent the representing relationship itself, which is what Pylyshyn (1978) called *metarepresentational* ability. By 4 years of age children not only have beliefs, for example, but they also have beliefs *about* beliefs, and they can attribute a belief to another. What evidence do we have that this is so?

THEORY OF MIND

Some time ago, Premack and Woodruff (1978) sought such evidence, not for young children, but for chimpanzees. They showed a chimpanzee videotapes in which a human actor was faced with some problem, such as trying to reach a bunch of bananas hanging from the ceiling, and then they gave the chimpanzee a pair of photographs, one of which depicted a solution to the problem, such as the actor's climbing onto a box. The animal's task was to choose one of the photographs; Premack and Woodruff showed that the chimpanzee usually chose the photograph depicting the solution. They interpreted their results by claiming that the chimpanzee possessed a *theory of mind*; that the animal attributed mental states to the actor, such as wanting to get the bananas, and chose the photograph that depicted a means to the desired end. They considered it appropriate to call this a *theory* of mind because the mental states attributed were not directly observable, and because the theoretical system could be used to make predictions about the actor's behavior, such as that he would climb onto a box. That is, Premack and Woodruff used the chimpanzee's predictions of the actor's behavior to infer the animal's possession of a theory of mind.

Critics were concerned whether it was reasonable to make that inference, or whether it was likely that the chimpanzee's predictions came from simple association, training, and so on. A number of critics (Bennett, 1978; Dennett, 1978; Harman, 1978) tried to envisage the basic test that would be required to demonstrate conclusively that an individual attributed mental states, such as belief, to another. The essence of their tasks is this: to show that someone understands another's belief, she must be able to appreciate that the other's belief may be different from her own, and therefore wrong from her point of view, but the other will act on the basis of that wrong belief. For example, the individual and the other observe some state of affairs, such as an object being hidden in a container, so that they share the same belief about its location. Then in the absence of the other, the individual sees the object moved to a new location that the other does not see. The individual knows the true location of the object; the real state of affairs in the world. The crucial question is: Does she also realize that the other does not know this, that the other thinks the object is in the original location and would look there to find it? The difficulty for primatologists, such as Premack and Woodruff, is to find a way to ask that question. However, if we are interested in children's ability to attribute beliefs to another, the problem is at least somewhat easier.

INVESTIGATIONS OF
CHILDREN'S THEORY OF MIND

Indeed, Wimmer and Perner (1983) developed this paradigm into a now well-known task for assessing children's understanding of belief. A story is acted out for child subjects, using dolls and toy furniture. A boy puts some chocolate into a blue cupboard and goes out to play. While he's out, his mother moves the chocolate to a green cupboard. The boy returns to look for the chocolate. The child subject is asked, "Where will he look?" The subject has seen the chocolate moved from the blue cupboard to the green cupboard, and she knows that is where it now is. When she's asked where will the boy look, what does she say? Up to about the age of 4, children say that the boy will look in the green cupboard, where the chocolate actually is, even though they remember that he put the chocolate in the blue cupboard in the beginning and then went out to play. They cannot see that the story child's beliefs about the situation would be different from what they know actually to be the case. Put another way, they cannot simultaneously tell the story in the landscape of action "The chocolate is in the green cupboard" and in the landscape of consciousness "The boy thinks the chocolate's in the blue cupboard."

In the same year that Wimmer and Perner published this study, a report of research into children's understanding of the distinction between appearance and reality was also published (Flavell, Flavell, & Green, 1983). At first this seemed a quite unrelated piece of work, but more recently a close relation has been established between the two. Flavell and his colleagues showed children some objects that had a deceptive appearance, such as a sponge that was painted to look remarkably like a rock. First, children saw the object at a distance and presumably thought it was a rock. Then they played with it and found out that it was a sponge. After that they were asked two questions, one about the object's appearance, what it looked like, and one about what it really was. Until about the age of 4, children said that it looked like a sponge, and it really was a sponge. Again the younger children seemed unable to tell a story on two landscapes simultaneously, the landscape of reality ("it's really a sponge") and the landscape of consciousness ("It looks like a rock," which is equivalent to "someone might think it's a rock").

So these two findings are not at all unconnected. In fact, Alison Gopnik and I (Gopnik & Astington, 1988) showed them to be closely related by asking children questions about another's mistaken belief, and about appearance and reality, for the same objects. For instance, concerning a sponge rock, as well as asking "What does this look like?" and "What is this really?" we said, "Nicky [a friend of the subject's] hasn't touched this, he hasn't squeezed it. If Nicky just sees it over here like this, what will he think it is?" We asked similar questions about other materials; for example, a picture of a green cat that appeared to be black when the children first saw it because it was covered with a pink filter (cf. Flavell et al., 1983). As in the previous studies, we found that children 4 years of age and older answered these questions appropriately, and further-more, there were significant correlations between total scores for the appearance-reality questions and for questions about the oth-er's mistaken belief, indicating that it is not simply a change that comes at about 4 years of age, but that individual children are more likely than not to acquire insight into both problems at the same time.

We also asked the children about their own mistaken belief. When they first saw the sponge rock at a distance, they would presumably think it was a rock, but when they played with it they would discover that it was a sponge; that is, their representation of the object would change. We wondered whether they would under-stand this representational change and remember their earlier rep-resentation, and so we asked, "When you first saw this, before you touched it or squeezed it, what did you think it was?" We used a variety of materials that were likely to produce an initial wrong impression, that is, a mistaken belief. As well as the sponge rock and the green cat that looked black, we showed the children a familiar candy box that actually contained pencils (Perner, Lee-kam, & Wimmer, 1987), two dolls clothed in one dress that appeared to be just one doll, and a picture book showing different animals' ears through peepholes, until the last one when the "ears" turn out to be the petals of a flower (cf. Chandler & Helm, 1984). The children were first shown the objects in their deceptive state, the true nature of the materials was then revealed, and after return-ing the object to its original state, children were asked about their first impression of it. A control task, asking about an earlier *physical* state of affairs in some different materials, ensured that they under-stood this question. Once again, we found clear evidence of develop-ment of understanding between 3 and 5 years of age; this time, children's understanding of their own mistaken belief. A majority of 3-year-olds reported that when they had first seen the deceptive objects they had thought that they were what they were later revealed to be (sponge, pencils, etc.) whereas a majority of 5-year-olds remembered and reported their original mistaken belief (rock, candy, etc.). Thus, even for their own beliefs, young children are unable to tell a story in the dual landscape. Once they know the real state of affairs, for example, "The 'rock' is really a sponge," they cannot tell the story, "I thought it was a rock."

In addition, scores on this task were significantly correlated with scores on the appearance–reality task and scores on the task asking about the other's belief. The correlations between these three tasks are perhaps the most interesting aspect of this study, providing evidence that there is a general change that underlies children's cognitive abilities at about the age of 4 years. It is this change that allows the child, for the first time, to comprehend representations as representations, and this ability enables the child to appreciate the dual landscape of a story.

THEORETICAL EXPLANATIONS OF CHILDREN'S THEORY OF MIND

What is this general change? One might want to argue that it is the ability to form counterfactual and hypothetical representations, such as that expressed by "Pretend this is a rock." But this cannot be the answer. Even 2-year-olds are not limited to forming only veridical representations of what is peceived; they can form hypothetical representations, for example in pretend play, as Leslie (1987) cogently argued. Alternatively, one might argue that it is the ability to distinguish these hypothetical representations from reality, to recognize them as not real. But this cannot be the answer either. Three-year-olds are very good at making distinctions between real objects and mental representations, such as imagination and dreams, as Wellman and Estes (1986) showed. Or perhaps one would argue that the change is due to the ability to talk about representations of representations, such as "He thinks it's in the green cupboard" or "I thought it was a rock" and so on. But nor is this the answer. Two- and 3-year-olds can engage in this kind of talk about mental events (Bretherton & Beeghly, 1982; Shatz, Wellman, & Silber, 1983).

So is my claim justified? Are children really unable to synchronize the two landscapes of narrative before they are 4 years old? I think so. What then is the change that occurs at about 4 years of age that enables children to understand others' false beliefs, their own earlier beliefs, the distinction between appearance and reality, as well as the dual landscape of a story? A number of theorists have suggested that a new understanding of the representational capacities of the mind develops at this time (Flavell, 1988; Forguson & Gopnik, 1988; Perner, 1988). For example, Perner argued that at about 4 years of age children acquire the metarepresentational ability to represent the representing relation itself, that is, to see representations *as* representations. Two-year-olds can form models of the world, including hypothetical models, and can compare these models to the world, so that they can engage in pretend play, for example, and can tell you that dreams are not real. They can also associate other people with models that describe alternative situations, so that they can understand another's pretense. But they cannot represent the *process* of modeling; they do not have a model of the other's mind representing reality, whereas 4-year-olds can represent this process. Thus, 4-year-olds, but not 2-year-olds, are able to see that another's belief is in fact his or her representation of reality. It therefore represents the real world for the other person, and is the world in which that person will act, even if the belief is mistaken, that is, if the model *mis*represents the real situation. This is what is needed to understand false belief, and to make accurate predictions about the other's behavior in the real world. And this is what is needed to synchronize the two landscapes of narrative. Four-year-old children can comprehend the landscape of consciousness as the story character's mental representation of the actual situation that is depicted in the story on the landscape of action. It is this understanding that is required to appreciate the dual landscape.

THE CREATION OF SUBJUNCTIVE REALITY

Once children are able to model the process of representing reality, they can understand the dual landscape of narrative, but how? How do they acquire competence with the two landscapes? A prior question is: What are the characteristics of these two landscapes; how is the dual landscape created? How is the language of narrative used to paint two landscapes simultaneously?

As I said at the beginning of this chapter, Bruner (1986) characterized good stories by their portrayal of a dual landscape, the landscape of action and the landscape of consciousness. He discussed the way in which this dual landscape is created by the production of the "special form of speech act that is a story" (p. 22), an idea adopted from Iser (1978). Iser argued that good stories are deliberately indeterminate; they do not present the hearer or reader with a fixed chronicle; rather they invite the reader to interpret the story, and in so doing to find its meaning. The meaning is not entirely dictated by the text.

Bruner mentioned three features of discourse that create the dual landscape by maintaining, in some sense, the indeterminacy of a fictional text, thus allowing the reader to determine its meaning for him or herself. Bruner called these features ways of "*subjunctivizing reality*," and that, he said, is "the key to the issue of discourse in great fiction" (p. 26).

What is a subjunctive reality? The term *subjunctive* is taken from subjunctive mood, which in traditional grammar is a category of verbal inflection contrasting with indicative and imperative moods (Levinson, 1983, p. 243). The indicative mood is the unmarked case, used in making statements that are not in any way qualified with respect to the speaker's attitude; the imperative mood is used to express orders and instructions (Lyons, 1968, p. 307). The subjunctive mood modulates such bald expressions by grammatically marking the speaker's attitude, so that facts and commands are expressed as possibilities or wishes or obligations. It is the difference between "You're here" (a statement) and "Come here" (an order) on the one hand, and "You might be here" (a possibility), "Would you were here" (a wish), and "You should be here" (an obligation) on the other. Thus, the subjunctive mood is associated not with bald facts, but with wishes and possibilities. And thus, Bruner's term *subjunctive reality* denotes a possible, not a certain reality; one that is not entirely determined by the storyteller, but is partly created by the listener.

The discourse processes that are used to subjunctivize reality are thus fundamental to the language of narrative, to the creation of the dual landscape of the fictional world. Children must acquire competence with these processes if they are to enter this landscape. Bruner (1986) discussed three of these processes: presupposition, subjectification, and the use of multiple perspective. Briefly, presupposition conveys information by implication, not by statement. It invites the listener to assume that such and such is the case, but without explicitly stating that it is so. Subjectification depicts the fictional world through the eyes of one of the characters, so the listener is not told how things are but how they seem to be. In a somewhat similar way, by using multiple perspectives, the storyteller does not present a single view of the fictional world, but a series of partly overlapping views that allow the listener to build up a complex picture. In each case, the meaning is not entirely determined by the text, but the listener is involved in its construction.

INTENTIONAL AND ILLOCUTIONARY VERBS

Bruner (1986) discussed the ways in which each of these three features is realized in fictional discourse. Although each can be achieved in a variety of ways, all of them can be achieved by using an intentional or illocutionary verb, and that is what I focus on here. These are the verbs used to characterize attitudes to propositions, which I referred to at the beginning of this chapter (p. 153), verbs such as *believe, desire, intend*. These propositional attitudes are mental states, or more precisely, intentional states, and these verbs are often referred to as intentional verbs.

Intentional is used here in its philosophical, rather than everyday, sense. The term was introduced into philosophy by Brentano (1874/1960) in a discussion of the distinction between psychological and physical phenomena. An intentional state is a mental state, such as belief, desire, or intention, which is directed at something outside the self. In Searle's (1983) terms, it is a mental state that has a representational content: For example, beliefs, desires, and intentions must be beliefs about something, desires for something, and intentions to do something. These are intentional states that can be distinguished from mental states, such as sensations of pain and pleasure, that have no content outside themselves; that is, a specification of the content of a sensation is just a description of the sensation, whereas a specification of the content of an intentional state is a representation.

Every intentional state consists of this representational content in a certain psychological mode (Searle, 1983). The same content can occur in different modes; for example, Henry can *believe* that Belinda loves him, *hope* that Belinda loves him, *want* Belinda to love him, and so forth. Different types of intentional state have different *directions of fit* in Searle's terms, between the mental representation and the actual state of affairs in the world. If Henry believes that Belinda loves him, his belief will be true if she in fact loves him. If his belief is false, he can make it true by changing the belief: a *mind-to-world* direction of fit. On the other hand, if he wants Belinda to love him, his desire is neither true nor false, but is fulfilled if she does and unfulfilled if she doesn't. If she doesn't love him, things are made to fit not by his changing the desire, but by Belinda's changing her feeling for him: a *world-to-mind* direction of fit. Not all propositional attitudes have directions of fit; if Henry is sorry that Belinda does not love him, then his sorrow contains a belief that she does not love him, but his sorrow is not true in the way that the belief is. For those intentional states that do have directions of fit, the states of affairs in the world that have the correct fit are called their *conditions of satisfaction*, and this is what is represented mentally.

Just as an intentional state has a representative content in a certain psychological mode, so a speech act has a propositional content expressed with a certain illocutionary force (Searle, 1969). Thus, there is a second set of propositional attitude verbs, those that characterize the illocutionary force of speech acts, verbs such as *doubt, demand, promise, persuade.* According to Searle (1979), the illocutionary force determines what kind of speech act is performed: *assertive* (e.g., stating, predicting), *directive* (e.g., ordering, questioning), *commissive* (e.g., promising, vowing), *expressive* (e.g., thanking, congratulating), or *declaration* (e.g., christening). Like intentional states, speech acts may contain the same proposition expressed with different forces; for example, "Henry is getting married" (assertive), "Who will marry Henry?" (directive), "I promise to marry" (commissive, if spoken by Henry), "Congratulations on your marriage, Henry" (expressive), and "I do" (declaration, if spoken by Henry at the wedding ceremony). And, again like intentional states, speech acts have a direction of fit between the expression and reality. Assertives have a *word-to-world* direction of fit; false statements, like false beliefs, can be changed to fit the state of affairs in the world. Directives and commissives have a *world-to-word* direction of fit; orders and promises, like desires, cannot be changed to fit reality. If they are unfulfilled, the world must be changed to fit them. Expressives have no direction of fit, because the speaker presupposes that the propositional content is already satisfied. Just as Henry's sorrow that Belinda does not love him contains a belief that she does not love him, so when I congratulate Henry on his marriage, the fact of his marriage is presupposed.

Notice that an intentional state and a speech act may have the same representational content, as for example, when Henry believes that Belinda despises him and he asserts, "Belinda despises me." The statement expresses the belief that Belinda despises him. The conditions of satisfaction are the same for the assertion and the belief, namely *Belinda despise Henry*, and the direction of fit is the same in both cases, namely word-to-world for the assertion and mind-to-world for the belief. In a similar way, the speech act of requesting expresses the intentional state of desire, and the speech act of promising expresses the intentional state of intention. In each case, the conditions of satisfaction, that is, the representational content, and the direction of fit are the same for the intentional state and the corresponding speech act. For example, if Henry asks Belinda to marry him, he expresses the desire that she marry him; the conditions of satisfaction of the intentional state and of the speech act are *Belinda marry Henry*, the psychological mode of the intentional state is desire, its direction of fit is world-to-mind, the illocutionary force of the speech act is request, and its direction of fit is world-to-word.

Thus, the performance of any speech act is necessarily an expression of the corresponding intentional state. But notice that, although it is paradoxical to assert a proposition and deny belief in that proposition (for example, "It's raining and I don't believe it's raining"—Moore's paradox), one does not necessarily have the belief that is expressed, because one may be insincere. Nonetheless, the belief (that one does not have) has necessarily been expressed (Forguson, 1968). This fact is of importance in creating subjunctive realities, in creating the indeterminacy of the narrative text. It allows the storyteller to report what was said, without committing him or herself regarding the speaker's actual psychological state. Belinda can say that Henry is charming, but whether she believes him to be so is left open. Belinda can promise to marry Henry, but whether she intends to do so can be left for the listener to determine.

Intentional verbs are also important in creating subjunctive reality using subjectification, that is, the depiction of the world through the eyes of one of the characters. The fictional world is not then represented directly but via the representational content of the character's intentional state, particularly intentional states with a mind-to-world direction of fit so the narrator tells how things seem to be, not how they are; for example, "Belinda thought Henry was pompous." These verbs are also important in creating multiple perspectives, from which the listener builds up a picture of the fictional world; for example, "Henry believed that Belinda was beautiful but Brian thought she was quite plain."

FACTIVE VERBS AND PRESUPPOSITION

I briefly mention some syntactic facts concerning these verbs that are important to their role in creating subjunctive reality or the dual landscape of a story. Intentional and illocutionary verbs take object complements; that is to say, an embedded sentence functions as the direct object of the verb. The embedded sentence is an expression representing the conditions of satisfaction of the intentional state or speech act expressed by the main verb, and it may take a variety of different surface forms. For example:

1. Henry thinks *that he bought a ring.*
2. Henry admits *buying a ring.*
3. Henry promises *to buy a ring.*
4. Henry knows *that he should buy a ring.*

And lest you think that the particular surface form of the complement is determined by the precise intentional or illocutionary verb that is the main verb of the sentence, consider these examples:

5. Henry remembers *that he bought a ring.*
6. Henry remembers *buying a ring.*
7. Henry remembers *to buy a ring.*
8. Henry remembers *that he should buy a ring.*

Remember is a *factive* verb. When a factive verb is used in the main clause, the speaker presupposes the truth of the complement clause (Kiparsky & Kiparsky, 1971). A factive verb can be identified by negating it and determining if the truth value of the complement clause remains unchanged; thus:

5 → 9. Henry does not remember that he bought a ring.

1 →10. Henry does not think that he bought a ring.

In examples 5 and 9 the truth value of *he bought a ring* is the same, but it is not the same in examples 1 and 10; thus, *remember* is factive in examples 5 and 9, and *think* is nonfactive in examples 1 and 10. What of the other examples?

6 →11. Henry does not remember buying a ring.

7 →12. Henry does not remember to buy a ring.

8 →13. Henry does not remember that he should buy a ring.

Miller and Johnson-Laird (1976) suggested that a *that*-complement in indicative mood (e.g., as in examples 5 and 9) and some gerundive complements (e.g., as in examples 6 and 11) assert or presuppose the truth of the complement clause, whereas an infinitival form (e.g., examples 7 and 12) or a nonindicative mood (e.g., examples 8 and 13) in the complement clause does not presuppose its truth. This would explain why someone hearing examples 9 or 11 would assume that Henry bought a ring, but on hearing examples 12 or 13 would not assume so. That is, factivity depends on the syntactic nature of the complement construction, not just on the semantics of the main verb. Furthermore, some verbs may not remain factive if a modal auxiliary is inserted in the main clause; for example, compare:

14. Belinda remembers that the ring is too small.
15. Belinda may remember that the ring is too small.
16. Belinda discovers that the ring is too small.
17. Belinda may discover that the ring is too small.

In examples 14, 15, and 16 the truth of the complement is presupposed, but not in example 17.

Other factive verbs that may be used to create subjunctive reality by triggering presuppositions are: *know, regret, realize, be aware that,* and so forth (see Levinson, 1983, p. 181); for example, 18 presupposes 19:

18. Brian is aware that Belinda will invite him to her wedding.
19. Belinda will invite him to her wedding.

There are other verbs, known as implicative verbs (Karttunen, 1971), that can be used to create presuppositions. Most of these are not propositional attitude verbs, but some are. For example, item 20 implies what item 21 says:

20. Brian forgot to send a gift.
21. Brian intended to send a gift.

Like factive verbs, implicative verbs allow the storyteller to convey something without saying it explicitly, and thus to retain the openness of the text that Bruner (1986) considers so important in fictional narrative.

CHILDREN'S COMPETENCE
WITH THESE VERBS

As already noted, children use some of these terms for referring to mental states and speech acts when they are only 2 or 3 years old (Bretherton & Beeghly, 1982; Shatz et al., 1983). *Think, know, remember, want,* are the most commonly used mental state terms, with *say, tell,* and *ask* for speech acts. Remember that this is before the age when children are able to understand the dual language of narrative. Once they are 4 years old and can understand this, do they understand the distinction between factive verbs like *know* and *remember* and nonfactive verbs like *think* and *say*? Are they able to perceive meanings that the storyteller conveys by presupposition? For example, would they understand the different presuppositions created by "The weaver knows that there is nothing there" and "The emperor thinks that there is nothing there"?

Earlier research suggests that they wouldn't (e.g., Harris, 1975; Scoville & Gordon, 1980), but a more recent, careful study (Abbeduto & Rosenberg, 1985) shows that 4-year-olds, but not 3-year-olds, do understand the presuppositions created by the factive verbs *know*, *remember*, and *forget*, and understand that *think* is nonfactive. Seven-year-olds have also mastered *believe*; no children between 4 and 7 years of age were tested. The standard way of assessing children's understanding of factivity presents them with affirmative and negative sentences containing a factive or nonfactive main verb and a *that*-complement, and asks them to judge the truth of the complement clause; for example:

"The emperor knows that he is in trouble."
    Is the emperor in trouble? Yes, no, or can't tell?
"The emperor does not think that the weavers are crooks."
    Are the weavers crooks? Yes, no, or can't tell?

Unlike earlier studies, Abbeduto and Rosenberg (1985) introduced the test sentence with a brief story that established the referents of the test sentence but gave no clue to the truth of the complement; nor could the truth be determined from world knowledge; for example, "I have a friend named Mary. Mary has a cat. Mary forgets that the cat is slow" (p. 626). Children were then asked, "Is the cat slow?" and had to respond with "Yes," "No," or "Don't know." Also unlike earlier studies, the children had been trained to use the three response options and were not included if they could not do so. In addition, they were given sentences without factive or nonfactive verbs, where the correct response was "Don't know" (e.g., "John found a mitten. Was the mitten blue?"). The fact that children of all ages answered these questions correctly shows that the 3-year-olds' wrong answers for items with *think* and *believe* were due to their lack of understanding of presupposition, not their unwillingness to admit ignorance.

It is interesting that children found it easier to understand presupposition when it was contained in a story context. This had already been noted by Macnamara, Baker, and Olson (1976), but their results had been criticized on the grounds that the story context provided the information needed to respond correctly, whether or not the children understood the presuppositions (Hidi & Hildyard, 1979). Abbeduto and Rosenberg's (1985) study shows that a story context is facilitating, even if it provides no information directly.

Indeed, it is likely that reading and listening to stories helps children acquire competence with propositional attitude verbs and their presuppositions. Subjunctive realities can be created using simple verbs such as *know, think,* and *remember* that children acquire before they are 4 years old. However, there are hundreds more of these verbs (Austin, 1975, p. 150) that are part of the narrative language. How do children acquire competence with these terms, many of which are rarely used in oral language? It is likely that they acquire them from reading, and particularly from reading stories.

Kirkwood and Wolfe (1980), in a study of the readability of books used in schools, sampled passages from a variety of science and language arts texts; the language arts materials were almost all stories. There are three or four times as many propositional attitude verbs used in these texts than in the science texts; for example, the verbs *know, think,* and *believe* occur 7 times in 10,000 words of middle school science texts, and 29 times in 10,000 words of middle school language arts texts. In addition, there is a greater variety of propositional attitude verbs in the language arts texts; for example, *advise, assure, convince, demand, doubt, fear, forget, guess, intend, request, suggest,* and *wish* all occur in the stories and not in the science texts. Thus, it is likely that children acquire competence with these verbs and their presuppositions from reading stories, and in turn this competence helps children appreciate the subjunctive reality of narrative. If children do not comprehend these verbs, they will not understand one of the crucial ways in which storytellers create presupposition, subjectification, and multiple perspective.

SUGGESTIONS FOR FURTHER RESEARCH

My suggestion, that children would not understand the dual landscape of narrative before they are 4 years old, was simply based on my own experience of reading to children. The suggestion is certainly supported by observations of children's understanding false belief and the distinction between appearance and reality at the age of 4, and by theoretical arguments concerning children's theory of mind. Furthermore, there is one empirical study that provides more direct support.

Baron-Cohen, Leslie, and Frith (1985, 1986) compared the performance of normal 4-year-old children with that of autistic children (mean age 12 years) and Down's Syndrome children (mean age 11 years) on a variation of the Wimmer and Perner (1983) false belief test. They found that the 4-year-olds and the Down's Syndrome children could attribute a false belief to another, but the autistic children were unable to do so, despite the fact that the latter group had a considerably higher mental age than either of the other two groups. They postulated that autistic children lack the basic metarepresentational ability required for a theory of mind. They also gave the children a picture sequencing task, in which children had to arrange four pictures in sequence and then tell the story. There were three types of story: causal–mechanical, descriptive–behavioral, and psychological–intentional. The autistic children performed better than either of the other two groups on the mechanical stories and as well as the 4-year-olds on the behavioral stories, but worse than either of the other two groups on the intentional stories. To understand these stories, but not the other two types, one had to be able to consider two landscapes: what was going on in the world, and what was going on in the minds of the characters. The autistic children seemed to be completely unable to attribute propositional attitudes to the story characters.

To my knowledge, this is the only study that explicitly links theory of mind and story understanding. It would be interesting to conduct a similar study that looked at normal children in the crucial 3- to 5-year period. It is remarkable how much is achieved during this time, and it would be interesting to discover whether the mastery of the dual landscape of a story is one of these achievements. I would certainly hypothesize that it is.

A related question is: When do children start to produce stories with a dual landscape? It wouldn't be surprising if it is later than when they first begin to understand them, but I think not much later. Most research on children's story production has focused on the structural aspects of the story, conformity to story grammar, knowledge of story conventions, and so on. Leondar (1977) claimed that "attributes of thought, feeling, or motive are entirely absent from primary narratives" (p. 181) that are characteristic of 5- to 7-year-olds. If this is so, it is quite remarkable. However, a cursory reading of the stories recorded by Pitcher and Prelinger (1963) from children 2 to 5 years of age yields a number of examples of such attributions, especially in the 4- and 5-year-olds' stories; for example, in one story a baby kitten is looking for his family, "And the baby was frightened when he saw the tiger. But he climbed into the mouth because he wanted to see if it was his family" (his family was hidden in the tiger skin)—(p. 151). The explicit use of the dual landscape is not so immediately obvious, but there are instances; for example, in another story two children meet, "And they ran home—and they didn't know it, but they were brothers and sisters" (p. 143). Indeed, one of the dimensions that Pitcher and Prelinger scored in their analysis of the stories was *action versus thought processes*. Although acknowledging that the number of attributions is quite small, they reported that "as age progresses [children] attribute more detailed processes of thinking and of feeling, affect, or emotion to the characters in their stories" (p. 158–159), which is what one would expect between the ages of 2 and 5 years, at least from the argument I advance here. Of course, Leondar's main interest was in story structure. Her analysis of primary narratives showed that they contain only four of Todorov's (1971/1977, chapter 14) five elements of narrative. The missing element is "the Aristotelian moment of recognition . . . less an action than a mental event . . . a change of knowledge or of motive" (Leondar, 1977, p. 181), and this does not appear in stories produced by children until they reach 8 or 9 years of age, according to Leondar. However, Leondar underestimates younger children's competence. The 5-year-old's story about the two children previously mentioned, continues: "The girl said 'What's your last name?' and the boy said, 'Anderson' " (p. 143). Then later on the story characters find a baby, and the story continues: "So they took him by the hand and said, 'What's your name?' 'Tommy Anderson.' 'Why we must be brothers or sisters!'. . . . Soon came a person like their mommy. 'Are these my brothers?' the little girl said. 'Yes, they are.' " Perhaps younger children are capable of producing simple transformations of knowledge or motive. It would be worth investigating more thoroughly.

CONCLUSION

I have emphasized the special importance of children's theory of mind to their understanding of narrative, and I have suggested that the metarepresentational ability to ascribe propositional attitudes to others is required in order to comprehend the two landscapes of a story: the landscape of action and the landscape of consciousness. This is not to say that children younger than 4 years of age do not appreciate fictional stories; indeed they do, and just as 2-year-olds can enter into pretend play, these younger children can enjoy stories of make-believe and fantasy. The crucial change that comes at 4 years of age is an appreciation of the dual landscape of narrative, and I have discussed the way in which intentional and illocutionary verbs can be used to create this dual landscape. These are verbs that create subjunctive realities, keeping meaning indeterminate, "so as to allow play for the reader's imagination" (Bruner, 1986, p. 35). Readers make their own interpretation, and, in some sense, construct their own version of the story. Readers can do this from great literature, from fairy tales, and even from tedious linguistic examples: *Did* Belinda marry Henry?

ACKNOWLEDGMENT

I am grateful to Nancy Torrance and David Olson for their critical reviews of this chapter.

REFERENCES

Abbeduto, L., & Rosenberg, S. (1985). Children's knowledge of the presuppositions of *know* and other cognitive verbs. *Journal of Child Language, 12,* 621–641.

Austin, J. L. (1975). *How to do things with words* (2nd ed.). Cambridge, MA: Harvard University Press.

Baron-Cohen, S., Leslie, A. M., & Frith, U. (1985). Does the autistic child have a "theory of mind"? *Cognition, 21,* 37–46.

Baron-Cohen, S., Leslie, A. M., & Frith, U. (1986). Mechanical, behavioural and intentional understanding of picture stories in autistic children. *British Journal of Developmental Psychology, 4,* 113–125.

Bennett, J. (1978). Some remarks about concepts. *The Behavioral and Brain Sciences, 1,* 557–560.

Brentano, F. (1960). The distinction between mental and physical phenomena. In R. M. Chisholm (Ed.), *Realism and the background of phenomenology* (pp. 39–61). New York: The Free Press. (Originally published in 1874)

Bretherton, I., & Beeghly, M. (1982). Talking about internal states: The acquisition of an explicit theory of mind. *Developmental Psychology, 6,* 906–921.

Briggs, R., & Haviland, V. (1974). *The fairy tale treasury.* Harmondsworth, England: Puffin Books.

Bruner, J. (1986). *Actual minds, possible worlds.* Cambridge, MA: Harvard University Press.

Chandler, M. J., & Helm, D. (1984). Developmental changes in the contribution of shared experience to social role-taking competence. *International Journal of Behavioral Development, 7,* 145–156.

Dennett, D. C. (1978). Beliefs about beliefs. *The Behavioral and Brain Sciences, 1,* 568–570.

Flavell, J. H. (1988). The development of children's knowledge about the mind: From cognitive connections to mental representations. In J. W. Astington, P. L. Harris, & D. R. Olson (Eds.), *Developing theories of mind* (pp. 244–267). New York: Cambridge University Press.

Flavell, J. H., Flavell, E. R., & Green, F. L. (1983). Development of the appearance-reality distinction. *Cognitive Psychology, 15,* 95–120.

Forguson, L. (1968). On "It's raining, but I don't believe it." *Theoria, 7,* 89–101.

Forguson, L., & Gopnik, A. (1988). The ontogeny of common sense. In J. W. Astington, P. L. Harris, & D. R. Olson (Eds.), *Developing theories of mind* (pp. 226–243). New York: Cambridge University Press.

Gagg, M. E. (1958). *The farm.* Loughborough, England: Wills & Hepworth.

Gopnik, A., & Astington, J. W. (1988). Children's understanding of representational change and its relation to the understanding of false belief and the appearance-reality distinction. *Child Development, 59,* 26–37.

Harman, G. (1978). Studying the chimpanzee's theory of mind. *The Behavioral and Brain Sciences, 1,* 591.

Harris, R. J. (1975). Children's comprehension of complex sentences. *Journal of Experimental Child Psychology, 19,* 420–433.

Hidi, S., & Hildyard, A. (1979). Four-year-olds' understanding of pretend and forget: No evidence for propositional reasoning. *Journal of Child Language, 6,* 493–510.

Iser, W. (1978). *The act of reading.* Baltimore, MD: Johns Hopkins University Press.

Karttunen, L. (1971). Implicative verbs. *Language, 47,* 340–358.

Kiparsky, P., & Kiparsky, C. (1971). Fact. In D. Steinberg & L. Jakobovits (Eds.), *Semantics: An interdisciplinary reader in philosophy, linguistics and psychology* (pp. 345–369). Cambridge, England: Cambridge University Press.

Kirkwood, K. J., & Wolfe, R. G. (1980). *Matching students and reading materials.* Toronto: Ministry of Education for Ontario.

Leondar, B. (1977). Hatching plots: Genesis of storymaking. In D. Perkins & B. Leondar (Eds.), *The arts and cognition* (pp. 172–191). Baltimore, MD: Johns Hopkins University Press.

Leslie, A. M. (1987). Pretense and representation in infancy: The origins of "Theory of Mind." *Psychological Review, 94,* 412–426.

Levinson, S. C. (1983). *Pragmatics.* Cambridge, England: Cambridge University Press.

Lyons, J. (1968). *Introduction to theoretical linguistics.* Cambridge, England: Cambridge University Press.

MacNamara, J., Baker, E., & Olson, C. (1976). Four-year-olds' understanding of pretend, forget and know: Evidence for propositional operations. *Child Development, 47,* 62–70.

Miller, G. A., & Johnson-Laird, P. N. (1976). *Language and perception.* Cambridge, MA: Harvard University Press.

Perner, J. (1988). Developing semantics for theories of mind: From propositional attitudes to mental representation. In J. W. Astington, P. L. Harris, & D. R. Olson (Eds.), *Developing theories of mind* (pp. 141–172). New York: Cambridge University Press.

Perner, J., Leekam, S., & Wimmer, H. (1987). Three-year-olds' difficulty with false belief: The case for a conceptual deficit. *British Journal of Developmental Psychology, 5,* 125–137.

Pitcher, E. G., & Prelinger, E. (1963). *Children tell stories.* New York: International Universities Press.

Premack, D., & Woodruff, G. (1978). Does the chimpanzee have a theory of mind? *The Behavioral and Brain Sciences, 1,* 515–526.

Pylyshyn, Z. W. (1978). When is attribution of beliefs justified? *The Behavioral and Brain Sciences, 1,* 592–593.

Scoville, R. P., & Gordon, A. M. (1980). Children's understanding of factive presuppositions: An experiment and a review. *Journal of Child Language, 7,* 381–399.

Searle, J. R. (1969). *Speech acts: An essay in the philosophy of language.* Cambridge, England: Cambridge University Press.

Searle, J. R. (1979). A taxonomy of illocutionary acts. In *Expression and meaning* (pp. 1–29). Cambridge, England: Cambridge University Press.

Searle, J. R. (1983). *Intentionality: An essay in the philosophy of mind.* Cambridge, England: Cambridge University Press.

Shatz, M., Wellman, H. M., & Silber, S. (1983). The acquisition of mental verbs: A systematic investigation of the first reference to mental state. *Cognition, 14,* 301–321.

Todorov, T. (1977). *The poetics of prose* (R. Howard, Trans.). Ithaca, NY: Cornell University Press. (Originally published in 1971)

Wellman, H. M., & Estes, D. (1986). Early understanding of mental entities: A reexamination of childhood realism. *Child Development, 57,* 910–923.

Wimmer, H., & Perner, J. (1983). Beliefs about beliefs: Representation and constraining function of wrong beliefs in young children's understanding of deception. *Cognition, 13,* 103–128.

7

The Narration of Dialogue and Narration Within Dialogue: The Transition From Story to Logic

C. Jan Swearingen
The University of Texas at Arlington

A good story and a well-formed argument are different natural kinds.
. . . It has been claimed that the one is a refinement or an abstraction
from the other. But this must be either false or true only in the most
unenlightening way.
—Bruner (1986, p. 11)

We have become accustomed to thinking of poetic language as
universal, "paleolithic" (e.g. (Friedrich, 1986, p. 26), as a prelap-
sarian mode of thought and language in which narrative is often
included. In this chapter, I contend that in several important senses
narrative is not timeless or unchanging. *Narrative* is far from ancient; examining its relatively recent genesis as a genre term and
as a concept can help explain the burgeoning diversity of narrative
forms that are emerging in the research of several fields. That
"narrative" is relatively neologistic is not to say that we shouldn't
continue to investigate the kinds and uses of narrative in culture,
language, and cognitive development. However, as we advance in
these areas of research, we can profitably begin to monitor the
recursion (Feldman, 1986) in our own concepts of narrative, a recursion that is shaped by the increasing scope and detailed diversity
of the data being gathered. Two elements in our concept of narrative

173

help account for the protean and elusive qualities of narrative thought and practice.

Approached as a metalinguistic concept and particularly as a stable description of broad shared patterns in language practice and thought, narrative is of very recent vintage. The first section of this chapter defines the complex origins of the current concept of narrative and suggests how this complexity can account for the instability of narrative as a descriptive genre. Today's uses and understandings of narrative bear traces of its conceptualization in 19th-century philology and folklore, in the patterns of the 19th-century novel given critical articulation only in the 20th-century "new" critics' appraisals of narration (cf. Kelber 1987a), and, only within this century, in studies of oral literature, oral composition, and narrative patterns in child language. Narrative has undergone particularly rapid expansion and redefinition within the past two decades (e.g., Bauman & Scherzer, 1974; Bruner 1986; Finnegan, 1977; Heath, 1983; Kermode, 1983; Lord, 1960; Mitchell, 1968, Scholes & Kellog, 1966). After examining the uses and meanings of narrative within these recent fields, the examination turns to the classical period when the term *"narratio"* was first used. The following points are developed. Classical evidence supports the view that the term narrative, up through the 1st century B.C., emerged in a context unrelated to storytelling, invention of tales, or well-crafted narration as we understand these modes today. *Narratio* first surfaced as a technical rhetorical term that denoted the part of an oration immediately following the statement of the issue or argument.

It was not until Cicero's era that the term "narrative" was extended to include pleasant, artful, or inventive storytelling. Even then, the telling of such stories, including histories, was regarded as a branch of rhetoric. Perhaps most surprising and thought provoking is Cicero's classification of argument as one kind of narrative, suggesting that sequentiality, whether of events or of ideas, was a defining characteristic of early narrative and logic alike. The diversity of Greek and Latin terms for story, storytelling, and history that were in use long before "narrative," raises many of the same questions for the narrative genres of antiquity that are being asked of today's uses and understandings of narrative.

What is narrated, in what sequence, and to what end—events, causes, meanings, inner mental states, speech, other stories? How is narrative received and understood? (Heath, 1983; Michaels & Collins, 1984). How do its hearers or readers construct virtual texts (Iser, 1978) and "take" meaning? (Barthes, 1977). Is understanding invariably a goal of the hearer or reader of narrative? (Ricoeur,

1976). Do hearers or readers in some cases neither take meaning nor seek understanding? If they are not taking meaning or seeking understanding, how do tellers of tales and listeners to stories define what they are doing? What are the cognitive, developmental functions of narrative, both for individuals (Bruner, 1986) and for cultures? (Goody, 1982; Havelock, 1982). Can we define forms of narrative that are universal—as genre (Feldman, 1987), as cognitive scaffolding (Bruner, 1986; Friedrich, 1986), or as a means of understanding self, others, and the world? What makes for a good story? What are the characteristics of a good storyteller? Are narrative arts and forms best learned by emulation or by formal teaching? These are among the questions being investigated in current studies of narrative; they were explored in antiquity as well.

Narrated speech, and in particular narrated dialogue, for reasons that remain elusive, is a prominent narrative mode in early Greek genres. Is narrated speech a vestige of earlier wisdom literature, or is what remains of wisdom literature—most of it fragmentary—itself a vestige of earlier narrated dialogue? This continues to be a matter of debate and conjecture, not only for the case of classical literature (Havelock, 1982), but for biblical scholarship as well (Kelber, 1983). Did the first written narratives impose new narrative conventions, sequences, and genres on oral discourse or are the early epics we have simply "fixation of a previously oral discourse"? (Ricoeur, 1976, p. 28). Havelock (1983) pointed out that one classical tradition believed the Homeric epics were not composed until the age of Pisistratus, and then by committee. Proponents of oral poetics (Tedlock, 1983) suggested that the ancient poetic devices of rhythm, meter, and rhyme are indebted to literate forms, to the eye seeing and composing a text as well as to the ear hearing rhythm and rhyme (Havelock, 1986; Tedlock, 1983). The diversity of these views exemplifies a growing pluralism within the consensus that narrative is a crucially important form and paradigm of thought and language.

The primary aim of this chapter is to document the recent genesis and complex origins of our modern concept of narrative. In developing the documentation, two contrasts are used to clarify what may initially seem to be a difficult distinction to make between the undeniably ubiquitous nature of storytelling and the concept of narrative. Using any of a number of modern definitions of narrative, we can identify stories that are, according to one of more of these definitions, not narrative. The story–narrative contrast can help isolate significant or problematic disparities between description and phenomena.

Narrative is sometimes *of* dialogue, and vice versa. The classical literary dialogue form has interlocutors tell stories. A narrative–dialogue contrast, or narrative–conversation contrast, can sharpen genre boundaries further, including the difficult distinction between dialogue and conversation.

Substantial portions of Greek epic narrative are structured not by narrated speech or by events in sequence but by dialogue, by reports (Maranhão, 1984) of exchanges, debates, or disagreements. The recordkeeping and reporting function of some narrative is distinctly different from literary qualities in narrative that allow it to be aligned with the poetic and the creative universals of language. In addition, ethnographers now speculate that one function of reported or narrated speech and dialogue was to model verbal behavior. Heath (1983) proposed a similar function for the narrative genres children bring with them to school, patterns that are often at odds with the schools' focus on explicitly topicalized, expository, "focused" stories (Heath, 1983, pp. 265–314). General consensus today holds that narratives of dialogue and reported speech function to model and script a diversity of discourse genres: conflict resolution, negotiation strategies, and inquiry into issues and subjects. The classical dialogue was, strictly speaking, a narrative of dialogues that dealt with an inquiry into issues. As a literary form, the dialogue allowed a broad array of subjects and points to be defined abstractly and articulated in propositional form, as arguments, but within the interlocutors' arguments often appear narratives. The arguments and narratives of interlocutors are coordinated antiphonally rather than being presented as an evolving linear statement. The literary dialogue remained a popular literary genre from the 4th century B.C. through the 19th century. Is it story or logic or both?

Plato's dialogues narrate abstract propositional arguments, but they are nonetheless narrated, and in their original settings they were used quite literally as scripts, as reader's theater where they were read aloud, then discussed. In their original settings, Plato's dialogues were closer to drama in form and performance than has been emphasized in many subsequent interpretations, where instead of honoring the fluidity of the views developed in a give-and-take dialectic, the views are rearranged as an integrated, systematic argument and given the freestanding, decontextualized form of modern academic expositions.

Contemporary studies of oral discourse, narrative, and conversation tend to label preliterate orality as preponderantly epic-narrative, and to examine contemporary orality within a literate society as conversational (Feldman, 1987). This obviously polarized and oversimplified classification system has obscured the need for delineating uncharted oral genres (Bauman & Scherzer, 1974; Feldman, 1987; Tedlock 1983), many of them tacit. Recent empirical studies increasingly demonstrate that conversation (Tannen, 1982b) and narrative (Tannen, 1982a) comprise multiple genres and use topics, events, and reported speech in different ways to relay information, express views, and resolve conflicts. Perhaps the most uncharted territory of all is the relationship between dialogue and conversation, both as observable phenomena and as theoretical models that we use to appraise both oral and written discourse.

THE ROOTS OF CONTEMPORARY
NARRATIVE STUDIES

Although now undergoing analysis and revision (Finnegan, 1977; Havelock, 1986; Horton & Finnegan, 1973; Ong 1982), the concept of oral literature has been an important contributor to recent narrative studies. Since its adoption by cognitive psychologists to define and examine modes of thought (Bruner, 1986), the parallelism between developmental, oral, tacit, and universal genres has contributed to valuable methodological convergences among several fields. It has led in particular to studies of narrative and logical modes of thought and to postulates defining mental templates that can be characterized as story on the one hand and argument on the other.

The fields of oral literature and ethnography of speaking have developed models of oral literature, composition, and performance drawn from Lord's (1960) analysis of contemporary Balkan singers of tales. Based on Milman Parry's (1928) conjecture that the Homeric epics were oral compositions and not composed in writing as had long been believed, Lord's work defined parallels in the form and composition of Balkan and Homeric oral epics. His analogy supplemented 19th-century literary concepts of universal poetry and the universality of story (Schlegel, 1968). It has been the Lord legacy more than any other, I propose, that has prompted the notion of the universality of narrative. The resulting momentum toward a unified field concept of narrative has already prompted valuable integrations of genre studies across several disciplines.

German romantic folklorists were among the first to propound the concept of the universality of poetry and poetic language, a universality in which they included stories. The key concept was not narrative genre per se, but story and voice, concreteness and vividness, imagination and creativity. In this century, both philology and folklore have been more interested in questions of form, composition, and textual transmission. In going back to Homer, Lord (1960) stretched the time frame for oral narrative back to the historical edge of preserved discourse per se, in effect to the edge of history itself. Though now questioned, the analogy between contemporary and Homeric oral composition and genres has, both subliminally and directly, supported the view that narrative, like the poetic, is both timeless and universal. The following reappraisal of Homeric precedents demonstrates that there was in that era neither a single term for nor a single form of narrative thought and language.

EPOS, MUTHOS, LOGOS

Pre-Socratic philosophers debated the nature of thought and language and through their discussions generated among our earliest formal and metalinguistic terms. These included definitions of kinds of *epos* (epic, traditional story) and *muthos* (fable, Aristotle's plot). Philosophical and rhetorical analysts named and defined distinctions between *muthos* and *logos* (statement), and between *logos* and *doxa* (traditional belief, opinion), providing us with a range of metalinguistic and metacognitive terms (see Yaden & Templeton, 1986). *Epos* preceded *muthos*, according to Aristotle's account of genre; merely episodic stories were supplanted by narratives organized thematically to convey an idea through plot. Emplotment, defined as the imitation of action, is the central distinction made between *epos* and *muthos* in Aristotle's taxonomy (Else, 1957). In today's terminology, both *epos* and *muthos* are narrative. The early Greeks did not group genres as narrative. They distinguished among story, fable, sequence of sayings, proverbs, maxims, and commonplaces. The earliest metalinguistic labels for what we now regard as narrative genres continue to defy confident translation, precisely because there was then no single designation for narrative. It was the poetic that Aristotle chose as the category of categories for literary discourse. Narrative was not adapted to designate a number of kinds of stories and storytelling until Cicero's era.

The Greek term that is the etymological ancestor of narrative surfaced relatively late in the period that saw the emergence of Greek literature, philosophy, and rhetoric. *Diegesis* (digest, summary of the facts or events) was adopted by the sophists to define that part of a rhetorical speech that immediately follows the statement of the case or main argument. *Diegesis* and its Latin translation, *narratio*, remained technical rhetorical terms. The kinds of narratives people practiced in exercises training them for rhetorical fluency slowly came to be regarded as useful and instructive in their own right, as literature in the beginnings of its modern sense. Aristotle is disdainful toward *diegesis* for reasons similar to his objections to *epos*: It is mere listing, summary, recounting with no plot, purpose, theme, or point.

The Latin root for the English "narrative" was activated when the writers of the first Latin rhetoric manuals adopted *"narratio"* to translate *diegesis*. "Narrative" accumulated some of its contemporary meanings gradually throughout antiquity, but at first outside the domain of *diegesis/narratio*. Aristotle's *Poetics* appraises genres stretching from Homeric epic narrative (c. 700 B.C.) through Plato's dialogues (c. 370 B.C.). Aristotle did not examine these genres as narrative, however. The category name he adopted is *poiesis*, which means made, composed, constructed, invented. Because it denotes fabrication, composition, and invention *poiesis* denotes the opposite of timeless, universal, mythic, ancient forms of language. It is from among an older group of terms and concepts that Aristotle drew his terms for what we now call narrative: *epos*—the Homeric word for story; *logos*—the Pre-Platonic (cf. Havelock, 1986) philosophers' word for proposition, ordered and ordering thought, but also used to mean story, fable, saying, and argument; and *muthos*, the Attic word for myth or traditional story that Aristotle adopted as his term for *plot* (Porter 1986).

The Pre-Platonics adopted *logos* to denote the consciously crafted statement, the logically wrought philosophical proposition that they distinguished from *doxa*, received beliefs and commonly held opinions (Havelock, 1963). *Muthos* and *epos* came to denote both the content type and the form of the Homeric epics, an equivocal usage that is one of several probable sources of the diversity in subsequent concepts of narrative. As *muthos, epos*, and *logos* came to be used as technical terms in systematic definitions they had, and continue to have, a recursive function. Writing drama after Aristotle had written the definitive statement of what drama should be was a different activity from writing drama when its conventions were more loosely transmitted among practitioners.

The fliting and fussing routines observed in young children (Heath, 1983) in Black English-speaking American culture are transmitted with great precision by emulation rather than by formal teaching. Mastery is achieved not through formal teaching but by the oldest informal teacher of all: an unresponsive or scornful audience. Like drama and rhetoric before they had been formally defined and technically analyzed, fliting and fussing routines are widely practiced and communally understood arts and, simultaneously, modes of thought. What will they become as their conventions and structures, their morphological contours and social functions alike, undergo definition, analysis, and naming?

Further study is needed to determine the scope and mechanisms of recursion that are activated by explicit metalinguistic and meta-cognitive terms. In particular, "narrative" itself, insofar as it is a metalinguistic term, can and should be examined with closer attention to the beliefs and assumptions of storytellers and story-hearers (cf. Iser, 1978). The early Greeks had no generic term for narrative and no single word for story or storytelling. They did have a word for making and maker, which they used generically to denote the poetic and the poets. How then did they understand and receive these makings? How does our current conceptualization of narrative shape our perception and understanding, especially of discourse or thought patterns that are unfamiliar?

It is probable that in some instances we label something narrative that is not understood as such by its speakers or hearers. The Greek epics were not primarily narratives or even good stories in their original settings. As far as we can tell, they would most likely have been understood as religion or memory by their listeners. The gospel of Mark employs a narrative form iterating the events of Jesus' life in a birth-to-death chronology of events. The birth-to-death chronology of the hero's life is unknown in oral epic (Kelber, 1987a, 1987b). The narrative form of biographical chronology that Mark used is uncharacteristic of his milieu and thus would have been new, perhaps even shocking to his listeners. These examples illustrate that even with so simple a concept as genre, we sometimes find ourselves in Luria's (1976) position, asking for a definition of something which, although "known" on some level, is not known or defined by its users in the ways we, as analysts, know and define. This raises the question of the extent to which genre is in the eye of the beholder, and the extent to which a given genre can be shown to be a widely distributed pattern of thought or language. The notions of tacit genre (Feldman, 1987) and oral poetics (Tedlock, 1983) help bridge this gap and open up new directions and methods for further inquiry.

Studies of language and literacy acquisition suggest that an important concomitant of literacy education today is the mastery of metalinguistic terms that are themselves part of the literate lexicon (Olson & Astington, 1986). These studies extend the delineation of logical patterns that are in the mind and those that are imposed by formal education. The ability to use the nouns *argument, point, view,* and *position* and the verbs *say, believe,* and *know* denotes explicit recognition of distinctions among kinds of discourse and content

(Feldman, 1986; Olson & Astington, 1986). Observing the genesis of these terms of course runs the risk of hypostatizing etymology. Such observation can also serve as a speculum that allows us a focused gaze through the looking glass to observe both the practice and the evolving theoretical language that are the ancestors of our explicit, metalinguistic, and theoretical concepts of narrative.

THE POETIC AND THE LOGICAL: NARRATIVE AND WHAT IS NOT

Among the Pre-Platonic philosophers, and most pointedly in Parmenides, there are recurrent debates about the pursuit of not-being, and the inquiry into what is not. Included in what is not are the poets' stories (*poiesis, muthos, epos*), traditional beliefs and received opinion (*doxa*), and the then-new logical device of stating contrary propositions for the purpose of analyzing the structure and truth of propositions, the *dissoi logoi*. Aristotle commented that the poets' "utterances are devoid of sense" (1975, p. 1404). The charge that the poets invent or imitate what is not is interestingly parallel to the modern notion that narrative, understood as making or telling a story, is a developmentally important ability to speak of what is not (Feldman, 1986). Today, narrative is often defined as a reference to what is not actually present or as the representation of an imaginary reality.

Plato's and Aristotle's works extend the Pre-Platonics' debates about what is not, but without linking what is not directly to narrative. There are repeated links made between the poets' stories (*muthoi, epoi*) fiction (*poiesis*), and falsehood (*pseudos*). Narrative per se is not at issue, in part because accounts or stories are lumped together with arguments and reasoned explanations in the wide range of meanings *logos* had assumed in this period. Plato's and Aristotle's treatments of what is and what is not include logical and linguistic appraisals of degrees of truth in different verbal representations of reality. Increasingly diverse distinctions were defined between the probable and the true, between what is likely to be believed and what can be proven, between history and poetry. From this period as well comes the notion, expressed by Aristotle, that "Homer taught the poets to lie," a formulation that is among the earliest equations between poetry and fiction.

The Pre-Platonic philosophers had a quarrel with the poets, a quarrel whose most famous culmination is Plato's banishment of the poets from the Republic. What remains a matter of lively debate

and conjecture is exactly who these poets were and why the philosophers felt such antipathy toward them. The control of what is was
clearly at issue, with the philosophers claiming that the poets'
stories were made up, and thereby not true. The poets, joined sometimes by the rhetoricians, claimed that the philosophers' analyses
were mere word-splitting and logic-chopping that tear apart what
is, never to put it back together again.

Plato's dialogues constitute a middle ground in this debate. They
are hardly transcriptions of informal conversation, but they aren't
syllogisms or treatises. They are neither exclusively narrative nor
syllogistically logical. The narrative frame to the *Theaetetus* (Plato,
1977) is particularly illustrative of the middle ground represented
by Plato's use of narrative as the vehicle for dialogue. The opening
passage to the *Theaetetus* recounts how the dialogue about to be
presented was recorded, defends its authenticity, and explains why
the transcriber has omitted the interlocutionary narrative convention *and then he said.* This editorial change was made, said the
transcriber, because omitting the interlocutionary narrative ren-
ders the dialogue more accurately.

Most significantly, perhaps, for the comparison of logic with
narrative and myth, Socrates used myths frequently in the dialogues, a practice that belies the generalization that Plato banished
the poets. When Socrates introduced a myth or anecdote, however,
he did so with a purpose other than storytelling in mind. In the
conclusion to the *Gorgias* (Plato, 1952) Socrates contends that what
men fear most is not death, but dying having done wrong. To prove
this point, he asks his interlocutors to listen to a story, "which you
will regard as a fable [*muthos*], I fancy, but I as an actual account
[*logos*]; for what I am about to tell you I mean to offer as the truth
[*alethe*]" (p. 523). He then proceeds to tell the Homeric story of the
judging of souls as they enter the underworld after death. At the
conclusion of the story, he tells Callicles that this "is what I have
heard and believe to be true; and from these stories, we must draw
a moral" (p. 524). In straight narrative the story tells the tale; in
Plato's dialogues the story is entered in defense of a point, and
from it an inference must be made, a statement that will then be
examined philosophically for its merits.

"DIEGESIS" AND "NARRATIO"

I have suggested that what we now examine as narrative forms and
thought were widely practiced in the period from Homer to Plato,
but that these were not defined or understood as narrative. I now

turn to a more detailed examination of the origin of the English word "narrative." A close appraisal of how Aristotle analyzed Homeric epic, dramatic dialogue, and philosophical dialogue provides the starting point for tracing the Greek *diegesis* from its humble origins as a rather limited rhetorical device through its translation and transformation in the Roman choice of *narratio* as its closest Latin cognate.

The Greek and Latin words that converged in the English *"narration,"* but not *"story"* (*muthos, logos, historia*), emerged first as technical terms within rhetoric, to define the part of a speech just after the proem, or introduction. In the *Phaedrus* (Plato, 1973) Plato listed the *diegesis* as one of the parts of a speech outlined in the technical rhetorical manuals of the 4th century B.C. The function of this part of a speech was to summarize, or digest the facts relevant to deciding the matter (*pragma*) at hand in a dispute. The relationship between this portion of a rhetorical speech and earlier concepts of story remains a matter of conjecture, though similarities can be observed between statements of facts defined as *diegesis* and the kinds of events recounted in the older *epos* and *muthos*.

In the Homeric epics, there is a high proportion of narrated dialogue in which we find counterposed views and debate of the kind that would later be analyzed and defined by rhetoricians. Aristotle (1954) observed that Homer speaks at one moment in narrative and at another in an assumed character (p. 1448). Within the narrated dialogues in Homer's *Iliad* there are additional narratives spoken by individuals. The *Iliad* is far from a sequential, chronological narration of events, the "merely episodic" plot that Aristotle deemed weak because it lacks probability and unity (p. 1452). The *Iliad* is a series of narrated dialogues. "But Pallas Athene laughing stood above him and spoke to him in the winged words of triumph . . ." (*Iliad* 21, 408–409). Aristotle's depiction of Homer as alternating between his own and a character's voice reveals a subsequent analyst's insight into composition, and an awareness that the *Iliad* is a composition under the control of an author, not simply the transcription of an ancient series of words and events.

Aristotle's analysis of Homeric and subsequent narrative not only develops distinctions among genres, but also develops a theory of authorial control. In these delineations, Aristotle employed a lexicon of metalinguistic genre terms that were, at the time, neologisms. He develops a ventriloquistic conception of poetic composition and performance that links the poet's to the actor's art and both quite directly to the rhetor's use of *ethos* (Aristotle, 1975), an "assumed" character (p. 1408). Aristotle's concept of *muthos*—plot, or fable—and his discussion of poetic and dramatic mimesis—"imitated actions and events"—are the concepts most cognate with current models of narrative and narrativity. It is the representation of something "out there" that shapes both the content and the motive of narrative, at least in many of today's characterizations. In Aristotle's appraisal, only the weakest poetry and drama "merely narrate [*diegesis*]" (*Poetics*, 1954, pp. 1458–1460). The "greater" works "imitate a unity" in all their particulars, a thematic and organic conception of plot and meaning. This judgment provides a context for understanding Aristotle's famous axiom that "poetry is something more philosophic and of graver import than history, since its statements are of the nature rather of universals, whereas those of history are singulars" (p. 1451). History, like "mere narration," (that is, *diegesis*) is not for Aristotle a particularly servicable vehicle for truth. Although this characterization of history is not universally true, particularly today, its truth in Aristotle's time suggests the extent to which history, like other forms of narrative, has undergone recurrent metamorphosis (cf. White, 1973; Kennedy 1980; Kelber 1987a, 1987b). The association Aristotle made between history and mere narration demonstrates further that he held recounting events (*diegesis*), in and of itself, in rather low esteem by the criteria of both art and epistemology.

"EPOS" AND "MUTHOS": STRINGING
TOGETHER VERSUS THEME AND PLOT

In the *Iliad*, a recounted sequence of dialogues and actions gradually forms a composite of events, agents, settings, outcomes, and judgments. The narration is neither temporally nor causally ordered. There are many flashbacks, dialogue recountings of previous relevant incidents that have some bearing on the issue immediately at hand. There is a thematic unity, but it is not developed in a sequential exposition. There is more than one moral to this story, but the many morals are woven together by the theme stated in the opening invocation: "Sing, Goddess, the anger of Peleus' son Achilleus" (*Iliad* 1,1). It is that wrath, and its diverse consequences, that is the warp of the story. The Pre-Platonics and Aristotle, developing the logical and artistic standards for later eras, deemed Homer weak on several counts. Aristotle finds no unity of plot (*muthos*), understood as the imitation of action presented in a coherent sequence and organized around a clearly defined theme. The Pre-Platonics are among the first to charge that Homer repeated lies; that is, that he told stories that no one any longer believed were true. Against the old poets and the new alike, philosophy, growing power, labeled the pretty fabrications of the poets fictions, pleasant pastimes. The one exception was dramatic imitation of action, which Aristotle maintains made poetry as paradeigma a better vehicle for truth than history. "Hence poetry is something more philosophic and of graver import than history, since its statements are of the nature rather of universals, whereas those of history are singulars" (p. 1451).

Modern literary practice and theory is less different than we might expect from the pluralism of narrative modes exemplified in the *Iliad* and subsequent Greek literature (Schneidau, 1987). Aristotle's analysis of this literature continues to influence contemporary concepts of genre. For this reason it is difficult to get behind and before Aristotle's analysis, to speculate about the composition and delivery, the assumptions and understandings that contexted epic and lyric. The Homeric composer and audience remain forever irretrievable (Havelock, 1986), an irretrievability that is now being posited for the biblical Gospels as well (Kelber 1987a, 1987b). The *Iliad* is narrative, but it was also song, bible, represented speech, action, judgment, theology, cosmology, wisdom, and model for action and behavior. *Epos* and *muthos* denote the ancient rhapsodist's art of singing through inspiration the canonical stories that survive for us in the written Homeric canon.

Modern studies of Balkan singers of tales have analyzed the processes of composition used by contemporary oral storytellers (Lord, 1960). Though their value is unquestionable, these studies establish necessarily conjectural parallels (Havelock, 1982) with the practice and tacit theory of Homeric bards (Havelock, 1986). That stories were and are told and sung, then and now, is indisputable. The way in which stories are understood by their listeners, and the beliefs their tellers or singers hold about the meaning and status of the story, bear much further investigation.

FROM EPIC TO DRAMATIC NARRATIVE

The balancing of rights and wrongs, the measuring of human souls by Dike—Justice—is explicitly defined as a theme in the Greek dramas. As in the Homeric texts, large portions of the dramas are taken up with dialogue within which events are recounted. In contrast to the thematically associative, flashback-laden pattern of the *Iliad*, the events depicted in the dramas are rendered sequentially, a plot pattern that would provide Aristotle with the raw material for a linear, chronological, and causal theory of dramatic plot (*muthos*) and action. The linearity of events in the Greek dramas has also led to the hypothesis (Kerckhove, 1981) that the strongly sequential pattern of Greek drama had the effect of rehearsing the Greek audience for linear sequences of thought and telling that are essential to reading written texts (p. 23).

Though not narrated, the Greek dramas are more chronologically sequential than previous epic narratives and contribute to a linear sense of story, Aristotle's plot or fable, which has subsequently been essential to definitions of narrative. By modern standards of narrative cohesion, the Greek dramas are more narrative than the Greek epics. Their implicit narrative (Porter, 1986) pattern consists of the arrangement of events in a unified causal and thematic series, a standard definition of narrative today, but one that first achieved centrality in Aristotle's concept of *muthos*. Aristotle's explication of the Greek dramas' difference from Homeric epic may have contributed to subsequent concepts of narrative in yet another way, defined in the concept of the *ktema*, or theme. Where the Homeric epics ramble from a thematic point of view, the dramas contain repeated key words, extended dialogues repeating and debating their meaning using conceptual-abstract terms that define the issue, topically: justice, vengeance, pollution, law.

The presence and structural importance of the *ktema* in Aristotle's analysis of plot cohesion and structure parallels the concepts of topic and point as they evolved in the analysis of nonliterary discourse. Initially defined within classical rhetoric, the notions of topic and point have remained remarkably stable. They figure prominently in contemporary studies of narrative and conversation (Feldman, 1986; Tannen 1982b). Aristotle's analysis of the *ktema* in Greek dramas indicates that explicit thematization was becoming simultaneously more perceptible and more frequently perceived. The dramatists introduced new ways of telling that stimulated new modes of understanding. The surfacing of the concept of theme itself is a prime example, as is the particular case of the theme of justice. Dramatic treatments of justice gradually converged in philosophic inquiries into the nature and finally the theory of justice, an analytical mode that would reach its classical culmination in Plato's dialogues (Havelock, 1938).

Caution is needed to avoid oversimplification by deriving from historical backward scanning an exclusively developmental understanding of genre. Modern postulations of the emergence of causal plot and topicalization as stages achieved should not be understood simply as an expected advance in a developmental sequence (Bruner, 1986)—either within the literature itself or in the modes of understanding the literature. Rather, we should attempt to also view these linear patterns as accumulating alternates which, after their emergence, coexisted with earlier ways of making and taking meaning (Barthes, 1977).

THE ROLE OF NARRATIVE "DIEGESIS" WITHIN THE RHETORICAL SPEECH

Rhetorical and dramatic modes influenced one another in Plato's and Aristotle's generation, a synergistic relationship that is immediately observable in the parallel between the dramatic theme and the rhetorical topic. The placement of the *diegesis* within the earliest rhetorical speech depended on an already topicalized mode of discourse in which one issue was at hand. It is in that context that the summary of the facts or events was recounted. Once the matter or issue or question or argument had been stated, narrated events and actions provided facts and evidence for deciding the issue. In the original setting of rhetorical speeches, the assembly or court, was one in which justice, judgment, and law had been placed only recently squarely in the human arena. No Necessity, Dike, or Olympian council, as in the Homeric epics; no Athena, as in many of the dramas, pronounces the final word. Athena, as it were, replaces Dike and is in turn replaced by the body politic, the polis. Consensus is achieved by debate and persuasion. The vote is taken after the speeches have been made. Narrative *diegesis* within the rhetorical speech recounts events after an issue is stated but before the judgment is made, an ordering of thought and use of narrative quite unlike either epic or dramatic narration.

The Greek terms of the 4th century distinguish between the hapsodist—literally, the stitcher—who sang or recited the Homeric canon, and the aoidos—the singer—whose singing was an act of inspiration, invention, and composition. Unlike the rhapsodist, the aoidos was part inventor, a maker of new stories (Goody, 1982, p. 209). The Greek verb *poie*, from which we derive *poet*, *poetry*, means to make, to craft, to invent. The distinctions drawn between rhapsodist and aoidos as poets indicates a new awareness of differences between those through whom the muses spoke and those who were good storytellers; between performance, understood as apt retelling, and art, newly understood as beautiful invention.

How these differences affected changes in basic thought patterns on the part of the singers, the tellers, and the listeners invites much further inquiry. "Sing Goddess, the anger of Peleus' son Achilleus" (*Iliad* 1,1) invites an already existing story to be brought to life by the telling. Saying that someone tells a story well reflects the same concept. By the time of the Pre-Platonics, the rhapsodists were frequently scorned as mere repeaters of old shadow pictures, as sleepwalkers leading others in dreams like pied pipers. By the 4th century B.C., Aristotle's era, *rhapsode* had a strongly pejorative connotation (Havelock, 1982). The *aoidoi* were singers of a different sort. They didn't just stitch; they embroidered, rearranged, and invented. They were composers, improvisationists, and artists. "Tell me the stories of Jesus./I want to hear./Things I would ask him to tell me,/If he were here . . . ," as the hymn has it, invokes narrative storytelling that is more conjectural and inventive than repeating a canonical text, regardless of whether that text is written or oral. In such narratives, the teller will embroider and adapt, and will be understood as embroidering and adapting, a core narrative so that it can instruct, reveal, or uncover. This second sense of narrative is the one that seems to inform the character of the *aoidos*. Only after its translation by the Latin *narratio* did the rhetorical *diegesis* begin to assume this sense. The emphasis on the maker, or constructor, of the story was one basis of the choice of *narratio* by the Latin authors.

The *Rhetoric ad Herennium* (1981) and Cicero's *On Invention* (1949) were among the conduits through which Greek rhetorical teaching was translated into Latin culture and teaching. In these first Latin rhetorical manuals, the term adopted to translate the Greek *diegesis* was *narratio*, to tell or relate, to give an account that reveals something, to recite or disclose. Unlike *diegesis*, with its narrower emphasis on listing or selectively retelling, *narratio*, at least initially, carried with it the messenger, storytelling, knowing and saying force that narrative is now alleged to have in many oral settings. "Tell us the story of what happened," is different from "Tell us the events salient to the current case or discussion; list." In addition, *narratio*, unlike *diegesis*, connoted a kind of knowledge and a way of knowing; it shares one of its Indo-European roots with *gnosis*.

The account, disclosure, and revelation meanings of the Latin *narratio* are particularly interesting illustrations of how difficult it is to translate so seemingly simple a concept as narrative from one language and culture into another. *Narratio* is closer to the Greek use of *logos* to denote illustrative anecdote or fable and *logoi lexai* to denote stories that tell or give an account than to *diegesis*. *Diegesis* had always needed something else around it to make it explanatory; *narratio* was itself an explanation.

Because *diegesis* was the term translated by *narratio*, it is worth reviewing Aristotle's (1975) consistently disdainful treatment of *diegesis* in the *Rhetoric*. "... 'Narration' (*diegesis*) is part of a forensic speech only; how in a political speech or a speech of display can there be narration in the technical sense?" (p. 1415). "In political oratory there is little room for narration, as nobody can narrate what has not yet happened. ... Any narration will be of past events used in making plans for the future" (p. 1417). It is noteworthy that Aristotle did not assign to narrative (*diegesis*) proper the status of poetry, that is, of the "imitation of imaginary events," which he restricted to fable, myth, drama, and poetry. Aristotle cautioned against linear narrative in most oratory, and recommended that narrative sections that depict "moral character" and "moral purpose" (1975, p. 1417) be placed intermittently (p. 1416) within other sections developing the theme or argument of the speech.

In Aristotle's discussion of the rhetorical example (*paradeigma*) (1975, pp. 1356,1368,1393) as a form of proof, we find more direct ancestors to the kinds of narrative listed by both the unknown *ad Herennium* author (1981) and Cicero (1949). "Examples are either historical parallels, or invented parallels." If invented, they are "either illustrations [*parabolai*] or fables [*logoi*]" (p. 1394). Aristotle's *Rhetoric* and other rhetorical treatises of the same period raise the question of how new the concepts and terms were. The practices, without question, go very far back. But was fable, for example, a new way of thinking about the status and meaning of traditional stories? It is certain that fable as a kind of rhetorical example was a new depiction.

The *ad Herennium* author's distinctions among narrative kinds and uses are detailed and rendered highly problematic by translation from well-established Greek technical terms into neologistic Latin terms for rhetorical devices and techniques, terms which were frequently being invented on the spot (Cicero, 1939, p. 25). The *ad Herennium* author and Cicero selected Latin words that

would most closely resemble the Greek technical terms. An extension of that selection continues today as we scrutinize how successfully the Greek and Latin pairs have been translated into English
in the translations of classical rhetorical texts completed, it should
be recalled, only within the last century. "Narration" today continues to denote a part within a rhetorical speech or composition, but
also a distinct kind of rhetoric or argumentation. In addition, as
"narration" and "narrator", it now defines the author's stance visà-vis a story being told, a role that is now being scrutinized not
only for the case of the literary author but in studies of the diverse
span of narrative conventions across widely different cultures. An
equally wide range of discourse forms that were considered separate in antiquity are now considered alike insofar as they are narrative in one or more of today's canons of narrativity. What were the
already burgeoning diverse meanings assigned to narrative in the
first century B.C.?

The rhetoric *ad Herennium* identifies three types of statement of
facts [*narratio*] (p. 23): (a) narratives whose goal is victory in a case
where a decision is going to be made, (b) highly selective narratives
whose goal is to discredit the opponent or enhance the credibility
of the speaker, and (c) narratives that are composed as practice
exercises, of three kinds: legendary, historical, and realistic. This
division among narrative practice exercises suggests that one function of composing narratives was training through the imitation of
existing narrative genres: epic, history, and reportorial representation of events. Though originally destined for use in rhetorical
performance, these practice narrative compositions also served as
models of literary composition. The alternations between the
sturdy but simple rhetorical *narratio* of public servants to the leisure practice of *narratio* as literature, and as an independent art, is
a cyclical process that has been termed literaturization (Kennedy,
1980) and can be observed within several classical periods, and in
the Renaissance as well.

The *ad Herennium* author's depiction reveals that between the
4th and 1st centuries B.C., the accounts of epic, fable, and plot
developed in Aristotle's *Poetics* had become fully integrated, if
somewhat confusingly, into the outline of the parts of a rhetorical
speech used in curriculum materials. It remains a matter of conjecture whether this conflation was the result of recognizing some
organic or essential similarities among *epos, muthos, mimesis,
poiesis,* and *diegesis,* or whether it resulted instead from the fragmented transmission of Aristotle's work. Whatever its sources, the
integration of poetic and rhetorical narrative paradigms suggests

a growing recognition that there were poetic and literary elements in rhetorical speeches, and persuasive capacities in narrative, even in nonrhetorical settings. Cicero's highly detailed and integrated account promotes dignity and substance within the narrative portion of the rhetorical speech (*On Invention*, Book I, 30).

Cicero's list parallels the *ad Herennium* list, but extends many definitions and descriptions within each category. The *ad Herennium* singles out narrative in support of the defense, against the opposition, and practice narratives of three kinds: legendary, historical, and realistic. Cicero listed (a) narrative of just the case and an explanation of the reason for the dispute; (b) narrative that digresses beyond the strict limits of the case in order to attack someone, to make a comparison, to amuse the audience, or to amplify the main point; and (c) narratives wholly unconnected with public issues, "recited or written solely for amusement." (p. 55) It is in this third group that Cicero listed many of the forms of literary and imaginary narrative, including history, which we continue to group together under narrative: "narratives concerned with events"—fabula, historia, argumentum; and "narratives concerned with persons" (p. 55). For these he provided rules of probability and verisimilitude. The Loeb translator's note to Cicero's discussion of history as a rhetorical genre exemplifies the surprise and even dismay that has recurred as the moderns rediscover that "history in antiquity was regarded as a branch of rhetoric, much to the disadvantage of history" (1939, p. 37).

Cicero's depictions suggest that the imaginary, the historical, and the argumentative had all come to be classed as subsets of rhetorical narrative in the teaching of the 1st century B.C. Up until Cicero's proposals that they become the centerpiece of a liberal arts curriculum, literature and history were regarded as leisure time activities and as practice for the more demanding tasks of rhetoric in the public arena. Even argument is listed by Cicero as a kind of narrative, yet another indication that sequentiality—whether of events or of ideas—was a defining characteristic of narration. Alternately, we might investigate further the consequences of a translation conundrum: *Logos* is translated by both *fabula* and *argumentum*.

CICERO'S INTEGRATION OF RHETORICAL AND HISTORICAL NARRATIVE

Between the 4th and 1st centuries B.C., epic, fable, narrative, and history coexisted within and outside of rhetorical theory and practice. Although regarded as leisure, entertainment, and rhetorical

practice, the production of narrative subgenres in this period generated a body of written exempla to which theorists and practitioners
alike could refer. It was through this process that the concept of
narrative genre may have emerged as a conscious element in composition and in reader comprehension alike, creating among the
first literate, and literary, possibilities of virtual text (Iser, 1978).
Increasingly sophisticated aesthetic evaluation was also made possible by the recursion (Feldman, 1986, pp. 8–13) going on, at a
cultural level, in genres of thought and language. Cicero's treatises,
as distinct from his youthful rhetorical manual, are indebted to
the paradigms of genre and topic that preceded them. They also
continue the recursive process by proposing, rather startlingly, that
the historian of the present day needs to learn a few things from
the orator.

  In Book I of *de Oratore* (Cicero, 1942) Crassus, who had in real life
been Cicero's childhood tutor, proposes that the fledgling orator
should read and memorize the history and laws of the past as a
storehouse of precedents. But in Book II, Antonius, who had been
another of Cicero's tutors, gives a brief history of history in which
he laments the paucity of Latin histories and particularly of rules
for its composition. He asks, "Do you see how great a responsibility
the orator has in historical writing?" The question implies that
there was very little historical writing of the kind Crassus has
recommended in Book I, and indeed there was very little in Latin.
Atticus and Varro were contemporaries of Cicero, and frequent
objects of his complaint that history should be more than mere
chronicle or annal (cf. White, 1973). Antonius, who is both a tradi-
tionalist and sceptical about the likelihood of change, propounds
a list of improvements that the orator can and should give the
historian.

  The nature of the subject needs chronological arrangement and geo-
  graphical representation; and since, in reading of important affairs
  worth recording, the plans of campaign, the executive actions and
  the results are successively looked for, it calls, also, as regards such
  plans, for some intimation of that the writer approves, and in the
  narrative of achievement, not only for a statement of what was done
  or said, but also for the manner of doing or saying it; and, in the
  estimate of consequences, for an exposition of all contributory causes,
  whether originating in accident, discretion or foolhardiness; and as
  for the individual actors, besides an account of their exploits, it
  demands particulars of the lives and characters of such as are outstanding in renown and dignity. (Cicero, 1942, Book II, 62–63)

The list Antonius provides is drawn from the new, improved conception of rhetoric that Cicero defined. As with the rhetorical speech, Antonius proposes, the historical text should be based on a considered reflection of the nature of the subject, should not just list but also express the author's approval, disapproval, and appraisal. The historical narrative should not be merely a statement of what was done or said but also a description of the manner in which it was done and an assessment of its causes. Finally, the text should describe the lives of those actors whose characters are outstanding and exemplary. The emphasis on actors not only makes an explicit analogy to dramatic categories, but also suggests that it was not the task of most history at that time to inquire into character, as both drama and rhetoric did. The history Cicero propounds here had yet to be written.

FROM STORYTELLING TO
TOPICALIZED TELLING

Like Plato's, Cicero's dialogue treatises exemplify what Aristotle termed intermittent narrative (1975, p. 1416) narrative occurring in small chunks within an explicitly, logically ordered discussion of topics. Is it topicality, perhaps, that more than anything else marks the sometimes elusive line dividing story from argument? The matter at hand, the issue, the subject, the point, culturally relative as these are (Tannen, 1982b) shape not only the virtual text of the reader's or hearer's understanding, but the actual text as well.

Antonius's exhortation vividly illustrates that not all histories look at the manner in which something was done, or at the character of the main actors, or at the causes of the events. The same thing can be said of narrative today. Even fewer histories—or stories— make the author's view explicit and one of the points of the text. Explicit topicality and the exposition of the speaker's or author's views or points are elements shared by narrative and non-narrative discourse, a kinship that is nicely elucidated in Aristotle's treatment of dramatic theme. Intrinsic, implicit, or tacit genre boundaries (cf. Feldman, 1987; Tedlock, 1983), which define narrative types, are better known than equivalent assumptions, which define topic within narrative (cf. Feldman, 1986). In cross-cultural studies of responses to narrative, and in the contemporary literary classroom as well, an amusing but also sobering pluralism is revealed when uninitiated readers are asked to talk about the point of a story (Bruner, 1986; Michaels & Cazden, 1986; Michaels & Collins 1984;

Heath 1983, Tannen, 1982b). The more diversities there are in tacit
and explicit concepts of narrative genre, the more we can predict
questions to students and among conversationalists: What's the
point?; Get to the point; What did you mean by that story? Those
students who bring with them to school the assumptions about
narrative and about points that they are expected to operate with
in the classroom are by third grade well ahead of those whose
narrative practices and assumptions don't match those of the
schools (Heath, 1983; Michaels & Collins, 1984).

The evolution of narrative patterns in child language development, and the cross-cultural study of narrative paradigms, is being
usefully supplemented by studies of metalinguistic awareness,
metalinguistic language, and metacognitive awareness and language (Feldman, 1987; Yaden & Templeton, 1986). "Jane hit the
ball," is narrative; "I think Jane hit the ball" expresses a mental state
about an event. The *I* referred to in the second, simple sentence
doesn't exist in some cultures, though it exists for very young children in our culture. Much further consideration should be given the
question of whether the self, or, in philosophical language, the
individual, is essential to metalinguistic and metacognitive consciousness. Increasingly, evidence supports the hypothesis that the
conscious self, the "Cartesian self" (Olson 1986b), and perhaps self-
consciousness itself, are activated and cultivated by forms of consciousness transmitted in metalinguistic language. Can we say that
in some senses the self as we know it doesn't exist in some cultures?

"Homer wrote the *Iliad*" is as revolutionary a statement as
"Homer taught the poets to lie." An individual is credited; the text
is treated as a composition and not as received wisdom from time
immemorial. In becoming conscious of making stories, of stories as
made things and of poets as makers, as fabulators, the early Greeks
quite literally invented invention, and with it the link between
narrative and what is not. Without this concept, we cannot observe
the intricate connectedness of narrativity to reflectivity (Feldman,
1986). It remains to be seen whether or not the concept of oral
literature itself, including the current understanding of narrative
within literary studies, psychology, and anthropology, is in part an
imposition of quite recent theoretical concepts onto nonliterate
individuals and cultures. Though such individuals and cultures
indisputably produce forms that we call narrative, much further
investigation is needed to determine how they understand and
name these forms.

One of the values currently ascribed to narrative in child language development is that it encourages thinking and talking about

the non-here-and-now (Feldman, 1986). Reflection in turn is observed to be a propadeutic for mental state expressions such as "I think Dad is coming." It is possible, however, for such conjectural modes of thought and for the language of the self not to emerge at all, as is the case in language communities that have few mental state or self-reference terms? In such cultures, we find few terms like *topic, argument,* and *point.*

Historical and cross-cultural studies should continue to examine not only the universality of narrative, but also the roles played by different narrative modes in developing the metalinguistic consciousness that appears to be a precondition for reflection and abstract thought. We may find that imagination and fiction are very narrowly western concomitants of narrative. We may discover further evidence not only that the distinction (Olson, 1986) between say and mean or between text and interpretation requires metalinguistic awareness and written texts, but also that say and even self,—seemingly self-evident phenomena—are also products of a tradition narrower and more recent than we yet realize. The surviving texts of the Pre-Platonics record what may have been among the first moments of debate about what is and what is not in our cultural tradition, an inquiry that prompted the evolution of our earliest metalinguistic and metacognitive terms for distinctions between truth and falsehood, logic and poetry, history and fiction. Narrative allows thinking and talking about what is not only when what is is implicitly or explicitly defined in some way: as truth, as physical presence, or as non-narrative itself. One hardy trace of this tacit consensus is simultaneously revealed and challenged when we say, "Well, let's stop all this talk; I want to tell you a story. . . ."

ACKNOWLEDGMENTS

Grateful acknowledgment is due Tullio Maranhão, of the Department of Anthropology at Rice University, and Thomas Porter, Dean of the College of Liberal Arts at the University of Texas at Arlington. Both read an earlier version of this chapter and made many helpful suggestions.

REFERENCES

Aristotle. (1954). *Poetics* (I. Bywater, Trans.). New York: Modern Library.
Aristotle. (1975). *Art of rhetoric* (J. H. Freese, Trans.). Cambridge, MA: Harvard/Loeb.
Barthes, R. (1977). *Image music text.* London: Fontana.

Bauman, R., & Scherzer, J. (Eds.). (1974). *Explorations in the ethnography of speaking.* New York: Cambridge University Press.

Bruner, J. (1986). *Actual minds, possible worlds.* Cambridge, MA: Harvard University Press.

Cicero. (1933). *Brutus, Orator* (G. L. Henrickson & H. M. Hubbell, Trans.). Cambridge, MA: Harvard/Loeb.

Cicero. (1939). *De Natura Deorum, academica* (H. Rackham, Trans.). Cambridge: MA: Harvard/Loeb.

Cicero. (1942). *De Oratore* Books I & II (E. W. Sutton, Trans.). Cambridge, MA: Harvard/Loeb.

Cicero. (1949). *De Inventione; De Optimo; Genere Oratorum; Topica* (H. M. Hubbell, Trans.). Cambridge, MA: Harvard/Loeb.

Cicero. (1981). *Ad Herennium* (H. Caplan, Trans.). Cambridge, MA: Harvard/Loeb.

Else, G. F. (1957). *Aristotle's poetics: The argument.* Cambridge, MA: Harvard University Press.

Feldman, C. F. (1988). Early forms of thought about thoughts: Some simple linguistic expressions of mental state. In J. Astington, P. Harris, & D. Olson (Eds.), *Developing theories of mind* (pp. 126–137). New York: Cambridge University Press.

Feldman, C. F. (1987, June). *Oral metalanguage.* Paper presented at the International Summer Institute for Semiotic and Structural Studies, Conference on Orality and Literacy, Toronto, Canada.

Finnegan, R. (1977). *Oral poetry: Its nature, significance, and social context.* Cambridge, England: Cambridge University Press.

Friedrich, R. (1986). *The language parallax.* Austin, TX: University of Texas Press.

Goody, J. (1982). Alternate paths to knowledge in oral and literate cultures. In D. Tannen (Ed.), *Spoken and written language: Exploring orality and literacy* (pp. 201–216). Norwood, NJ: Ablex.

Havelock, E. (1938). *The Greek concept of justice.* Cambridge, MA: Harvard.

Havelock, E. (1963). *Preface to Plato.* Cambridge, MA: Harvard University Press.

Havelock, E. (1982). *The literate revolution in Greece and its cultural consequences.* Princeton: Princeton University Press.

Havelock, E. (1983). The Linguistic task of the presocratics. In K. Robb (Ed.), *Language and thought in early Greek philosophy* (pp. 7–82). LaSalle, IN: Monist Library of Philosophy.

Havelock, E. (1986). *The muse learns to write.* New Haven: Yale University Press.

Heath, S. B. (1983). *Ways with words.* New York: Cambridge University Press.

Homer. (1951). *Iliad* (R. Lattimore, Trans.). Chicago: University of Chicago Press.

Horton, R., & Finnegan, R. (Eds.). (1973). *Modes of thought.* London: Faber & Faber.

Iser, W. (1978). *The art of reading.* Baltimore: Johns Hopkins University Press.

Kelber, W. (1983). *The oral and written gospel.* Philadelphia: Fortress Press.

Kelber, W. (1987a). Biblical hermeneutics and the art of communication. *Semeia, 39,* 97–105.

Kelber, W. (1987b). Hermeneutical reflections on the gospels. *Semeia, 39,* 107–133.

Kennedy, G. (1980). *Classical rhetoric and its christian and secular tradition from ancient to modern times.* Chapel Hill: University of North Carolina Press.

Kerckhove, D. de. (1981). A theory of Greek tragedy. *Sub Stance, 29,* 23–36.

Kermode, F. (1983). *The art of telling. Essays on fiction.* Cambridge: Harvard University Press.

Lord, A. (1960). *Singer of tales.* Cambridge, MA: Harvard University Press.

Luria, A. R. *Cognitive development: Its cultural and social foundations.* In M. Cole (Ed.); (M. Lopez-Morillas & L. Solotaroff, Trans.). Cambridge, MA: Harvard University Press.

Maranhão. T. (1984). The force of reported narrative. *Papers in Linguistics, 17* (3), 235–266.

Michaels, S. & Cazden, C. B. (1986). Teacher/child collaboration as oral preparation for literacy. In B. Schieffelin & P. Gilmore (Eds.), *The acquisition of literacy: Ethnographic perspective* (pp. 132–154). Norwood, NJ: Ablex.

Michaels, S., & Collins, J. (1984). Oral discourse styles: Classroom interaction and the acquisition of literacy. In D. Tannen (Ed.), *Coherence in spoken and written discourse* (pp. 219–244). Norwood, NJ: Ablex.

Mitchell, W. J. T. (Ed.). (1968). *The value of narrativity in the representation of reality.* Chicago: University of Chicago Press.

Olson, D. (1986a). The cognitive consequences of literacy. *Canadian Psychology, 27* (2), 109–121.

Olson, D. (1988). Mind and media: The epistemic functions of literacy. *Journal of Communication 38,* 27–36.

Olson, D., & Astington, J. (1986). Children's acquisition of metalinguistic and meta-cognitive verbs. In W. Demopoulos & A. Marras (Eds.), *Language learning and concept acquisition* (pp. 184–199). Norwood, NJ: Ablex.

Ong, W. (1982). *Orality and literacy.* New York: Methuen.

Plato. (1952). *Gorgias* (W. C. Helmbold, Trans.). New York: Bobbs-Merrill/Library of Liberal Arts.

Plato. (1973). *Phaedrus* (Walter Hamilton, Trans.). Harmondsworth, England: Penguin.

Plato. (1977). *Theaetetus, Sophist* (H. N. Fowler, Trans.). Cambridge, MA: Harvard/ Loeb.

Parry, M. (1928). *L'Epithete traditionelle dans Homère.* Paris: Societé Editrice des Belles Lettres.

Porter, T. E. (1986). Drama as text: Mythos and praxis. *Word, 37* (1–2), 93–110.

Ricoeur, P. (1976). *Interpretation theory: Discourse and the surplus of meaning.* Ft. Worth, TX: Texas Christian University Press.

Schlegel, F. (1968). *Dialogue on poetry and literary aphorisms* (E. Behler & R. Struc, Trans.). University Park: Pennsylvania State University Press.

Schneidau, H. N. (1987). Let the reader understand. *Semeia, 39,* 135–145.

Scholes, R., & Kellog, R. (1966). *The nature of narrative.* New York: Oxford University Press.

Tannen, D. (1982a). Oral and literate strategies in spoken and written narratives. *Language 58* (1), 1–21.

Tannen, D. (1982b). The oral literate continuum in discourse. In D. Tannen (Ed.), *Spoken and written language: Exploring orality and literacy.* Norwood, NJ: Ablex. (pp. 1–16).

Tedlock, D. (1983). *The spoken word and the work of interpretation.* Philadelphia: University of Pennsylvania Press.

White, H. (1973). *Metahistory.* Baltimore: Johns Hopkins University Press.

Yaden, D. B. & Templeton, S. (Eds.). (1986). *Metalinguistic awareness and beginning literacy.* Portsmouth, NH: Heinemann.

8

The Principle of Relevance and the Production of Discourse: Evidence from Xhosa Folk Narrative

David Gough
University of South Africa

In this chapter I explore some aspects of the production of discourse, specifically of narrative discourse. In particular, I demonstrate that evidence from Xhosa folk narrative (*intsomi* [sg.] *iintsomi* [pl.])[1] suggests that there is a single, fundamental principle underlying discourse production, which I refer to as the *principle of relevance*. Furthermore, I show that this principle helps to explain the phenomenon of narrative creativity that is manifest in the individual creativity a narrator brings to the performance of a traditional tale. Creativity is a central feature of Xhosa folk narrative performance.[2]

---

[1]Xhosa is a Bantu language spoken in the southeastern tip of southern Africa by about 6 million speakers. Extensive pioneering research into Xhosa folktales has been carried out by Harold Scheub (1975). Although our approaches are quite different, Scheub's ideas have played an invaluable role in the formation of my own.

[2]The notion of narrative creativity has been of central interest to folklore studies for many years. Many theories have been postulated to explain how individual narrators bring their own artistic improvisation to traditional tales with the result that different performances of the "same" tale may display a good deal of variation.

RELEVANCE AND THE COMPREHENSION
OF DISCOURSE

In recent research, Sperber and Wilson (1986) emphasized the importance of what they termed the principle of relevance in the comprehension of discourse.[3] According to Sperber and Wilson, this principle is "the single principle governing every aspect of comprehension" (Sperber & Wilson, 1982, p. 74). In basic terms, the principle of relevance states that hearers expect their speakers to be relevant, their comprehension being based and calculated on this assumption. In general, an utterance is deemed relevant if it has implications or is informative within a particular context. In expecting speakers to be relevant, hearers thus expect them to be informative to the context that is operative at the time.[4] As a brief illustration, successive sentences in this chapter have implications to the context of this chapter as a whole, but to no other, and a reader's interpretation is based on this assumption.[5] (For a more in-depth discussion of relevance, see Sperber & Wilson, 1986, pp. 119–123. The principle of relevance itself is discussed more formally in Sperber & Wilson, 1986, pp. 155–163.)

RELEVANCE AS A PRODUCTION PRINCIPLE

Sperber and Wilson based their exploration of the principle of relevance on discourse comprehension, to the exclusion of discourse production. I claim that relevance is equally important to the production of discourse. In many, if not most instances, following this principle presents no problems to speakers; in general, it appears that speakers experience no trouble in producing utterances that are consistently informative to their discourse contexts. In certain contexts, however—for instance, ones with which the speaker is

---

[3]The importance of relevance for discourse comprehension was originally postulated by Grice in terms of his conversational maxims (for a review see Leech, 1983, pp. 30–34). The most thorough and formal exposition of Sperber and Wilson's views is to be found in Sperber and Wilson (1986).

[4]Viewed from a different angle, an utterance would be deemed relevant if the hearer can infer new information from the content of the utterance when combined with available contextual information (any such previous utterances or the hearer's encyclopedic knowledge).

[5]Contrarily, the proposition, "I have broken my leg," although possibly true, would not be relevant at this point, as it would have no implications in the context of this chapter.

not familiar—the problem of being relevant may be very real. In such situations, the feeling arises that one is out of one's depth. It is, indeed, in such cases that the importance of relevance as a production principle in discourse becomes accessible to investigation. This is also true with the production of Xhosa *iintsomi*, which present intriguing evidence for the principles underlying narrative production. Before we investigate *iintsomi* themselves, however, we first examine the process of reminding, which, as we shall see, is fundamental to the principle of relevance. I initially discuss this process with reference to conversational discourse.

CONVERSATION, REMINDING, AND RELEVANCE

Interlocutors involved in everyday conversation are involved in the activity of discussing a certain topic or certain topics. Conversations have, in this regard, a topic framework: the area or areas discussed by the interlocutors involved (see Brown & Yule, 1983, pp. 75–79 for an in-depth discussion of topic framework). Discussing a particular topic within this overall framework—such as old age or marriage—intrinsically involves for the interlocutors the activation of a particular body of information that forms the context of the conversation at the time. I term such active contextual information—which may involve, inter alia, some domain of the knowledge, beliefs, and experience of the interlocutors, and/or some part of their environment—a *contextual domain*. Once one contextual domain has been determined at a certain point of a conversation, it makes accessible to each of the interlocutors certain personally experienced episodes of that domain, which then form the basis of a contribution they may make to the conversation. As conversations may cover more than one topic, any number of contextual domains may be involved.

To illustrate these introductory points, consider the following list that summarizes successive contributions made in an attested conversation. The interlocutors involved in this conversation were, inter alia, E. P, M, and D.

E: Eating of horses.
P: Eating of monkeys.
M: Eating of worms.
D: Eating of dogs.

The contextual domain here—that is, that part of the interlocutors' knowledge that is made active at this point—can be seen to involve strange things people eat. Each of the interlocutors in the preceding example related some personally experienced episode made accessible through this domain, and their contributions are thus consistent with this domain. Importantly, if D, for example, had to make a contribution concerning, say, the robbing of a bank without any other indication, his contribution would not be so consistent. Such a contribution is, however, unlikely to occur, and in this way the contextual domain operating at any point naturally acts as a constraint on the potential selection of information for expression.

How individuals select information for expression in terms of the constraints set by the contextual domain is, it appears, through a process of reminding. The type of reminding relevant at this point of our discussion involves the perception by speakers of shared features between some previous contribution (i.e., their input or cause of the reminding process) and some information stored in their memories that then becomes amenable for expression (i.e., their output or result of the reminding process). In that D, for example, was reminded by previous contributions of an episode concerning the eating of dogs, there are obvious similarities between the previous contributions and that episode that make it accessible. In that such similarities are not apparent between the contributions and, say, an episode concerning the robbing of a bank, it would be unlikely that this episode would become accessible to D; that is, D would not be reminded of it. I refer to this type of reminding as inter-contextual reminding. (For an extensive discussion of the importance of reminding for cognition, see Schank, 1984.)

The perception of shared features between some input (the cause of the reminding process) and some information in memory (the result of the reminding process) that makes such information accessible is based on the contextual domain that is established at a certain point in the conversation. In the foregoing conversation, for example, the interlocutors involved heard contributions concerning the eating of horses, monkeys, and worms. The contextual domain established in order to understand the implications of these contributions was, as we have seen, in terms of strange things people eat. Given this delimited domain in memory, certain experiences of the interlocutors stored in terms of this domain become accessible. Once such information becomes so accessible, reminding can be said to have occurred.

Conversations do not always revolve around one particular topic, and may thus involve more than one contextual domain. Conversations in this regard may exhibit a conversational flaw, so that what possibly forms the topic of conversation at the end of a conversation appears quite unlike the one discussed at its beginning. To account for one type of this drift of topics and the accompanying change of contextual domains, we examine another contribution made in the foregoing conversation.

H, another interlocutor in the conversation, was reminded by M's contribution concerning the eating of worms of some personal experience of coming across a very large earthworm while on holiday. This episode that H was reminded of did not directly relate, as we may see, to the contextual domain of strange things people eat, which was operative at the time, as she made no reference to eating whatsoever. Instead of this overall domain, it appears that it was part of M's contribution itself that formed the contextual domain in terms of which H's reminding experience occurred. In that M's contribution was about worms, it defined a particular domain of information in H's memory concerning worms, thus making accessible the episode she finally contributed. This episode was thus not consistent with the contextual domain of strange things people eat, but it was consistent with a contextual domain established by part of the previous contribution. In this way, features or details of contributions (such contributions offered in terms of the overall contextual domain) may, in themselves, potentially form the contextual domain for later contributions as interlocutors latch onto such features in place of the contextual domain previously operative. I term this process *subcontextual reminding.*

Subcontextual reminding, as well as inter-contextual reminding, may and does occur within one contribution as well as across contributions. When subcontextual reminding occurs to a great extent in interlocutors' contributions, they will be perceived as rambling. Rambling occurs when one incident the interlocutor recounts forms the contextual domain for another, and so on.

There appear to be, then, two types of reminding that operate in conversation; two ways, that is, in which relevant information is made accessible to interlocutors. In the one—intercontextual reminding—episodes are made accessible to interlocutors through one established domain of information or contextual domain. In the other—subcontextual reminding—a specific feature from a previous contribution becomes, in itself, a contextual domain for an interlocutor that then makes an episode stored under this domain accessible to that interlocutor. Such subcontextual reminding results in a shift in the contextual basis of the conversation. Metaphorically, in intercontextual reminding the spotlight remains focused on a particular scene (i.e., the contextual domain) highlighting its details (i.e., the episodes that are made apparent to the individual speakers). In subcontextual reminding, on the other hand, the spotlight zooms in to focus on a specific detail that then forms a scene with its own associated details. (In this respect, the distinction between inter- and subcontextual reminding may also be seen in terms of overall or global versus local coherence.) In intercontextual reminding, all episodes are globally coherent to one contextual domain. With subcontextual reminding, on the other hand, a subsequent episode may be locally coherent to a detail of a previous episode, but not globally coherent to the contextual domain operating up to that point. Contributions following such an episode may be globally coherent to the new contextual domain that is so established. Conversations thus move from one area of discussion to the next in a connected and coherent way, disconnected breaks in topic being marked occurrences.

Reminding intrinsically involves relevance. Given that a contextual domain operating at a particular point defines a certain area in the interlocutor's memory, the information made accessible through this domain must necessarily have implications for this domain. In this regard, the selection of irrelevant information—information that would have no particular implications for the domain at hand—is effectively prevented, as such information could not be made accessible through that domain. Reminding, as it were, acts as the process that ensures the selection of relevant information and ensures that the principle of relevance is maintained.

RELEVANCE, REMINDING, AND THE *INTSOMI*

One of the hallmarks of the *intsomi* tradition is narrative creativity. Performances of *iintsomi* do not involve the bland and verbatim recall of previously internalized tales. Especially with accomplished narrators, each performance of an *intsomi* results in a creative and individual work of art. Each *intsomi* performance is unique and is the result of the narrator's tradition, imagination, and the immediate circumstances of the performance situation.[6]

---

[6]For an alternate discussion to the one to be discussed here on the nature of narrative creativity manifest in Xhosa narrative (see Scheub, 1975).

The basic memorial units involved in the production of *iintsomi* are what I term *tale chunks*. These are coherent stretches of narrative information in a narrator's memory. One of the main factors underlying the phenomenon of narrative creativity I have just discussed is the fact that the narrator is free (within certain limitations) to choose and combine tale chunks in the creation of his or her *intsomi* performance as a whole. Furthermore, individual tale chunks may form the basis of tales themselves. On one occasion, thus, a completed *intsomi* may consist, say, of tale chunks A, B, and C. In another performance, tale chunk A may be selected but may be followed by tale chunks D and E instead of B and C. Furthermore, tale chunk A may form the basis of a tale by itself. In each of these cases, the tale chunks are suitably adapted to form complete and coherent tales. Unlike the Western tradition where one cannot, for example, "tack on" *Cinderella* to *Little Red Riding Hood*, there is no concept of a fixed or "correct" text as in the Xhosa tradition.[7]

In my examination of the production of *iintsomi*, I devote my attention to an in-depth analysis of the text presented in the appendix (originally narrated by a female narrator). In this tale, a tale chunk concerning a girl forgetting her skirt after collecting clay (to be termed the girl tale chunk) and a tale chunk concerning a dog that makes various requests to a girl (to be termed the *dog tale chunk*) are presented as forming one *intsomi*. Each of these chunks may be present in various manifestations in other tales, with or without other tale chunks. The girl tale chunk need thus not occur with the dog tale chunk.

The problem of initially selecting a tale chunk from the many the narrators have in memory is apparently one of the most arduous and conscious tasks they have. This is especially apparent in the various surface cues of planning as discussed by Chafe (1980), such as stumbling, self-correction, and hesitation. These often characterize the opening of tales, where they are more prevalent than anywhere else. In many cases this results, it seems, from a narrator selecting a tale chunk that is not recalled very well. This is manifest,

---

[7]According to Scheub, the basic unit of *intsomi* composition is the image. An image is a discontinuous or abstract mental picture that the narrator has distilled from previous performances he or she has witnessed. Narrators have a "repertoire" of such images (Scheub, 1975, pp. 46–47). During the composition of a particular *intsomi*, the narrator selects images through a "complex process of cueing and scanning." It is through this process that the images are "recalled and objectified." The process must be seen in the light that "nothing is memorized," and that the performer is free to make changes to the images (Scheub, 1975, p. 90). For a critical review of Scheub's views, see Gough (1986, pp. 146–152).

to a certain extent, in lines 1–3 of the narrative in the appendix, where the narrator has to backtrack to include the information that there were specifically four girls. This is relevant information, as later on in the tale one of the girls (the heroine) asks three others individually to accompany her to the river. Such planning features are also manifest in the subsequent dog tale chunk at line 31. Between this line and line 35, certain disfluencies and restarts can be seen to occur as the narrator attempts to recall the new tale chunk. The original tape recording also shows that marked pausing occurs at this point.

Once tellers are in their stride and the tale chunk is fully available, their telling is characterized by a far greater smoothness, as we see in the narrative in the appendix. Occasionally, however, inexperienced narrators may simply drop a tale chunk they are experiencing difficulty remembering and proceed to select another one.

Once a tale chunk has been selected and expressed, the initial chunk in our example being the girl tale chunk, it becomes pertinent to ask how narrators select the next one in their performances. The answer to this question is in terms of subcontextual reminding. As we have seen, subcontextual reminding describes the process where some part of the preceding discourse determines, in itself, a contextual domain in the mind of the speaker, in terms of which a particular body of information is made accessible to him or her. We noted that such reminding may occur both as the result of a discourse contributed by a previous speaker or as the result of the discourse a current speaker is constructing. It is naturally the latter situation that would be applicable to the production of *iintsomi*.

The process of subcontextual reminding appears to occur initially between lines 30–40 in the appendix narrative, an area where there is some evidence of discourse planning. Here the girl's traveling at line 30 can be seen to determine the contextual domain in the narrator's memory through which the following arrival-at-a-house incident is made accessible. This incident, in turn, determines another contextual domain through which the dog tale chunk is similarly made accessible. Both these cases are examples of subcontextual reminding, in that what the narrator selects to express appears to be determined by the memorial context established by some previous detail.

Other tale chunks may have also been made accessible through the contextual domains operative at this point in the tale. Thus, for example, the homestead at which the girl arrives could have been that of an ogre or *izim*, and a tale chunk concerning the adventures with the ogre could have been told (as indeed a number of similar tales demonstrate). Other tale chunks that do not fall under the contextual domains operative could not, however, be made so accessible. In this regard, the contextual domain determined by some previous detail acts as a general constraint in terms of which tale chunks may be selected. As more than one tale chunk may be made accessible through one contextual domain, there need be, however, no fixed pattern of selection. Indeed, the variety of tale chunks selected in this way contributes to the fact that there is no fixed tale as such in the *intsomi* tradition.

In my discussion of convesational discourse, I pointed out that an episode that is made accessible to a speaker by a particular contextual domain necessarily has implications and is relevant to that domain. The latter holds true for the aforementioned selection of tale chunks, where the tale chunks of which the narrator is reminded are indeed relevant to their contextual domains. Thus, in this narrative, for example, the girl's arrival is quite consistent with her traveling, and, furthermore, that it is the house of a dog at which she arrives is similarly consistent with the fact that she arrives at a house at all. There is, however, an inherent danger at such points. This danger is that the process of subcontextual reminding as the method of tale chunk selection culd lead to irrelevance in terms of the tale as a whole. As I noted in my discussion of conversation, the subcontextual reminding process ignores any contextual domain broader than the one determined by some preceding detail. In the production of *iintsomi*, however, there is such a broad contextual domain—the contextual domain that involves the tale as a whole, beyond the individual tale chunks. If the subcontextual reminding process (which, as I have noted, would ignore such a broad contextual domain) occurs without check, there is no guarantee that anything in particular would unite the selected tale chunks as having implications for the tale they constitute as a whole. Although subsequent tale chunks would have implications to some preceding detail, they would not necessarily have implications for the broader contextual domain of the overall tale. The extreme result of unchecked subcontextual reminding is *iintsomi* that appear to be simple exercises in remembering tale chunks, each successive one not relating in any global way to the ones that precede.

It is obvious that competent narrators, like the narrator of the text under examination, begin tales by selecting a tale chunk without knowing their final destination. They do not necessarily know, in other words, due to the nature of the subcontextual reminding process, what other tale chunks they will select (if any), and thus how their tales will end. What is needed and what is learned by the more competent narrators are certain basic constraints operating over the subcontextual reminding process. Such restraints are, it appears, in terms of intercontextual reminding.

Intercontextual reminding, as we have seen, involves the selection of information in terms of a single overall contextual domain. In the production of *iintsomi*, subcontextual reminding may result in creativity and variety, but it is potentially counterproductive to overall coherence. In order to preserve such coherence, a narrator needs to take account of the context of the tales he or she is creating as a whole. The narrator needs to be also aware of the fact that the first tale chunk selected necessarily limits the number of choices he or she can make to continue the story in a relevant way. In this regard, tale chunks subsequently selected must be modified by the inclusion or exclusion of certain information to fit the total production. Such information allows the tale chunks to have implications and be relevant to the contextual domain determined by the tale as a whole. Intercontextual reminding thus intrinsically involves improvisation and the exploitation of individual imagination.

In the appendix narrative, the largely improvised final section of the tale can be seen to be the result of intercontextual reminding. The dog's demise at the end of the tale, for example, constitutes an effective resolution to the tale as a whole. Furthermore, the reintroduction of the girls who were involved at the beginning of the tale (now given the role of agents in the resolution) gives the tale an overall unity. Such information could only be accessible to the narrator in question if she was aware of the broad contextual domain set by the tale she was creating. Given such awareness, she is in the position to select certain information that rounds off her tale in a coherent way and that has implications for the tale as a whole.

Given the fact that *intsomi* productions may involve a number of tale chunks, successful intercontextual reminding is not a trivial accomplishment. Inexperienced or poor narrators do not seem to be in a position to maintain a consistent orientation to one overall contextual domain, and their tales thus generally lack the cohesiveness that characterizes the productions of more competent narrators.

Acting over the production of an *intsomi*, then, complex processes of reminding and the associated principle of relevance explain a central property of the tradition alluded to earlier—the notion of narrative creativity through personal improvisation. The principle of relevance associated with reminding of various degrees of complexity forms part of the narrator's narrative competence, with which he or she is born or is particularly gifted. It is best demonstrated, thus, in tales told by good narrators and is the hallmark of narrative excellence.

SUMMARY AND CONCLUSION

In this chapter I explored the process of reminding and the associated principle of relevance in the composition of Xhosa folk narrative, and I suggested the importance of these notions for the creativity and coherence manifest in the tradition. I distinguished two types of reminding that operate in *intsomi* production—subcontextual and intercontextual reminding. Subcontextual reminding is the process whereby the tale chunks that make up a tale are selected. In subcontextual reminding, a particular detail at the end of a tale chunk reminds the narrator of the commencement of another. This occurs through the detail establishing the conceptual context (or contextual domain) in respect of which the following chunk becomes accessible. In this way, subcontextual reminding is responsible for the potentially large variety of tale chunks that may be selected to form a tale. This variety is one of the hallmarks of the creativity manifest in the *intsomi* tradition.

Intercontextual reminding, on the other hand, describes the process whereby narrators add their own details and personal improvisations to the traditional tales. Although the tale is not fixed in advance and may be made up of a number of (potentially discrete) tale chunks, narrators strive to create a unitary work of art that forms a coherent unit, all its parts being relevant to the context of the tale as a whole. This is achieved through the narrators' keeping in mind the context of the tale as a whole. In so doing, narrators obtain access to information that will bind the individual tale chunks together to form a coherent whole. Such addition of personally improvised information is a further hallmark of the creativity manifest in *iintsomi*.

The cognitive process of reminding is of relevance to other domains of discourse production besides the production of *iintsomi*, in which it is made particularly apparent. It also appears to opeate in conversational discourse as the basis for the offering of relevant contributions. Interlocutors are enabled by this process to make relevant contributions to a conversation as a particular domain of their knowledge is made active. Episodes attached to this domain of knowledge are made accessible by this activation. As in *intsomi* production, episodes become accessible through both inter- and subcontextual reminding. In intercontextual reminding, interlocutors stick to one domain of knowledge, all episodes reminded of being consistent with and made accessible through this domain. Subcontextual reminding, in turn, explains the gradual and connected movement of the contextual bases of conversation as one detail from a previous contribution forms the contextual domain for the next speaker.

Research into discourse production more generally will reveal the importance of reminding as a central process of retrieving relevant information as well as an important factor in the creativity and coherence that may be manifest in a discourse.

APPENDIX

1. *kwathi ke kaloku ngantsomi*
   Now for an intsomi.
2. *yaxiintombi*
   There were some girls.
3. *zaya kukha imbola.*
   They went to collect clay.
4. *yaziintombi zane.*
   There were four girls.
5. *zahamba*
   They traveled.
6. *xa zifikileyo ekukheni imbola*
   When they had arrived at the place of collecting clay,
7. *zafika zayikha zayikha*
   they arrived and collected and collected.
8. *xa zibopha le mbola zahamba zagoduka*
   When they had secured the clay, they traveled and went home.
9. *enye esithubeni*
   One, after a while,
10. *kanti ilebele umbhaco wayo*
    discovered she had forgotten her skirt.
11. *yathi kwenye intombazana ndikhaphe*
    She said to one of the girls, "Accompany me.

12. *ndiyothatha umbhaco wam ndiwulibele phezu komngxuma*
I'm going to go and get my skirt. I forgot it above the hole.

13. *ndincede mntakadadobawo*
Please, child of my father's sister."

14. *wathi ndakuba ndingumntakadadoboyihlo noba andiyanga*
She said, "Even though I'm the child of your father's sister, I'm not going."

15. *waphinda kwenye*
She went to another

16. *wathi ndincede ndikhaphe*
and said, "Please accompany me."

17. *ndilibele umbhacho wam phezu komngxuma*
I forgot my skirt at the top of the hole.

18. *ndincede mnt—ndincede mtana womnakwethu*
Please, child of my brother."

19. *wathi ndakuba ndingumntana womnakwethu—*
She said, "Even though I'm your brother's child—

20. *ndakuba ndingumtana womnakwethu noba andiyanga*
Even though I'm your brother's child, I'm not going."

21. *wathi ndincede mntakamama wamagqibilo ndikhaphe*
She said, "Please, mother's last born, accompany me.

22. *ndiyothatha umbhaco wam*
I'm going to fetch my skirt.

23. *ndiwushiye phezu komngxuma*
I left it above the hole."

24. *wathi ndakuba ndingumtana kamama noba andiyanga*
She said, "Even though I'm mother's child, I'm not going."

25. *wahamba wajika*
She traveled and turned.

26. *xa efika phezu komngxuma*
When she arrived above the hole,

27. *yafika kukho isilwanyana*
she arrived and there was an animal.

28. *sathi sondela*
It said, "Approach!"

29. *hayi wayoyika wancama washiya*
No, she was scared, and gave up and left.

30. *waphinda wahamba ethwela umthwalo*
Again she traveled carrying a load.

31. *kwahlwa esendleleni*
It became dark while she was on the road.

32. *kwala kumnyama*
While it was dark—

33. *kwala xa—kwanti—*
While—

34. *wabona umzi—okanyi—*
She saw a house which—

35. *unomlilwana omncinci*
which had a tiny little fire

36. *othi kanyi kanyi*
flickering 'kanyi, kanyi'—

37. *wayofika*
She went to arrive.

38. *xa efika wankqonkqoza kulo mzi*
When she arrived, she knocked at the house,

39. *wathi nkqo*
she went 'knock.'

40. *kanti ngumzi wenja*
But it was the homestead of a dog.

41. *yathi hawu hawu ngaphakathi*
It said, "Woof, woof come in!"

42. *wangena*
She went in.

43. *xa ehlala egumbini*
While she was sitting in the room,

44. *le nja isuka ithi*
the dog said,

45. *hawu hawu ndiphothulele*
"Woof, woof, grind for me!"

46. *athi yena zange ndiyiphothulele nja nasekhaya*
She said, "I have never ground for a dog, even at home."

47. *ithi hawu hawu ndakutya*
It said, "Woof, woof, I'll eat you!"

48. *wahamba wancama waphotula*
She traveled and despaired and ground.

49. *yavubisa inja*
The dog made porridge.

50. *xa igqiba -i- xa igqiba ukuvubisa*
When it was finished making porridge,

51. *yathi hawu hawu yiza uze kutya*
It said, "Woof, woof, come, you must eat!"

52. *wathi zange nditye nanja nasekhaya*
She said, "I have never eaten with a dog, even at home."

53. *yathi ndakutya*
It said, "I will eat you!"

54. *wancama waza kutya*
She gave up and came to eat.

55. *xa begqib'ukutya*
When they had finished eating

56. *yathi inja hawu hawu yizolala*
the dog said, "Woof, woof, come and sleep!"

57. *wathi zange ndilale nanja nasekhaya*
She said, "I've never slept with a dog, even at home."

58. *yathi hawu hawu ndakutya*
It said, "Woof, woof, I'll eat you!"

59. *wahamba waya kumbatha enjeni*
She traveled and went to sleep with the dog.

60. *kwakusa ngomso inja ivulele iinkomo*
Early next morning the dog released his cattle.

61. *iyahamba iya kwalusa*
He was going to go and herd.

62. *uma ijonga le ntombazana*
When the girl looked,

63. *ezi nkomo ziihagu*
these cattle were pigs.

64. *yaziqhuba ke*
It drove them then.

65. *yahamba yayokwalusa*
It went to go and herd.

66. *yathi ke uzoph- uzopheka iinkobe uphothule*
It said, "You must cook the maize you ground."

67. *wavuma le ntombazana*
The girl agreed.

68. *kwaba mzuzu se iziphekile iinkobe apha eziko*
After a while, having cooked the maize here at the fireplace,

69. *yaxhwitha unwele*
she pulled out a hair,

70. *yalu- yalombela apha embundwini weziko*
and hid it here in the hearth.

71. *yathatha elinye inwele*
    She took another hair,

72. *yalibeka emva kwecango*
    and put it behind the door.

73. *yathatha elinye inwele*
    She took another hair,

74. *yalembela phantsi kweenkuni egoqhweni*
    and buried it under the woodpile.

75. *ngoku yath- yathatha impahla yahamba yagoduka*
    Now she took her possessions and traveled and went home.

76. *nxa ibuya inja isizaneed komo*
    When the dog came back with the cows,

77. *ithi hawu hawu yiza nethunga*
    it said, "Woof, woof, bring the pail!"

78. *lithi eli nwele liseziko*
    The hair at the fireplace said,

79. *ndisakhwezela*
    "I'm busy making a fire!"

80. *hawu hawu yiza nethunga*
    "Woof, woof, bring the pail!"

81. *lithi eliya lisegoqhweni*
    The one at the woodpile said,

82. *ndisachola-chola*
    I'm busy gathering!"

83. *hawu hawu yiza nethunga*
    "Woof, woof, bring the pail!"

84. *liyathetha inwele elisemva kwecango*
    The hair behind the door spoke,

85. *lithi ndisaya emlanjeni*
    saying, "I'm busy going to the river."

86. *hayi ke akude kuphume mntu*
    So then at length, with no one coming out,

87. *wavalela iinkomo*
    it closed up the cattle

88. *wabheka endlini*
    and went to the house.

89. *uyathetha ke hawu hawu yiza nethunga*
    It spoke then, "Woof, woof, bring the pail!"

90. *ndisachola-chola*
    "I'm busy gathering!"

91. *kuthetha unwele oluphandle ezikweni*
    spoke the hair outside, at the fireplace.

92. *hawu hawu yiza nethunga*
    "Woof, woof, bring the pail!"

93. *ndisakhwezela*
    "I'm busy making a fire!"

94. *kuthetha inwele liseziko*
    spoke the hair at the fireplace.

95. *hawu hawu yiza nethunga*
    "Woof, woof, bring the pail!"

96. *ndisemlanjeni*
    "I'm at the river!"

97. *hayi wancama*
    Well, it gave up.

98. *wakufika pha akukho mntu*
    When it arrived there, there was no one.

99. *ngoku ulanda ekhondweni*
    Now it followed the trail.

100. *ahambe ayilande intombazana*
     It traveled and followed the girl.

101. *nxa efika ebukhweni*
     When it arrived at his in-laws,

102. *ufika ahlale phandle*
     it arrived and sat outside.

103. *xa ehleli phandle*
     While it sat outside

104. *athi ndifuna umkam*
     it said, "I want my wife."

105. *kweziwa neentombi zane zalapha zonke zone*
     All those four girls here came.

106. *kwathiwa ngowuphi*
     It was said, "Which one is it?"

107. *wathi ngulo*
     It said, "It's this one."

108. *bathathwa ke basiwa kulaa ndlu*
     They were taken and taken to that house.

109. *bancokola bancokola*
     They chatted and chatted.

110. *abanye bahamba baphuma washiwa nomkakhe*
     Some moved and went out and it was left with its wife.

111. *nxa ehleli umkakhe kanti*
     While his wife was staying yet

112. *abanye naba phandle*
     here are the others outside.

113. *kuse- kusesilapha isithunga*
     A torch was already there.

114. *ku- kuzatshiswa le ndlu*
     This house was to be burnt.

115. *ngokuba iboniwe yinya ayingomntu*
     As it was seen that it was a dog, not a person.

116. *kwasuka waphuma le ntombazana ngathi iyokuchama*
     The girl went out as if she was going to urinate.

117. *kwalayithwa esi sithungu*
     The torch was lit.

118. *yakhal' inja*
     The dog cried out

119. *yathi*
     hawu hawu ndatsha ebukhweni
     hawu hawu ndatsha ebukhweni
     hawu hawu ndatsha ebukhweni
     hawu hawu ndatsha ebukhweni
     and said,
     "Woof, woof, I'm burnt amongst the in-laws!
     Woof, woof, I'm burnt amongst the in-laws!
     Woof, woof, I'm burnt amongst the in-laws!
     Woof, woof, I'm burnt amongst the in-laws!"

120. *phela phela ngantsomi*
     The intsomi is ended.

REFERENCES

Brown, G., Yulle, G. (1983). *Discourse analyses.* Cambridge: Cambridge University Press.

Chafe, W. (1980). The deployment of consciousness in the production of a narrative. In W. Chafe (Ed.), *The pear stories: Cognitive, cultural, and linguistic aspects of narrative production* (pp. 9–50). Norwood, NJ: Ablex.

Gough, D. H. (1986). *Xhosa narrative: An analysis of the production and linguistic properties of discourse with particular reference to iintsomi texts.* PhD dissertation, Rhodes University, Grahamstown, South Africa.

Leech, G. N. (1983). *Principles of pragmatics.* London: Longman.

Schank, R. (1984). *Dynamic memory: A theory of reminding and learning in computers and people.* Cambridge: Cambridge University Press.

Scheub, H. (1975). *The Xhosa NTSOMI*. Oxford: Clarendon Press.
Sperber, D., & Wilson, D. (1982). Mutual knowledge and relevance in theories of comprehension. In N. Smith (Ed.), *Mutual knowledge* (pp. 61–131). New York: Academic Press.
Sperber, D., & Wilson, D. (1986). *Relevance: Communication and cognition.* The Hague: Mouton.

9

The Rhetoric of Narrative: A Hermeneutic, Critical Theory

Michael McGuire
California State University, Long Beach

The existence of this volume, like the colloquium held at the University of Georgia in early spring, 1987, bears witness to the facts that narrative is a topic of marked interest to many disciplines and that it is open to many lines of inquiry. Fascinating as psycholinguistic or sociolinguistic analyses can be, they leave unexplored many questions about the persuasive social influence of narratives among adults. Our discussions in Athens more than once raised the question, "What is the potential of narrative to influence social-political attitudes?" That question, which is the heart of a rhetoric of narrative, remains unanswered by other disciplines. Because there may be some confusion about the concept of a rhetoric of narrative, I begin with definition, showing the connection of rhetoric to hermeneutic and critical theory.

Rhetoric is a theory of language that explains its potential to inform and persuade (Bryant, 1953, 1973). Aristotle (1954) conceived of it as the counterpart of dialectic and a branch of politics—one of the practical arts, which has as its special task discovering means to persuade. According to Aristotle, rhetoric is the art concerned with arguments based on probabilities, as opposed to demonstrations of certainty; its realm is that of human social action and judgment, and its purposes include strengthening the democratic *polis* by maximizing the rationality of citizens' arguments. Aristotle was no more sanguine than Plato (1952, 1956) about the teachings of some sophists with regard to a rhetoric of high-style, ostentatious ornament, and the unimportance of knowledge (truth) relative to belief (appearance). Aristotle wanted to make rhetoric as rational—as probable—as possible for its social contexts: Athenian courts, legislative assemblies, and public celebrations or occasions. In his *Rhetoric*, which prescribes types of probable argument, Aristotle identified two "universal" forms of "proof" suited to these social contexts: *enthymeme*, which is a term for quasi-logical arguments, deductive or inductive; and *paradeigma*, which consists in narratives used to inform or persuade by their analogical quality and concreteness (McGuire, 1982a, 1987).

In the 2,000 years since Aristotle's foundational work, rhetorical theory has embraced, and been embraced by, literary theory, philosophy, and psychology (Ehninger, 1968). The "rhetoric" of any discourse—using the term in its serious-theoretical rather than its popular-pejorative sense—is the didactic and hortatory aspects of the work. It is clear, for example, that Sinclair's *The Jungle* and Swift's *Gulliver's Travels* have such aspects, beside whatever aesthetic qualities they possess, and ought to be considered rhetorically. Burke (1945, 1957) took the position that all literature must be viewed as rhetoric; and Barthes (1972) noted that rhetoric is the theory of language that shaped literature and its study until both were "ruined" by rationalism and positivism.

Similarly, nearly all philosophical works, even those purporting to be pure demonstrations, are not written for the mind of God, but to affect human judgment and behavior. All argument is addressed to some audience, and even scientific writings can be taken as having significant rhetorical dimensions and functions for their audiences (Kuhn, 1962; Overington, 1977). Nevertheless, the rhetoric of philosophy may be most evident in the works of writers like Nietzsche or Sartre, or in what is called practical philosophy (Riedel, 1972). Rhetoric also has high relevance to hermeneutic philosophy and critical theory, insofar as those branches of philosophy are concerned with analyzing language to understand its social power.

The Yale group's (Hovland, Janis, & Kelly, 1953) investigations of persuasion show an obvious connection between rhetoric and psychology, but the connections can be traced historically back to Aristotle's discussions of types of human character and emotions in the *Rhetoric*. Rhetorical theory concerns cognitive operations of the mind, both the highly emotional (hatred, grief) and the highly rational (syllogism, induction), as they are put into or brought about by language. The line of research on counterattitudinal advocacy stimulated by Festinger (1957) reveals a psychology of one type of rhetoric. The undeniable interest of psychology in persuasion makes psychology relevant to rhetoric, and vice versa.

The rhetoric of narrative, then, is the theory of how narrative can be used to persuade and to inform. The purely informational aspects of language (if such exist) are within the provinces of linguistics and grammar as well. What differentiates a rhetoric from them? Rhetoric is concerned, not alone with issues of meaningful language in the abstract, but more with the question, How may language be made meaningful and informative to some real, particular audience—to people with specifiable traits and purposes beyond linguistic competence? And rhetoric is concerned with what and how units of language longer than sentences have meaning (McGuire, 1977). Finally, as opposed to grammar and much of linguistics, rhetoric is concerned with the social structures, the contexts, in which and because of which utterances take on both the forms and meanings that they do (Geissner, 1986; McGuire, 1982b).

Both logic and psychology are useful in rhetorical analysis of discourse, because whatever one prefers or avers, both reason and feeling may lead to conviction and behavior. Social contexts in which discourses occur are essential components to understanding their persuasive potential (Gadamer, 1967), even though some discourses transcend their original, real-historical, generative contexts and speak persuasively to later times and different places and people (Bitzer, 1968; Hoy, 1978).

A rhetorical theory is inherently a hermeneutic theory, because it must interpret the potential meanings of discourse, as well as assess how those meanings are possible. This doesn't mean that only one meaning, or a true meaning, can be attributed to a discourse. Indeed, it may be that no interpretation ever can be "the" correct one, but only a probable, well-argued one based on the evidence available, as Hirsch (1967) admitted. However, a general rhetorical theory of narrative is both possible and useful, because it raises not the question of what a particular narrative means or what effect it has, but questions of how narrative as a form has potentials to inform and persuade that differ from other language forms. Such a metatheory is the purpose of this chapter. I examine first some sociological aspects of narrative that concern the use of the form for rhetorical purposes. Then I consider the operations of narrative language, including the potentials of such grammatical categories as narrating persona and direct discourse. Finally, these two levels of analysis are synthesized to suggest a rhetorical theory of narrative.

A SOCIOLOGY OF NARRATIVE

Because rhetorical discourse is inherently for and in public, rhetoric always has a social side. Although it may have been sufficient for Aristotle to specify the three types of rhetoric as judicial, legislative, and ceremonial, and for later theorists to add preaching, such a category system is replaced in this century by sociological theories not taking such structures as given (Berger & Luckmann, 1967; Habermas, 1967, 1968). The contemporary point of view holds that such social structures are often created by language, and that language is a storehouse of knowledge for institutions and for culture or society itself. Not only may this point be demonstrated with regard to language systems and their vocabularies, but with regard to huge bodies of discourse that are or are not accessible to some particular segments of society. Such considerations belong to a sociology of narrative.

Both literary and social theorists have observed the tendency of some types of discourse to form (be collected into) aggregates. Frye (1957) underscored the tendency particularly in regard to myths, but did not speculate about who does the collecting or why. Critical theorists observe that social and economic interests are involved in assembling and disseminating such collections (Habermas, 1968). Berger and Luckmann (1967) showed how such collections, whether mythological, theological, philosophical, or scientific legitimize and perpetuate beliefs and behaviors. These collections of discourse house commonplaces or lines for argument, and their rhetorical functions involve both message making and institution perpetuation.

From the perspective of a sociology of knowledge, the rhetoric of narrative is functionally significant indeed, for it is part of what informs people about the world and persuades them what to do in it, and how to evaluate behavior. Those who do not know our narratives do not participate in the same world we do. Our allusions wasted on them, we stare at them and wonder as Zarathustra did when he met the old saint, can it be that they have heard nothing of this, that god is dead? We detect that they are foreign or alien, and not part of our society. Communication with them is impaired, because knowledge is not shared.

What needs discussion and has received none is the question, Who has access to what? The narratives that form aggregates under social guidance are not equally available or intelligible to the whole population of a modern, industrial society. The narratives that form enclaves collect unevenly. Hand this book to your auto mechanic. Try to read his latest instruction manual. We all know that technical knowledge collects in pools for specialists. Then try instead to hand this book to the campus minister, or the Accuracy in Academia student in the front row of your lecture, and see if the same results occur. They do not, because access to knowledge, to belief, and to attitude differs in any modern society. Ignoring, for now, the Marxist imperative for equal access, we note that access to and agreement with narrative collections characterize the social roles that people live. These collections are parts of the knowledge that glues any culture together. Collections of stories to which we have access and with which we agree establish our faith in the social systems in which we believe and act as auto mechanics, college professors, or butchers, and our roles are thereby reinforced.

As large aggregates of narratives become important parts of the social stock of knowledge and serve to legitimate institutions, their rhetorical dimensions become clear if not central to all understanding and interpretation. These collections of narratives pull people together and push them apart. Their social power as a function and effect merits our attention before we pass on to how the form of narrative itself gets power.

When Jimmy Swaggart struts and frets his hour, he waves in his hand a Bible, a collection of narratives that are his unalterable, certain truth. All other narratives—and he names several, such as films and music lyrics—pale in comparison. Members of the audience are left with the choice, Truth or Falsehood; Good or Evil; Us or Them. But what traits do the members of a Swaggart audience really share, or how very different from one another can they be? The elderly widows, young children, truckers, sales clerks, and businesspeople become one through sharing in Swaggart's narrative on a narrative. Those who do not join in are cast out. If you're not part of the solution, radicals used to say, you're part of the problem. But is the urge for truth experienced by Swaggart's audience greater than the urge for truth felt at the same hour by colleagues in chemistry labs and library carrels? When people pursue the truth, they may be after very different things, committed to different stories and different methods.

As a second case in point, the Klaus Barbie trial is taking place as I write this chapter. In Germany interest is low, but in France, the public attitude is fear and loathing—they do not want to know about the trial, hear about it, read about it, or see it on TV. This peculiarity perplexed me until I heard an interview with Barbie's attorney by the American wire service AP. The lawyer commented on the lack of media coverage in France and explained it by saying that a great myth is believed in France, and perhaps elsewhere, that during World War II there were very few French collaborators, and hordes of swarming resistance fighters—The Marquis—just waiting for DeGaulle to return. The facts, of course, are dramatically different: The French were more than acquiescent to their Nazi conquerors; they were cooperative. Many French collaborators, said the attorney, today hold high government and business positions, and will not come forward to identify this "butcher of Lyon," because to do so could be self-incriminating. The lawyer critiqued the French story of how it was. He also shed light on how powerful such stories can be: Not everyone in France who knew Barbie is either dead or holding a cabinet post. The modern, mass-social person, helpless then to resist a Klaus Barbie, is helpless now to admit he or she didn't. Victims of revised history, they fear to speak to lose its dignity and their own.

What do such different examples show us? Even when narratives collect into aggregates, they are not accessed uniformly by populations. Not everyone reads the Bible or the auto mechanics' bible or the butchers' bible. The Marxist fear is that access to collections of knowledge is not equal for all people. Although I do not dispute that observation, I prefer to focus on its facticity, not its causes. Narratives collect into recognizable bodies because recognizable social groups control them, not vice versa. A sociology of narrative ultimately may be written to show which groups have access to what narratives, and what groups collect and distribute particular narratives.

Finally, the mobility of narratives from medium to medium is an aspect of a sociology of narrative that discloses access. The ubiquity of TV in American homes may or may not have undercut such traditional narrative media as novels and newspapers; surely these same televisions have brought films and religious programs and more, as well as their own products, both entertainment and news, to vast audiences. Moreover, some collections of narratives that originated in that medium have been and are retold with such frequency that their characters and world structures pervade the public consciousness more than all the novels of American literature added together: We live in a cable world where children cannot help but find and "learn" from "Gilligan's Island," Ricky and Lucy

Ricardo, what fun the Korean War was in a MASH unit, and more. It has become difficult to find public school graduates who have read a single novel by Faulkner or Melville, seen or read a play by Williams or Miller. This is not a question of taste, but of media availability and choices by consumers, programmers, and adver-tisers.

A sociology of narrative is not a sociolinguistics of narrative. To be sure, there are differences in idiom, code, and more, among persons who believe in the same stories and who, for the purposes here, are therefore in the same group. Such people might retell their shared stories in slightly or dramatically different ways. Tellings, however, are conventions not entirely related to social adherence. From one scientific point of view, Baptists, Roman Catholics, Con-gregationalists, and Presbyterians believe too many of the same stories not to be considered a group. (From a point of view within those groups, say, in Ireland, that's not so.)

If narratives can and do tell us as groups what to believe and why, then how they get their power is of immense importance. Given a number of narratives competing for our attention and loyalty, what things make one more compelling than another? Al-though being raised in a tradition is a factor for any individual, such a response ignores transformations of belief that people make and locates all the reasons for believing in the person, and none in the narrative. Surely there are interactive effects, at least, that merit some consideration of why and how narratives are persua-sive. Such considerations require detailed analysis of narrative in terms of linguistic categories.

A GRAMMAR OF NARRATIVE

The ground to cover in outlining a grammar of narrative may seem familiar and firm at first glance. What is there, after all, besides first and third person, direct and indirect discourse? What there is is a confusion of terminology and a set of vocabularies, if not also concepts, that vary with one's own discipline and focus. Besides efforts at formal definitions of narrative modes (Bickerton, 1967) and general treatments of narrative as a kind of language (Genette, 1980; Scholes & Kellogg, 1966), literary theorists have assessed the relationship between fictional narration and consciousness (Cohn, 1978; Humphrey, 1955; Peper, 1966), between narration and the presentation of reality, mimetic or not (Abrams, 1953; White, 1980), and the possibilities of narrative in nonlinguistic media (Chatman,

1978). Most of these discussions center on the expressive rather than the impressive possibilities of narration; that is, literary theorists and critics naturally tend to concentrate on the form's ability to speak for an author, not its ability to speak to an audience. Although there have been some studies of narrative as a practical and persuasive form (Kirkwood, 1983; Ochs & Burritt, 1973), theory is this area remains inelegant (McGuire, 1982a). It seems reasonable to consider the likely interactive effects of the syntactical features of narrative to search for possible effects they would have in combination.

The first question is, What types of narrative exist? From the point of view of rhetoric, there are three kinds (McGuire, 1982a). First, there are historical narratives, which are intended and recognized to report actual events. Second, there are literary narratives, which posit a fictive universe and are neither intended nor interpreted as reports of actual events. Finally, there are invented narratives, which, although they do not report actual events, are intended to be taken as reports of actual events.

Historical narratives may be reports of actual events and real people, but they are not the things themselves. Historical narratives are inherently rhetorical: They do not present, but represent events and persons—they interpret. We may leave aside questions whether such documents as statistical abstracts are either narrative or interpretive, and consider instead stories about factual information. Whether or not an objective narration is possible (I think it unlikely), audiences recognize some narratives as about reality. How, then, is historical narrative as a type detected by readers or hearers?

A first answer is that the sociology of narrative would show us what stories different groups of people acknowledge to be stories about real events and people. That is, events and people acknowledged to have been (or be) real are collected together in a common stock of knowledge: World War II really occurred; the Soviet Union is real; there really will be elections in the United States in November, 1992. Historical narrative is not recognized by a grammatical feature like tense, but by content units accorded the status of reality, that is, existing independent of our attitudes and volitions (Berger & Luckmann, 1967). This clarifies the fact that historical narratives are a category only in relation and contrast to literary narratives.

Literary narratives are stories that groups share that are agreed to contain content units referring to the unreal—and deliberately so. A sociology of such narratives would be extremely complex, showing that different people have access to Homeric epics, TV soap operas, Shakespeare plays, best-sellers, Marvel comics, Hitchcock films, and oral fables and jokes. Textual or narrative structure does not distinguish literary from historical narratives; an epistemic structure that involves the acknowledgment or disavowal of reality does. That structure is socially conditioned, and cognitively complex. Young children may have difficulty discerning the reality or unreality of the Flintstones (Palmer & Door, 1980); some adults manifest the confusion with regard to Mr. Whipple and J. R. Ewing. Literary narratives still may have rhetorical functions, because they may be used to persuade audiences that this is what reality is like—not that Captain Ahab is real, but that he shows the disastrous consequences of obsession; not that the fox and crow in Aesop's fable really conversed, but that they reveal the types of the flatterer and the vain; not that Lake Wobegon exists, but that it represents places that do. Although the definitive trait of literary narrative is the acknowledgment that its story is not real or true, the possibility of fiction being confused with fact is the very nature of the invented narrative, our third type.

Invented narrative is fiction passing itself off as historical narrative. These narratives are not literary, because they lack the social status as such. No group recognizes these stories as fictions, because they are spontaneous inventions of narrators, at least inceptionally, and if they pass at all into a shared stock of knowledge, it is after that passage that the stories are interpreted as history or literature. The sermons of Norman Vincent Peale are filled with such stories; Ronald Reagan has a fondness for telling stories; presumably the story of George Washington's late cherry tree is an example of this kind of narrative. An unfriendly name for these stories is lies. Yet no one attacks Peale's ethics on their account. Patrick Henry's most famous speech originated in this way from a historian's pen, but it is now accepted as history, and no one seems to care about debunking. It is worth noting that narratives of this category may come to be regarded as either history or literature, or they may simply pass away after the moment when they are invented and recounted. Much of the best of human conversation consists in inventing narratives for which no purpose beyond the moment, or conviviality, exists. Doubtless too, the worst of human perjury, the most damaging and ruinous stories, belongs to this type: fiction passing for fact.

But why are some narratives believed and others not; given the competition among narratives offering different representations of reality, what makes some narratives more persuasive than others? Why were Nazis more successful than Marxists in the relatively open field of competition (for extremist arguments) called the Weimar Republic? Why did Ronald Reagan survive accusations no less serious than those that ended the Nixon Presidency? Why does Sanka outsell generics?

These questions, having the very different answers that they must, may help us understand the persuasive powers of narratives of different kinds. The Nazis triumphed partly because the social structure precluded Marxist victory (too, many imperialists held judicial and other posts). Reagan was perceived as moral by Americans—a man from whom they would want to buy a used car. Generic decaffeinated coffee is not endorsed by Marcus Welby or anyone else; it simply exists, usually in packaging so bright it calls attention to itself and its purchaser, saying, "We're cheap." Neither environment nor source credibility nor message content is a sufficient explanation alone. The interaction between the receiver of a message, its source, and its content is essential to explain fully why one narrative persuades where another fails. Thus, the sociology of narrative never can be overlooked in explaining actual cases of narrative rhetoric.

Can we look beyond cases to see whether, other things being equal, specific linguistic factors make a narrative more convincing than its competitors? We can, by looking in two different directions. First, we must distinguish between the verbal and epistemic structures of narrative (McGuire, 1982a). Second, we must consider the effects of the verbal structure of narrative on its ultimate meaning, or epistemic structure (McGuire, 1987).

The verbal structure of a narrative is simply its linguistic existence, a text, *parole*. If the text is written, then the language is plain to see. If a question arises, such as, did Plato say so-and-so in section 229 of *Phaedrus*, we can look and see. We may discover a printer's error by this technique. Such analysis of language discloses things like the length of a narrative, its tenses, the persona of the narrator (e.g., first or third person), and the use of direct or indirect discourse. In sum, this analysis discloses objectively verifiable characteristics of narrative as a verbal structure—as a piece of language with particular, even measurable dimensions. But this describes only the empirical reality of language, and not its meaning—not its social reality.

What, then, is the epistemic structure of a narrative? We can build the epistemic structure of a narrative only by following the admittedly, avowedly different directions of structuralism and hermeneutics, which lead us to two different epistemic structures, both important. Just as Langue (an entire linguistic system) must be inferred from parole, all epistemic structures of language must be inferred or built from pieces of discourse. The epistemic structure of a narrative is not in the narrative itself. The two epistemic structures of every narrative exist, one after narration, one before narration. The after-narration epistemic structure is the meaning of the narrative inside some listener's or reader's head. The before-narration epistemic structure is both the thoughts and intentions of the narrator and the langue in which the narrative participates. The epistemic structure of Mann's *Dr. Faustus* includes not only his anti-Nazi intentions and his fascinations with Nietzsche, but a langue of Goethe's and Marlowe's and Berlioz's *Fausts* (Heller, 1968; Levi-Strauss, 1963; McGuire, 1977).

Here, then, I break from Hirsch (1967, 1976) by addition: Not only the author's intentions constitute an epistemic structure of a narrative against which interpretations can be measured, but the participation of a narrative in a langue of earlier texts and thoughts is necessary to the interpretation of that particular narrative, even if the author, unlike Mann, was ignorant of those texts and thoughts. From the point of view of rhetorical usefulness, a narrative probably succeeds better if it taps a well of familiar pretexts and thoughts than if it does not. Like a sentence in a language, a narrative is an empirical manifestation of an invisible system that nonetheless must be there, or the sentence would not, could not, function effectively. To select a simple illustration, it would not matter whether we named a new beauty cream Venus or Medusa unless potential customers have access to narratives that make one preferable to the other. There can be a sort of langue of content units, just as there must be for all words of a language; sometimes that langue consists of one or more narratives.

I argued elsewhere (McGuire, 1987) that two types of presence created by grammatical features of narratives affect and help to explain their persuasiveness. First, grammatical features increase or decrease the presence of the narrator in a narrative; second, grammatical features increase or decrease the presence of a narrative to an audience. A narrator is more present within a narrative when using first person narration than third; when using direct discourse instead of indirect discourse; and the narrator is more present within an historical than a literary narrative. In fact, the presence of the narrator at all in literary narrative may be viewed as inappropriate, unless the narrator is also the author; even then, as Dostoevsky showed, it may startle. If the narrator has high credibility, higher presence should produce more persuasion; a narrator with low credibility should decrease this presence. What is the presence of a narrative to an audience, and what increases and decreases it? How present a story is to an audience depends on several things. First, the general level of concrete detail—raised by direct instead of indirect discourse—raises the presence of the narrative to the audience. Second, the personae of narration affect its presence for an audience. The most present narration is second person; for example, Perry Mason saying to the witness, "And then you told Mr. McCloud what you thought of his offer, didn't you? And he threatened to report you to the police, so you killed him, and switched briefcases with Dr. Thomas so that he would be blamed. . . ." If one hears such a narrative that is personal and historical, it must indeed have high presence. Such narratives are less common than first and third person narratives, which have lower presence, but first is usually higher than third. A narrator's presence may allow the audience to "see" better, and adds a realism to the events, like eyewitness testimony. However, it is impossible to say whether literary or historical narratives have more presence to an audience, because the question is unintelligible but makes us consider something else of great importance.

A literary narrative of high familiarity has more presence for an audience than a historical one of relative obscurity, and vice versa. *Star Trek* has higher presence for most Americans than the biography of Aaron Burr; but Watergate has more presence than *The Sorrows of Young Werther*. However, as the familiarity and presence of a narrative of one of these two types increases, the epistemic structure of the story becomes fixed, and its informative and persuasive potentials are thereby delimited.

People who deliberately attend to literary narration are doing so to be entertained; they interpret the narration as more or less valuable in connection with that function. It is a function fulfilled by different things for different people, but it is an effect—an afterstory epistemic structure of narration. They may be informed or persuaded by the fiction, but those are not their purposes, and they may be reluctant to accept information from literary narrative. Everything there can be made up. History, on the other hand, even when exciting, is not attended to for entertainment, but for information and persuasion. It is real, and we should learn from it and be able to judge from it.

Accordingly, a poet may succeed with a line like "nibble again fish nerves," but an advocate almost certainly will not. The audience of historical narratives expects them to make sense and to be presented with a view to application by analogy. Bad narrators accordingly receive the responses: "Yeah, but what's the point?" and "So what's this got to do with anything?" (Good narrators may also get those responses from bad audiences.) Verisimilitude is not required of literature in the same way it is of history.

Rhetoric sees both facts as such, and advises play with these epistemic structures. The essential structure underlying narrative as a rhetorical device is analogy. Two or more things are compared—usually a present, recent, or future state of affairs about which there is uncertainty, and a past, literary, or invented state of similar affairs. The clear and often familiar narrative orients its audience to the uncertainty in question. "See things this way," it says, and "Here are the likely causes and effects of these circumstances." In sum, narrative shows things as they might be or have been. Aristotle believed that historical narratives, because known to be true, are better persuaders than the other two types; no evidence supports that claim, and there is a naivete in the assertion, as if all narrations of past fact seem equally accurate or true. But the idea of things as they might be accounts for the persuasive value of well-constructed narrative. The probability of narrative arguments is their plausibility as portrayals of types of events, people, and circumstances. The underlying faith to which they appeal is, Nothing ever changes; history repeats itself; there is a human nature and a natural order. (Not all narratives appeal to all of these possible beliefs, of course.) A rhetorically successful narrative, accordingly, must either be familiar to its audience (a sociological issue) or plausible for its audience as a typical story of how things are, and clearly comparable to the problematic uncertainty that it is intended to clarify. But what underlies and explains perceived plausibility? With that question, we begin our synthesis of the foregoing into a rhetoric of narrative.

THE RHETORIC OF NARRATIVE

Since its systematization by Aristotle over 2,000 years ago, rhetoric has been concerned with the "invention" or discovery of arguments—including narratives. But, although it is easy to specify topics of quasi-logical argument (e.g., cause–effect), there is no systematized statement in over 20 centuries of thought regarding the invention of narrative. A reader casually acquainted with Aristotle's *Poetics* might assume wrongly that it is such a system. The question of genres has been systematically resolved—what makes a tragedy, a comedy, and so forth—but that is a question about the formal features of narrative, not its content or rhetorical application. And genre theory does not explain how or why tragedies or comedies are conceived in the first place; it offers only a description of what they look like afterwards.

The rhetorician wants narratives, not alone entertaining, but informative and persuasive. The persuasive potentials of narrative have been acknowledged by all; but their invention by an advocate has not been clarified. Aristotle's claim that literary training and an eye for resemblances are required is small help. For quasi-logical arguments based on such topics as cause–effect, contradiction, definition, induction, and more, a plethora of lines to argue is available. But for the invention of narratives, for a theory of their argumentative qualities, no such system exists. What would such a system look like?

First, such a system would incorporate a thorough grammar of narrative that would have three dimensions: (a) narrating personae (first singular or plural; second person [in some languages, divisible into types]; third person; third person omniscient); (b) mode of discourse (direct, indirect, or both); and (c) type of narrative (historical, literary, or invented). Some narratives might require or preclude particular combinations of these three variables, but the three variables together are a model of narratives: historical, first person, direct discourse; literary, third person omniscient, indirect discourse; and so on. These formal features of narrative may be systematically described.

Second, a rhetoric of narrative must offer some criteria and descriptions of persuasive and informative effects. Although one rhetorical critic undertook to elaborate criteria for narrative rhetoric (Fisher, 1984), his account seems both hasty, on one hand, and fraught with self-contradiction on the clearest issues (Warnick, 1987). Only a hermeneutical approach that considers a narrative in its tradition as well as in its particular context(s) of use can do this adequately (Gadamer, 1975). This necessitates seeing the langue of narrative and seeking to construct its other epistemic structures. A rhetorical theory of narrative will not be fully testable, then, but will always have speculative dimensions.

Finally, such a system would assume and go beyond the poetic ideas of tragedy and comedy as types, of catharsis as an effect. How can a tragedy argue? As a beginning, we know that some tragedies argue against pride, ambition, avarice, or obsession. Other narratives argue for perseverance, skill, charity, or loyalty. They argue by showing positive or negative outcomes that result from some trait or action. Adam and Eve wanted knowledge, so out they must go; Ahab was obsessed with that white whale, and ruined everything; Robin Hood fought evil with great skill and aided the poor, and so succeeded; the fox got the meat away from the crow by deceptive flattery, so beware of flatterers.

Already these very simple examples show why no one has systematized the invention of narrative. In the last case, why not derive from the fable the moral to be a sycophant? And doesn't Robin Hood, an early antihero, seem "good" only because we think we're on his side when he robs and kills? These two examples raise what might be called the Jesse James Paradox: Because (partly due to social interests and backgrounds) people identify differently with characters and stories, few characters, traits, or actions will be praised or blamed universally within a society. (Those that are come from and comprise the realms of mythology and theology, both of which deal in absolutes and the supernatural or divine: gods and devils.) Loyalty cannot be appealed to as a form, because it must be loyalty to someone or something, and the object of loyalty makes it good or bad. Some people who oppose abortion because killing is wrong advocate capital punishment. Ethical judgments are conditioned by social frameworks, and are not absolute, abstract judgments of traits, people, or acts.

When we view narratives as teachers or persuaders, it is necessary to understand that the form's almost unlimited potential to create appearances is harnessed and directed by the advocate's didactic intentions. The rhetoric of narrative involves the epistemic structure of the narrative, which earlier was seen to be the meaning or interpretation of the narrative for an audience. That complex epistemic structure arises both from content and from form and conventions (issues such as mode or medium of presentation, e.g., writing, speaking face to face, radio). Part of that epistemic structure is the tale's reflection on the teller; the narrator's presence in the narrative increases this effect, but it is invariably present. The credibility of a narrator is affected by the narrative and its presentation: Competence, trustworthiness, and dynamism, not to mention homophily and likeableness, all are affected both by the content of one's story (even if it is not about oneself) and one's delivery.

Moreover, sociological factors of familiarity from access affect a historical or literary narrative's usefulness as an informative or a persuasive example. The rhetorical use of narrative depends on appealing to narratives that seem to be or are familiar and that reinforce the advocate's position. The advocate must have some knowledge of the tradition and effects of the story to use it to achieve the effect desired. That echoes Aristotle's advice that literary training—and history—facilitates the discovery of narratives for rhetorical purposes.

Because the logical aspect of rhetorical narrative is analogy or comparison, narratives must be chosen or created to fit the situations, characters, or events about which they are intended to inform or persuade. It is possible that narratives are reducible to propositional form—but that reduction strips the narrative of many of its most appealing features. A rhetorically used narrative, as a comparison or analogy, is reducible, not to propositional form, but to metaphor. That is, one may assert either with an extended, detailed narrative or a condensed metaphor that, for example, Fawn Hall was the Rosemary Wood of the Reagan era, or that Oliver North played Faust to Poindexter's Mephisto. These metaphors not only fit but also shape or interpret the persons, actions, and situations that are their objects.

In the end, then, a dialectical relationship exists between narratives and attitudes or beliefs. Narratives give people many of their beliefs and attitudes, or at least shape them. Beliefs and attitudes toward both the narrator and the content or objects of narration can be influenced by narratives. On the other hand, narratives must draw on previously existing knowledge and beliefs to shape attitudes, and narratives must participate in the langue of previous narratives in order to seem plausible to an audience, especially if that langue is part of the audience's knowledge. Narratives may expand or add to a stock of knowledge, or they may interpret new information for incorporation into a body of knowledge by showing how and where it fits. Some narratives make universal assertions or claims, but more commonly narratives are used to express the new or unfamiliar in terms of comparison with the known or familiar.

REFERENCES

Abrams, M. H. (1953). *The mirror and the lamp*. New York: Oxford University, Press.
Aristotle. (1954). *The rhetoric and the poetics of Aristotle* (W. R. Roberts & I. Bywater, Eds. and Trans.). New York: Modern Library.
Barthes, R. (1972). To write: An intransitive verb? In R. De George & F. De George (Eds.), *The structuralists: From Marx to Levi-Strauss* (pp. 154–162). New York: Anchor Books.
Berger, P., & Luckmann, T. (1967). *The social construction of reality: A treatise in the sociology of knowledge*. New York: Anchor Books.

Bickerton, D. (1967). Modes of interior monologue: A formal definition. *Modern Language Quarterly, 28,* 229–239.

Bitzer, L. (1968). The rhetorical situation. *Philosophy and Rhetoric, 1,* 1–14.

Bryant, D. C. (1953). Rhetoric: Its functions and its scope. *Quarterly Journal of Speech, 39,* 401–424.

Bryant, D. C. (1973). *Rhetorical dimensions in criticism.* Baton Rouge: Louisiana State University Press.

Burke, K. (1945). *A grammar of motives.* Engelwood Cliffs, NJ: Prentice-Hall.

Burke, K. (1957). *The philosophy of literary form.* New York: Vintage Books.

Chatman, S. (1978). *Story and discourse: Narrative structure in fiction and film.* Ithaca, NY: Cornell University Press.

Cohn, D. (1978). *Transparent minds: Narrative modes of presenting consciousness in fiction.* Princeton: Princeton University Press.

Ehninger, D. (1968). On systems of rhetoric. *Philosophy and Rhetoric, 1,* 131–144.

Fisher, W. (1984). Narration as a human communication paradigm: The case of public moral argument. *Communication Monographs, 51,* 1–22.

Frye, N. (1957). *Anatomy of criticism.* Princeton: Princeton University Press.

Gadamer, H.-G. (1967). *Kleine Schriften.* Tuebingen: J. C. B. Mohr.

Gadmer, H.-G. (1975). *Wahrheit und Methode: Grundzuege einer philosophischen Hermeneutik* (3rd ed.). Tuebingen, Germany: J. C. B. Mohr.

Geissner, H. (1986). *Rhetorik und politische Bildung* (4th ed.). Frankfurt a.M: Scriptor.

Genette, G. (1980). *Narrative discourse: An essay in method.* Ithaca, NY: Cornell University Press.

Habermas, J. (1967). Zur Logik der Sozialwissenschaften. *Philosophische Rundschau,* Beiheft 5.

Habermas, J. (1968). *Erkenntnis und Interesse.* Frankfurt a.M.: Suhrkamp.

Heller, E. (1968). Faust's damnation: The morality of knowledge. In *The artist's journey into the interior and other essays* (pp. 3–44). New York: Vintage Books.

Hirsch, E. D., Jr. (1967). *Validity in interpretation.* New Haven: Yale University Press.

Hirsch, E. D., Jr. (1976). *The aims of interpretation.* Chicago: The University of Chicago Press.

Hoy, D. C. (1978). *The critical circle: Literature, history and philosophical hermeneutics.* Berkeley, Los Angeles, and London: The University of California Press.

Humphrey, R. (1955). *Stream of Consciousness in the modern novel.* Berkeley and Los Angeles: University of California Press.

Kirkwood, W. G. (1983). Storytelling and self-confrontation: Parables as communication strategies. *Quarterly Journal of Speech, 69,* 58–74.

Kuhn, T. (1962). *The structure of scientific revolutions.* Chicago: The University of Chicago Press.

Levi-Strauss, C. (1968). *Structural anthropology* (C. Jacobson & B. G. Schoepf, Trans.). New York: Basic Books

McGuire, M. (1977). Mythic rhetoric in Mein Kampf: A structuralist critique. *Quarterly Journal of Speech, 63,* 1–13.

McGuire, M. (1982a). Some problems with rhetorical example. *Pre/Text, 3,* 121–136.

McGuire, M. (1982b). The structure of rhetoric. *Philosophy and Rhetoric, 15,* 149–169.

McGruire, M. (1987). Narrative persuasion in rhetorical theory. In H. Geissner (Ed.), *On narratives: Proceedings of the 10th International colloquium on speech communication* (pp. 163–178). Frankfurt a.M.: Scriptor.

Ochs, D. J., & Burritt, R. J. (1973). Perceptual theory: Narrative suasion of Lysias. In G. P. Mohrmann & C. J. Stewart (Eds.), *Explorations in rhetorical criticism* (pp. 51–74). University Park: The Pennsylvania State University Press.

Overington, M. A. (1977). The scientific community as audience: Toward a rhetorical analysis of science. *Philosophy and Rhetoric, 10,* 143–163.

Palmer, E. L., & Door, A. (Eds.). (1980). *Children and the faces of television: Teaching, violence, selling.* New York: Academic Press.

Peper, J. (1966). *Bewusstseinslagen des Erzaehlens und erzaehlte Wirklichkeiten: Darqestellt an amerikanischen Romanen des 19, und 20, Jahrunderts, insbesondere am Werk William Faulkners,* Leiden: E. J. Brill.

Plato. (1952). *Gorgias* (W. C. Helmbold, Ed. and Trans.). Indianapolis: Bobbs-Merrill.

Plato. (1956). *Phaedrus* (W. C. Helmbold & W. G. Rabinowitz, Eds. and Trans.). Indianapolis: Bobbs-Merrill Company, Inc.

Riedel, M. (Ed.). (1972). *Zur Rehabilitierung der praktischen Philosophie, 1.* Freiburg: Verlag Rombach.

Scholes, R., & Kellogg, R. (1966). *The nature of narrative.* New York: Oxford University Press.

Warnick, B. (1987). The narrative paradigm: Another story. *Quarterly Journal of Speech, 73,* 172–182.

White, H. (1980). The value of narrativity in the representation of reality. *Critical Inquiry, 7,* 1–30.

10

Narrative in Psychoanalysis: Truth? Consequences?

James Walkup
State University of New York
Health Science Center at Brooklyn

Clinical psychoanalysis is now in the midst of a conceptual revolution that has been waiting to happen for at least two decades. The regime under siege traces its lineage to Freud's metapsychology. The banner that has quickened and mobilized the long-standing discontent is narrative theory.[1] Now that the battle has been joined in earnest, the time has come to ask three questions: How is it that narrative transformed loose, dissenting alliances into a full-scale faction? Just what conceptual territory is held by each side? What can we expect to be the future course of the conflict?

---

[1] A good case can be made that a clear-cut victory for narrative theory would amount to the first successful paradigm shift within orthodox psychoanalysis. By no means are narrative theorists the first to attack the metapsychology or to complain about the distortions introduced by positivism but, in the past, schism, not revision, has been the result. The reasons for this are probably as much sociological and institutional as they are intellectual

Nevertheless, the temptation is best resisted to begin the discussion with such familiar phrases as paradigm shift, revolutionary science or (Kuhn, 1962). To do so would require an examination of sociological issues too far afield from the main topic, and, worse, beg the controversial question of the extent to which this is a conflict between two competing scientific models or (as some would have it) between scientific and nonscientific accounts.

Within the analytic community, the two most influential advocates of the narrative approach are Spence and Schafer. Prior to the development of working theories of the psychoanalytic narrative, important philosophical development of the concept came from Sherwood, a physician working in philosophy of science, and from two philosophers, Habermas (1971) and Ricoeur (1970, 1978). Common to all these men (with the partial exception of Sherwood) is a conviction that scientistic assumptions of traditional theory leave it unable to do justice to a constitutive characteristic of psychological reality. Different versions of the complaint are offered, but in one way or another, a mechanistic account of mind is usually pitted against what we might call a moral account of mind, though often the latter is expressed in the less dramatic language of intentions, meanings, actions, and so forth. (Habermas, 1970, 1971; Ricoeur, 1981; Schafer, 1976, 1978; Sherwood, 1969; Spence, 1982a).[2] In what follows, I discuss the two analysts, plus the preceding theorists, with the exception of Ricoeur (who is treated in Walkup, 1984). Both analysts have been widely criticized on a number of different grounds (Spence by Eagle, 1984; Schafer by Meares, 1985; Sass, 1988), but I focus on a single complaint, voiced by two critics disturbed by scientific shortcomings of narrative theory, the philosopher Grunbaum (1980, 1984) and the psychologist Eagle (1980). In particular, both men argued that the narrativists' concern with the form (rather than the faithfulness) of narratives leads to a failure to be loyal to Freud's (1917) insistence that theory and interpretation must "tally with what is real" (p. 452).

The primary purpose of this chapter is to give a history of the turn toward narrative in psychoanalysis, but this history cannot be told without some attention to the debates that surround it. No one can read the exchanges between Eagle (1984) and Spence (1983)

---

[2]Because we now know Freud to have been well acquainted with the main outlines of many of these distinctions (see McGrath, 1986, chap. 3), it is no longer credible to condemn (or excuse) Freud for a naive positivism. What will need to be explained by the full story of the development is how and why psychoanalysts recently decided to worry about the venerable distinctions.

Eagle (1980b, p. 420) cited these distinctions as a source. Eagle (1980a) gave an extensive review of both the issues and literature involved. There is no need to repeat this effort here, so I have limited my discussion to a short summary, plus a few likely sources not mentioned by Eagle.

Another tradition of philosophical criticism dates from Popper's (1962) charges that psychoanalysis is a pseudoscience. Its influence on narrative theory has been largely negative. For a detailed refutation of this charge, see Grunbaum (1984).

without being impressed with the resiliency of the misunderstandings that plague this debate. An atmosphere of frustration, even futility, accompanies their efforts to agree on the nature of the differences or how to settle them. Corrections accumulate, yet never seem to move toward any cumulative conclusion. When one party uncovers an implicit assumption of the other, it works like a yank on a tangled knot, tightening, rather than untying it.

The key to these misunderstandings lies, I suspect, in what the debaters want from a theory. So, before I begin my historical account, I mention two quite distinct cultural aspirations that have motivated the use of theory. A theory can be asked to provide an accurate representation of the facts of the matter. In addition, it can be asked to do other things as well: increase our ability to predict and control phenomena, answer questions, free us from ignorance, and so forth. The contrast is between the image of theory as a faithful model of reality versus the image of theory as a tool (as Francis Bacon saw it, for example). There will, of course, be those who insist that this distinction is sophistic, that the representational and instrumental aspects of theory go together. However, even if we were to accept (quite implausibly) that accuracy and power always go together, for those who see theory as a tool, accuracy is a means to increase predictive power, and for those who see theory as a representation, prediction is important because it confirms accuracy. In the history of narrative theory in psychoanalysis, the combinations of the two motives have been complex and often unstable.

In the next section, I use this distinction to provide some landmarks to orient the reader as I tell the story of the development of narrative theory. In the criticism and cognition section, I briefly describe an important criticism from the Eagle/Grunbaum case against the narrativists. And, finally, in conclusion, I summarize the debate in terms of the framework I have developed, use the summary to imagine the future of the debate, and then return to psychoanalysis to suggest a couple of facts about its cultural meaning that invited the turn to narrative theory.

NARRATIVE THEORY IN PSYCHOANALYSIS

Simplifying somewhat, there are two major trends that have come together in psychoanalytic narrative theory, one dating from Witt-

genstein, the other from hermeneutics and critical theory.[3] In what
follows, I follow the first trend up until the late 1960s, then cover
a similar period for the second. I use this date because it coincides
with the publication of the important two books that used narrative
to characterize psychoanalytic explanation, Sherwood's (1969) *The
Logic of Explanation in Psychoanalysis*, and the English translation
(1971) of Habermas' *Knowledge and Human Interest*.

The first trend comes from English language philosophical critics
of psychoanalysis (MacIntyre, 1958; Peters, 1958) who rely on a
distinction between causal explanations and reason-giving explanations to argue against the appropriateness of metapsychological
explanations. This was followed by the proposal that narrative
explanations offer an alternative to the strict dichotomy between
reasons and causes (Sherwood, 1969).

CAUSES, REASONS, AND MUDDLES

Many of the arguments against the language of causality in psychoanalysis can be found in Wittgenstein's (1982) remarks on Freud,
made in the 1930s and 1940s.[4] Although Wittgenstein is known to
have admired Freud, he believed Freud's writings contained "a
muddle between a cause and a reason" (p. 10). For Wittgenstein,

---

[3]A third, more recent influence not treated in this chapter is the flowering of
interest in psychoanalysis by a new generation of humanists, who have analyzed
implicit narrative and rhetorical strategies in psychoanalytic texts, as well as applying analytic concepts to literary texts (e.g., Marcus, 1974). Obviously, this movement
is a natural outgrowth of the influence of hermeneutical and aesthetic notions insofar
as these experiment with setting aside scientific denotative or referential concerns
and read Freudian cases as if they were works of fiction. (Of course, this similarity
need not imply that a given humanist is not in agreement with Freudian scientific
claims.)

[4]Because these are available only through notes published later, direct influences
on the next generation of philosophical critics require a measure of inference.
Memoirs of the period make clear that the intellectual atmosphere was thick with
Wittgenstein's ideas. Additionally, many of these remarks do little more than explicitly apply to Freud a general argument found in the second portion of his *Philosophical Investigations* (1953). Therefore, he can be considered an available source of the
argument described in the text (about reasons and causes) well in advance of his
published remarks (Ambrose, 1979; Barrett, 1966; Moore, 1959). Page numbers in
the text are taken from material reprinted in Wollheim and Hopkins (1982). See also
Hopkins (1982).

That Wittgenstein's influence was, in important respects, Kantian has been widely
accepted in the last two decades (Engelmann, 1967). (See, however, Bartley, 1973,
for a contrary view.)

the difference lay in the fact that when a person's reason for acting is being investigated, his or her agreement plays a crucial role, whereas when a cause is being investigated, experiments are needed. Talk of metapsychological regions, Wittgenstein said, "sounds like science, but in fact it is just a means of representation" p. 10, emphasis removed). He thought that, despite this confusion, analysis might still claim therapeutic power. Interestingly, Wittgenstein's account of this power pointed toward a theme that has been picked up in the debate over narrative.[5] When one is beset by troubles, he explained, one's situation may initially seem "too foul to be a subject of a tragedy [a]nd it may then be an immense relief [if] it can be shown that one's life has the pattern rather of a tragedy. . . ." (p. 9).[6] (He gave no hint that he believed this therapeutic power might itself be an object of scientific investigation—an issue raised by Eagle (1980b) and Grunbaum (1984)–and the attitude expressed in the last portion of his *Philosophical Investigations* makes it doubtful that he would accept this.)

For the next generation of English language critics of analysis, reasons (or purposes or motives) were often seen as the only correct explanation of human action, so that when we know a person's goal, plus what he or she believes to be the steps needed to achieve

---

[5]Tracing the direct influence of Wittgenstein on the contemporary psychoanalytic debate over narrative is no easy matter. Schafer (1980) cited Wittgenstein as an influence on his own action language theory (1980, p. 9), claimed to make use of Wittgenstein's ideas on epistemology (1983, p. 124), and directly responded to criticisms of free association that appear in the Wittgenstein's published conversations (Schafer, 1978). Sass (1988) and Meares (1985) gave reasons for doubting that the affinity between Wittgenstein and Schafer has much substance. (See also Schafer's, 1985, response to Meares.) In contrast, several arguments in Spence's (1982b) case against the verdicality of the patient's narrative strongly resemble many of Wittgenstein's complaints, yet without having been influenced by them (Spence, personal communication). Situating Wittgenstein is no easier on the other side of the argument. Although Eagle (19773b) cited with approval. Wittgenstein's (1982) separation of an interpretation's validity from its persuasiveness, Wittgenstein does not figure prominently in Eagle's (1973a, 1980a, 1980b, 1984) negative evaluations of the use of narrative and/or motivational accounts. And Grunbaum (1984) specifically disassociated his arguments from Wittgenstein's.

[6]There is less to this connection than meets the eye. The heart of Wittgenstein's account of psychoanalysis does not lie here, in the retelling of the patient's painful story with the aid of the new mythology Freud offered, but in the more subtle appreciation of the logical consequences of the means of representation offered by psychoanalysis. Specifically, Wittgenstein stressed the analogies with the aesthetic. So it is not the narrative per se—which can be taken in more and less historical, scientific, or aesthetic ways—but the logical affinities between psychoanalytic representations and aesthetic ones.

it, we need only fit his or her action into this scheme. Once a given action has been assigned a place in this psychological landscape of motive and belief, we know all there is to know about the action.[7] Events, on the other hand, are explained by citing causally necessary and sufficient conditions. (Events can include, say, neural events, but there will always be a logical gap between the two levels of explanation.) Psychoanalysis, these critics charged, erred in trying to have it both ways. By adding together the two types of explanation, the argument went, it ended up empty-handed.

As the evidence cited in Eagle (1980b) makes clear, the turn to narrative is one among several efforts to use some form of the distinction as a wedge to split off a natural science model, usually located in the metapsychology, from clinical psychoanalysis.[8] It is easy to see how the reason/cause split might fit comfortably with narrative theory—indeed, Schafer's argument often moves effortlessly between the two, as if the logic was identical in each case—but nothing about the former requires use of the latter. Historically, neither the psychoanalytic theorist most associated with this effort (G. S. Klein, 1976) nor the main philosophers who urged this distinction on psychoanalysis (e.g., MacIntyre, 1958; Peters, 1958; Toulmin, 1954) had much to say about narrative in their discussions of the matter. It is therefore ironic that, despite the obvious fit between reason-giving explanations and narrative explanations, the latter were introduced precisely to oppose the use of reason versus cause arguments in these discussions.

SHERWOOD

Sherwood (1969, p. 190) credited Farrell (1961) with an early introduction of the term narrative into philosophical discussions of explanation in psychoanalysis. In the same footnote, Sherwood

---

[7]If we are trying to understand how the Kantian cause/reason debate turned into the narrative debate, this description of reason-type explanations is worth noticing. With a little stretching, this formal explanatory structure (which actually dates from Aristotle's practice syllogism) can be seen as a highly schematic narrative form. This stretch is less implausible when we consider the proliferation of script and schema theories of narratives that postulate similar slots to be filled in by instantiations.

[8]It is easy to agree with Grunbaum (1984) that the hermeneutical versus natural science dichotomy does not line up neatly with the division between clinical analysis and case studies versus the metapsychology (or, as it is sometimes formulated, the legacy of Freud's *Project for a Scientific Psychology*). Moreover, Grunbaum showed

also cited affinities between his work and the use of narrative as an explanatory term in the philosophy of history, where the reason versus cause debate had recently surfaced with renewed intensity (Gallie, 1964).[9] It seems likely that Sherwood's use of narrative took hold precisely because he used it to address, and transform, the issues raised for psychoanalysis by the reason versus cause debate.

Sherwood objected to the earlier generation's use of reason versus cause arguments in discussions of psychoanalysis. Instead, he set out to change the terms of the dispute. Two important steps were taken. First, he emphasized that all explanation, whether it mentions causes or reasons, needs to be seen in the context of the puzzlement it is intended to relieve. The question to be answered lays down logical limits on the form possible answers may take. Second, he introduced into the discussion Hart and Honore's (1959)

---

how much trouble Habermas caused himself by relying on an old-fashioned, overly simple view of the complexity and heterogeneity of natural science (1984, pp. 1–94). Had he chosen to do so, he could also have charged Habermas with an analogous oversimplification of traditional hermeneutic methlology that portrays it as in need of deepening for use in the depth hermeneutics proper for psychoanalysis. (See Seebohm, 1977a, 1977b.)

[9]It is interesting to note that many of the current controversies and confusions about narrative in psychoanalysis first appeared in philosophy of history. In particular, a parallel can be seen in the complex irony of the way an early defense of the use of narrative form led to what some take to be a surrender of any claim that historical knowledge can be compelled by the facts of the matter.

Dray (1963), Gallie (1964), Morton White (1965), and Danto (1965) made the early case for narrative and against Hempel's (1942, 1962) call for the search for causal laws in history like those in the natural sciences. Mandelbaum (1967), Goldstein (1976), and others opposed them because they felt that narrative was essentially a medium, one medium, for organizing historical findings that could not themselves be identified with a genre or style of presentation. In the early 1970s, White's (1973) *Metahistory* supported the narrative counterattack by drawing on literary studies of the narrative form. The terms of the dispute began to undergo subtle changes at this point. The focus turned from the nature of actions and events—whether or not they are deterministically predictable—to descriptions. A couple of titles suggest the direction of the shift: Mink's (1978) "Narrative Form as a Cognitive Instrument" and White's (1981) "The Value of Narrativity in the Representation of Reality." More and more, the suspicion took hold that the coherent story told by the historian was not found, but made, that "narrative form in history, as in fiction, is an artifice, the product of individual imagination" (Mink, 1978, p. 145, quoted in Carr, 1986, p. 10). The irony here is that the most hard-headed opponent of narrative in history can now nod in agreement with White, seeing this identification with fiction as a vindication of an initial distrust and, no doubt, as a well-deserved visitation on those who traffic with relativism. The danger, as Lawrence Stone put it in a review of the debate, is that the turn to narrative may lead to storytelling for its own sake (1979, p. 23). My summary here draws heavily from Stone (1979) and Carr (1986).

use of the broad category of "casually relevant factors" (p. 107).[10]
Within this category, there is a major conceptual division between
a heterogeneous group of primary observables (physical events,
feelings, states of affairs, etc.) and two terms (i.e., cause and reasons)
we introduce when we are called on to pick out certain observable
events to answer a question.[11] Thus, the major conceptual split
divides observables from both causes and reasons.

In this scheme, a cause or a reason is not a specific item we find
in experience, it is a role we ask something to play in making
sense of an incongruity. Causes and/or reasons order observables in
accordance with the explanatory purposes the psychoanalyst
brings to them. Depending on the purpose at hand, the same primary phenomenon might be cited as either a cause or a reason.
(For example, a blow received in an adolescent confrontation with
a father might be the cause of a scar and the reason for running
away from home.)

Here narrative enters, for picking out candidates for the title of
cause or reason requires "a logical commitment to a theoretical
structure or framework or narrative in which the phenomena in
question are no longer considered independent entities but interre-
lated parts of a single unified process or sequence of events" (Sherwood, 1969, p. 169). Sherwood concluded that the subject matter
of psychoanalytic explanation—the incongruity to be explained—
is found in an individual life history. Thus, "the logic of psychoanalytic explanations . . . resolves itself into the logic of psychoanalytic
narratives. . . ." in which bits of behavior are fit together in a comprehensible whole (Sherwood, 1969, p. 191).

The puzzle or question is a life story with zones of damaged or
incomplete coherence. The job to be performed by theory is to guide
the selection and organization of the primary observables of a life.

---

[10]Grunbaum (1984) argued in his criticism of Habermas that the category of
"causally relevant factors" is a more scientifically adequate one than cause (p. 1ff.).
The use of an old-fashioned picture of a cause as a necessary and sufficient condition
contributes to an oversimplification of the differences between explanations in the
natural and human sciences.

[11]This does not imply that Sherwood does not distinguish reasons from causes,
only that the more important conceptual divide lies between primary events and
explanatory terms. Reasons can be distinguished from causes by virtue of the fact
that the former "are those causally relevant factors which become causally relevant
precisely because they are taken into consideration, or responded to, by the individual . . . [though it is unnecessary for] . . . the reason to have been consciously formulated" (1969, pp. 160–161). (In response to criticism, Sherwood, 1973, backed off
this way of stating the matter.)

The outcome is increased coherence. Specifically, Sherwood offered a three-tiered system for evaluating an explanation that asks that a possible explanation (a) prove itself appropriate by properly situating itself in a frame of reference within which it addresses a puzzle; (b) prove itself adequate by drawing the relations needed to solve the puzzle; and (c) prove itself accurate (i.e., free of false propositions). Notice here that accuracy—faithful representation—is only one of three criteria.

By emphasizing that an explanation has a job to do—solve a puzzle, draw together relations—Sherwood took a small step twoard a more instrumental view of theory. He recognized this shift and worried about it, because he insisted he was concerned with "the logic of explanation, *not* the psychology of persuasion." However, once narrative theory is to be judged by any criterion other than accuracy, the door has been opened for agnosticism about the referents of the narrative (such as we find in Schafer, 1981, and, to some extent, in Spence, 1982b). There exists an unclarity about a possible conflict among criteria: specifically, what is one to do when choosing between an explanation that does its job well (addresses the puzzling aspect of a life by drawing the necessary relations among events) versus one that does this less well but is more reliably free of false propositions. The overall problem can be seen in one of the criticisms made in Eagle's (1973a) review of Sherwood: Appropriateness and adequacy are criteria that could just as well apply to accounts that are not empirical.

HERMENEUTICS AND CRITICAL THEORY

A second trend comes from the development, in continental philosophy, of hermeneutics, the science of text interpretation and from subsequent reactions to it. In this case, narrative theory did not grow out of an effort to meet Kantian criticisms of psychoanalysis, although loyalty to a Kantian regard for freedom certainly inspired antagonism to psychoanalysis on the continent (see Walkup, 1986). Rather, when psychoanalysis attracted attention from continental philosophers, it came from phenomenologists who complained about its positivism (Merleau-Ponty, 1962), existentialists who denounced its determinism (Sartre, 1956), and critical theorists of the Frankfurt School, who tempered similar criticisms with a sympathetic interest in using analytic findings as an index of the psychic price extracted by capitalism (Jay, 1973; Walkup, 1984). Unlike the

work of MacIntyre (1958), Peters (1958), and the others Sherwood
(1969) answered with his use of narrative, these continental critics
did not constitute a sustained conversation on psychoanalysis.
Hence, it is no surprise that their criticisms did not form the context
in which Habermas (1971) brought narrative into the discussion.
Therefore, I describe only as much of the development of hermeneutics as is needed to follow what Habermas (1971) said.

For most of its history, hermeneutics was primarily a method
(i.e., philosophical and logical rules for interpreting documents and
other human traces). This phase is usually thought to have reached
its fullest expression in Schleiermacher's general theory of interpretation, which produced what is called "the hermeneutic circle."
This term points to the continual path the mind travels in unravel-
ing a text—from part to whole and back again, from word to sentence, sentence to text, from text to authorial and cultural context—
using each level of enrich and correct the others. Crucial to this
view is a strict division between the human and natural sciences.

Habermas's insistence that psychoanalysis differs from hermeneutics needs to be understood in the context of his relation to
critical theory and the work of the Frankfurt School (Jay, 1913).
For Habermas, as for members of this group such as Marcuse,
Adorno, and Horkheimer, the understanding of psychoanalysis is
part of a comprehensive political and intellectual project among
left-wing intellectuals in the 1930s. Questions arose from a loss of
faith in Marx's scientific predictions of economic collapse and class
revolt. Why had the working class failed to revolt? What were the
sources of the subjective impediments to class consciousness?

A new type of criticism began to develop. Indictments of the
institutions and practices of capitalism were joined by an indict-
ment of a style of thinking associated not simply with capitalism,
but with the enlightenment. This style was instrumental, techno-
logical, and concerned with efficiency, prediction, and control. Its
reductive simplicity—the whole of reality could be described as a
set of means-end relations—gave to it an insidious imperialism,
allowing it to invade every aspect of culture. The dilemma posed
by this style of criticism is that the critic must wonder where, in
people so misshapened by this logic, he or she is to find the spark
of resistance to it.

Psychoanalysis provided a partial answer. Adorno (1968) wrote
that psychoanalysis could be viewed as an index of the psychic
price extracted by the prevailing instrumental logic:

> The time lag between consciousness and the unconscious is itself the
> stigma of the contradictory development of society. Everything that

got left behind is sedimented and has to foot the bill for progress and enlightenment. Today it harbours even the demand for happiness. . . . (p. 80)

In a characteristic turn of thought, Adorno also condemned those aspects of psychoanalysis that reflect the prevailing positivism he criticized: "Under its deadly medical gaze, unfreedom becomes pertrified into an anthropological constant, and the quasi-scientific conceptual apparatus thereby overlooks everything in its object that is not merely object—namely, its potential for spontaneity (p. 81). Thus, although Adorno and the others anticipated few of the details of Habermas's use of narrative, their influence can be seen in the demands made of psychoanalysis by the role it is given in a larger intellectual project. Habermas (1971) followed this tradition by asking that analysis be purged of its positivism and that it provide some critical perspective on a potentially dehumanizing instrumental view of knowledge and theory.

HABERMAS

Habermas, like the hermeneuticists, divided the sciences. Whereas Sherwood (1969) introduced narrative in conjunction with his insistence on the essential unity of all forms of explanation (they all serve purposes), *Knowledge and Human Interests* (Habermas, 1971) introduced narrative in conjunction with his insistence on protecting an essential diversity of knowledge, based on the different purposes (or human interests) it can serve. Unlike Sherwood, Habermas wrote from within a tradition in which a stress on the unitary form of explanations is identified with positivism and instrumentalism.

Habermas proposed three rough divisions of knowledge, based on the cognitive interest served. First, the empirical–analytic sciences are guided by an interest in prediction and control. Second, the historical–hermeneutical sciences are guided by an interest in communication and the clarification of meaning within a normative order. Thus far, Habermas's division is essentially similar to the neo-Kantian tradition of distinguishing between causal (empirical analytic) and reason-giving (historical hermeneutic) accounts. Habermas did not, however, claim analysis for the hermeneutic tradition, a fact that would be impossible to guess from the persistence with which Habermas found his approach labeled hermeneutic (e.g., Grunbaum, 1984, p. 1; Schafer, 1980, p. 44). He argued that psychoanalysis has elements of both, but belongs to neither.

Instead it serves a third, altogether different interest: neither prediction and control, nor clarification of meaning relative to norms,
but human emancipation.

In Habermas' vocabulary, psychoanalysis is a form of "depth hermeneutics," in which analyst and analysand seek "mutual understanding about the meaning of incomprehensible symbols" (1971,
p. 254).[12] What makes it "deep" can be seen in the comparison with
Dilthey (1961). Whereas the interpretation of a text uses part/whole
relations between passages and larger units (corpus, genre, etc.) to
reconstruct its meaning, psychoanalytic interpretation must uncover meaning that is not only latent, but disguised. Simple hermeneutic analysis might be fooled by the cunning surface coherence of
psychopathology. Only when stereotyped behavior, linguistic devia-
tions, or a breakdown of the usual integration of word, action, and
gesture are present does the analyst recognize that a symbol attached
to some forbidden impulse has been split off from the symbol system
(e.g., the wings of a butterfly or the roman numeral V might loose
their ordinary meaning and attach themselves to a fear of castra-
tion). The analytic work consists in cracking the code of this private
significance, using what Habermas called "systematic analysis" to
return the (resymbolized) symbol to public discourse: "The What,
the semantic content of a systematically distorted manifestation,
cannot be 'understood' it if is not possible at the same time to 'ex-

---

[12]Because Habermas identified himself with the heritage of the Frankfurt School,
it might seem strange that, even though he followed their lead in assigning psychoanalysis a special emancipatory role in his theory, he chose Dilthey, not a critical
theorist, when he tried to cure psychoanalysis of its positivism. Although Habermas
may be doing no more than picking up on Horkheimer's (1939) article that compares
Freud favorably to Dilthey in his mastery of subjectivity, another reason can be
found in his desire to adopt a middle-of-the-road position in the cultural battle over
mechanization. He turned to hermeneutics, even though it had little contact with
psychoanalysis, because early critical theory went overboard in its rejection of
positivism. Habermas felt full loyalty to critical theory—something akin to Marcuse's later work—would have required him to surrender the opposition between
natural sciences and human ones. In contrast, most versions of hermeneutics marked
off a preserve for the human sciences, where special methods could be called on that
promised to restore what the mechanization of the mind threatened to dissolve: in
Dilthey's phrase, "the patterned quality of a life." Yet loyalty to the spirit of early
critical theory demanded that coherence not be uncritically presupposed, so hermeneutics needed supplementing.

For a more detailed summary of Habermas and his intellectual sources, see
Walkup (1984), which forms the basis for the account given here and includes a
contrast between his work and that of Ricoeur. On Habermas and psychoanalysis,
see also Dallmayr (1972) and McCarthy (1972).

plain' the Why, the origin of the symptomatic scene" (1970, p. 209). The symptom, the privatized symbol, must first be brought into relation to the scene in which it was split off. Thus, the response of Freud's patient, the Wolfman, to the sight of butterfly wings would be viewed in the context of the scene in childhood when he saw a butterfly and imagined the loss of his finger (Freud, 1918). Only when the frozen symbolic elements have been returned to their original context can be symbol recover the flexibility that allows the patient to use it to express intentions again.

Systematic analysis is narrative analysis in at least three senses. The first is suggested by the word *scene* in the preceding quotation, for the analyst relies on an essentially narrative technique, scenic understanding. She or he coordinates the structure of three scenes: the symptomatic scene enacted in the world (e.g., conflicts at the office), the transference scene in the consulting room (e.g., lateness, struggles over appointment times, competitive associations), and a scene in early childhood (e.g., battles over autonomy, impulse frustration).[13] Where a desymbolized element or relation is missing from one scene, it can be inferred by consulting its approximate counterparts in one of the other two scenes. So the analyst reasons in a narrative fashion. Realizing that, in the patient's symptomatic scene and his or her transference scene, expressions of aggression are followed by retribution, the analyst who hears stories of childhood aggression will listen for the punishment that follows.

Second, narrative plays a more directly explanatory role, as one of three theoretical guidelines for the semantic analysis.[14] Specifically, the analyst uses a theory of deviant socialization that takes the form of systematically generalized narratives, expressed in nontechnical language, which provide a schematic story into which individual names and circumstances gleaned from the patient's associations can be fit. For example, the oedipal story provides a series of slot or roles, as well as relations among the roles. So,

---

[13]These are my examples, not Habermas'.

[14]The other two guidelines are: (a) an amended description of pathologically distorted communication in which it is described as a regression to prelinguistic paleosymbols, which lack a distinction between sign, semantic content, and referent; and (b) a normative ideal of unconstrained communication in which motives can coincide with symbolized intentions, where no wish or impulse need be exiled from socially shared discourse.

Although the application of this general narrative resemble the deductively derived hypotheses of the "empirical sciences, . . . narrative explanations differ from strictly deductive ones in that the events or states of which they assert a causal relation is further defined by their application. Therefore general interpretations do

upon hearing of a male patient's conflict with a powerful male, the analyst would listen with a question in mind: Who or what is the forbidden object of desire?

Third, at the most general level, narrative gives content to a notion of freedom that justifies Habermas's (1971) assignment of psychoanalysis to a cognitive interest in emancipation. For Habermas, psychopathology controls the individual through the "causality of fate and not of nature, because it prevails through the symbolic means of the mind. Only for this reason can it be compelled by the power of self-reflection" (1971, p. 256).

This phrase about fate comes from Hegel and suggests the influence of 19th century German philosophy. Too complex to be briefly summarized, this tradition has a few features that must be mentioned. Freedom, the self, the public sphere, and even reason itself, are partly constituted by language. So the recovery of freedom from psychic compulsion and the truth of the account that enabled the recovery have meaning only in the context of language, the public symbol system. The emancipation wrought by psychoanalysis is essentially that of a *Bildungsroman*, the German novel of the education of consciousness through experience. By confronting and being transformed by what at first appears to be quite foreign, the subject moves from a limited, particular point of view to a more universal one, recognizing an element of unrecognized kinship between what had seemed wholly other and heretofore unrealized aspects of him or herself.

In this case, the wholly other is the unconscious, what Freud called the internal foreign territory. A desymbolized symbol is radically private, hence unfree. This identification recalls Arendt's (1958) rendering of the "original privative sense" of privacy in the Greek *polis:* "deprived of all things essential to a truly human life . . . of the reality that comes from being seen and heard by others, . . ." and, above all, exiled to a realm governed by "necessity" (pp. 58, 64). To be subject to unconscious influence is to suffer a loss of freedom, a deprivation by desymbolization that can be reversed only when a correct understanding has assumed explanatory power, simultaneously enlightening the subject and returning him or her to voluntary control of thought and action.[15]

---

not make possible context-free explanations" [as in the empirical sciences] (Habermas 1971, p. 273).

[15]Here we should recall Eagle's (1980b) careful segregation of the accuracy of an interpretation from its causal power. It is characteristic of the essentially Hegelian model Habermas retained that enlightenment, power, and freedom should coincide as phases of a single process.

At this point, an interpreter of Habermas faces a dilemma, because Habermas intended to introduce a reformist categorical framework. It is correct to conclude that Habermas, like Sherwood, in some sense backed away from a standard of accuracy—from Freud's (1917) demand that an account "tally with what is real" (p. 452)—if only because other considerations are introduced alongside it. Sherwood argued that explanations must be judged not only by their accuracy, but also by how effectively they answer the question they address and how thoroughly they draw together the various pieces. Habermas, (1971), too, introduced a consideration besides accuracy: emancipation. Yet Habermas defined emancipation rather negatively, as (among other things) the negation of any instrumental purpose, of any attempt to do something. Sherwood might accept that he asked that an analytic account not only be accurate, but that it serve as the means to other ends (e.g., solving a puzzle). Habermas might agree that accuracy per se is not an adequate standard, but he would quickly add two things: first, that the end served (emancipation) is so different from other ends that it is in a class by itself and cannot be considered instrumental in the sense I have been using and, second, that the self that is understood is partly constituted by its increased understanding, so that a self that has increased its own freedom has, in a sense, accurately understood a heretofore unrealized fact about itself.

Neither for Habermas nor for Sherwood has the movement away from the accuracy standard been wholehearted. Each retains a modified version of it. Sherwood aspired to accuracy, which is defined as the absence of false propositions, then asked that it be combined with other standards derived from the purpose served by the explanation. Habermas aspired to uncover a true text beneath the dissembling text of consciousness, which, when revealed, commands assent at the same time as it contributes to the individual's freedom from unconscious determination. In both cases, tensions remain, but this early stage in the development of psychoanalytic narrative theory is properly contrasted with the next, fully-developed stage in which a standard of empirical accuracy is jettisoned altogether by Schafer and given a quite different role to play by Spence.

SCHAFER

In his most recent book, Schafer (1983) said that, although there are differences, "[my] discussion owed much to Habermas's penetrating analysis of the linguistic and narrative aspects of psychoanalytic interpretation" (p. 234).[16] Chief among these debts is a wish to banish the rule of necessity from psychic affairs, replacing it with freedom.

Schafer's work is thoroughly immersed in the cause versus reason debate described earlier. Following early English language critics of Freud, Schafer (1976) decided that psychoanalysis should make a clean break with the language of its mechanistic past, adopting instead the "new [i.e., action] language" advocated by the following "fundamental rule": "Actions," he stated, "do not have causes" (p. 369). Causal language, the passive voice, and all idioms of determinism abet the disclaiming of action, which needs to be reclaimed. Schafer's disclaimed action, like Habermas's desymbolized symbol, has been exiled to a realm governed by necessity, and, with the help of language, is to be recovered.

In Schafer's most recent work, narrative has been moved into the foreground and asked to aid in the battle against two additional kinds of compulsion frequently found in psychoanalytic thinking. First, it is frequently thought that events of the past, carried in memory, cause pathogenic states that are relieved by the lifting of repression and realignment of psychic forces. In some versions (e.g., Habermas, 1971), the analyst uses a normative life history—an abstract scheme of standard conflicts and developmental milestones with slots to be filled in with individual details—to aid the fact-finding expedition into the past. Not Schafer. Narrative is fundamentally an organizing concept for describing what happens in the psychoanalytic dialogue itself: It is a story that begins in the middle and has two levels. Somebody (an analysand) tells something to somebody else about him or herself and about others, and that second person (the analyst) tells it back. This dialogue itself becomes the subject of a first order history of the exchanges. Only secondarily does the analyst construct the analytic life history of the patient.

For Schafer, the analysis initiates a movement between the presenting complaint and the present account of the past. Borders blur, so that, according to Schafer:

> The autobiographical present is found to be no clear point in time at all . . . more and more it seems to be both a repetitive, crisis-

---

[16]A deep incompatibility between Habermas and Schafer can be traced to the former's continuing allegiance to the work of the Frankfurt School (Horkheimer, Adorno, Marcuse; see Jay, 1973; Walkup, 1984). In this essentially romantic tradition, a negative valence is given to the effort to dominate nature, within and outside

perpetuating misremembering of the past and a way of living defen-
sively with respect to a future which is . . . imagined . . . on the model
of the past. (1980, p. 238)

Although the phrase has a paradoxical tone to it, Schafer emphasized the extent to which a past is chosen. This takes place within
the unfolding narrative of the analysis itself.

Second, psychoanalysis, in common with many sciences, has
often maintained that theory choice is strictly determined by evi-
dential demands. Even when it is acknowledged that evidence and
theory intermingle, theories are usually justified by some general
scientific/methodological principle. Not for Schafer, who quite deliberately chose to describe the choice among theoretical languages
as a narrative choice. Each is to be judged, not by its truth, but by
how well it suits the purposes for which it is deployed.[17]

The instrumental goal of theory use could not be more clear. The
human purposes to be served by a theory override considerations
of accuracy. Despite Schafer's avowed reliance on Habermas, this
aspect can also be connected to Sherwood's insistence that evaluation of an explanation (or, for Schafer, a narrative strategy) needs
to be made with due consideration given to the context in which it
is offered. Sometimes Schafer made the demands of context sound
weak indeed, as he did when he referred to Freud's *preference* for a
positivist theory (see footnote 21). (Recall Freud's chronic references to his compelled obedience to the evidence. How he would
have fumed at such a word.) Although nothing in Schafer's work
implies that contextually variable purposes served by a given narrative can be capricious, little is said about any limits that might
apply.

---

the individual. The attempt to objectify and control the inner life produces a redou-
bled alienation. And although it is clearly not Schafer's intention to objectify, the
action language he so values claiming of responsibility, it is hard to see how an ideal
of control can avoid the self-fragmentation of inner mastery/inner slavery that so
repelled the Frankfurt School.

[17]The connection between narrative and Schafer's pragmatism about theory
choice is not immediately obvious, but it makes sense if we take him as giving
narrative a foundational role, at least within psychoanalysis, providing "a point of
view on points of view" (1981, p. 3). Viewed in this way, narrative is a kind of limit
that cannot be exceeded, so that even the most dogged attempts to articulate non-
narrative approaches, specifically, "Freud's positivist version," can be seen as "his
[Freud's] preferred narrative strategy" (p. 4).

Interestingly, this elevation in status for narrative bears a remarkable resem-
blance to a central feature of Dilthey's work. Prior to his work, it had been a
methodological approach. He saw it in a more Kantian vein, as a kind of metatheory

Schafer would probably respond that he need not supply any
general theory of possible purposes of narratives: these will vary as
analytic situations vary. Although this may be a logically adequate
reply, it leaves itself open to a complaint about the form in which
it is put, plus a couple of practical questions it leaves unanswered.

The complaint is that a familiar pragmatist attitude toward theory has been combined with narrative theory, but it is not clear
that much is gained by adding the one to the other. Stated otherwise, why did Schafer not simply say it is fine to let context and
purpose govern theory choice? Why do we need to see this as a
choice of narrative strategy? Is not the theoretical value of the
concept of narrative endangered by expanding it to cover so many
things?

One wonders if the amalgamation of pragmatism and narrative
is entirely stable. This can be seen in a practical question. Schafer
has yet to offer much guidance for someone trying to decide whether
a narrative choice that opts for a thoroughgoing non-narrative
metapsychology may not be better than a narrativist account. If
freely chosen purposes determine which is superior, Schafer will
be hard-pressed to persuade an analyst whose chief purpose is to
translate action descriptions into scientific language.[18]

Problems have arisen in the discussion of analytic purposes. Specifically, for the analyst who wishes to follow Schafer, two purposes
that might be served have become entangled: Is a more coherent,
critically aware, and less metaphorically contaminated theory to
be created (regardless of its relation to clinical work), or is a less
self-deceptive, healthier, and more insightful analysand to be, if
not created, then at least promoted (whether or not the practices
that do so are vouchsafed by a clear-headed theory)?

Despite Schafer's emphatic, repeated insistence that action language is a new language for psychoanalytic theory (not therapeutic
practice), his critics take him to be doing both (e.g., Spence, 1982b).

---

of the human sciences that not only produced knowledge, but also critically outlined
its limits (see Seebohm, 1977a, 1977b).

[18]My proposed alternative may sound sophistic. Schafer could easily (and reasonably) have concluded that such an old-fashioned analyst is an improbable conversational partner and that it is no great loss to be unable to convince him or her.
However, there is a better case to be made. The value of the metapsychology might
lie exactly in the discontinuities that divide it from commonsense (essentially moral)
descriptions of actions. From this point of view, Freud was an unintentional avant-
gardist who provided a fresh look at experience by reframing it in an alternative
language. This is, in effect, an attempt to reclaim Freud's narrative preference as a
rhetorical style without going along with the faith he brought to it.

As Sass (1988) documented, Schafer must bear at least a measure of responsibility for his ambiguity because, despite his repeated disclaimers, he called action language the "native tongue of psychoanalysis" (1976, p. 361), its verbal products the "locutions of insight" (p. 146), and the narrative that results one that belongs to "a more reliable narrator" (1980, p. 44; cited in Sass, 1988, pp. 18, 20).[19]

SPENCE

On the surface, Spence's theory is an attempt to free psychoanalytic interpretation from an unrealistic demand for accuracy, but a look just beneath the surface shows that the attempt is partly driven by a chronically unsatisfied wish for a different kind of accuracy.

Spence differs in at least two ways from the other three figures discussed (Sass & Woolfolk, 1988). In one way or another, Sherwood, Habermas, and Schafer wrote from within the context of the reason versus cause debate. And for the latter two—in some sense, perhaps for all three—the trend to be opposed is the application to the psyche of the reductionism, mechanism, and determinism each associated with causal (and more specifically metapsychological) explanations. Not surprisingly, all three therefore emphasized the significance of narrative for psychoanalytic theory and for theories about psychoanalytic work—not for the conduct of analysis per se.

Spence parted company on both counts. He had a different opponent and a more practical set of concerns. He opposed what he believed to be bankrupt theories of perception and memory. Spence rejected a theory of the mind as a passive recoder of events that, once they have been laid down as memory traces, can be recovered during analysis. Unlike the other writers, he was not especially worried that such a theory is causal. Rather, he highlighted a practical conflict in the necessity to put nonlinguistic experience into words.

The early argument of Spence's (1981) book blends pessimism based on this practical conflict with optimism about new theoretical possibilities. He began with a discussion of empirical work by Loftus on the frailty and malleability of memory, evidence that suggests that the way an analyst words his or her question is likely

---

[19]My account of Schafer, as well as my understanding of him, is indebted to Sass (1988).

to bias the record of the historical past. Also, Spence brought up a couple of concrete questions (meant to point to the analyst's shaping influence) that are similar to some mentioned by Wittgenstein (1982) in his lectures. Spence asked why, if we can translate a dream into words, we cannot retranslate in the other direction (1981, p. 383). The clear implication of this asymmetry is that words inevitably misrepresent memories—memories that, "if true, tend to resemble photographs"—and that the linguistically distorted rendering replaces the original (1982a, pp. 56–57). Spence also asked how the analyst knows when the train of free associations has arrived at an appropriate destination. The answer is simple: He or she cannot (1982a, p. 78).

Free association also points up another source of distortions, this time a social one. In the two-person conversation of psychoanalysis, the closer an analysand approximates truly free association, the more incomprehensible he or she becomes to the analyst. "If he is truly free and veridical in his reporting, he cannot be understood" (Spence, 1982a, p. 85). So, if the analysand is to be understood, the associations must be worked over in two ways. First, the analyst must actively search out meaning by applying conventions of psychoanalytic interpretation (thematic unity, transference, etc.) and an awareness of unspoken context. The result of this first level of synthesis is more coherent than the associations themselves. The problem is that only part the synthetic process can be reproduced in the public communication of the material to the profession. (This led Spence to worry that "our best evidence is a well-kept secret," 1982a, p. 237). The fragmentary associative text must also be naturalized by the addition of a second level, the kind of narrative framework described by Sherwood.

Having doubted the feasibility of producing historical truth and acknowledged the powerful influence on the developing dialogue played by factors that have nothing to do with veridicality, Spence proposed two new ways to view interpretations. First, they are exercises in freedom, aesthetic experiences, to be judged by their appeal and persuasive power, not their informational, denotative content. Second, they are therapeutic agents, pragmatic statements, designed not to state a true proposition but to bring about the truth of the proposition expressed, statements to be judged as we would judge a tool, by how well it helps us realize a goal (Spence, 1982a, chap. 10).

This formulation has led to an uneasiness about narrative in recent papers. According to Spence:

Narrative coherence [that] is needed to make the case report more accessible to the outside reader, . . . must not be used to provide an explanation of the events in the case. . . . [It] . . . can obviously add to the plausibility of the account but this feature must be sharply distinguished from its logical force. (1986, p. 16)

Spence saw a "serious and deep-lying conflict of interest" between narrativization and explanation. He devoted the last section of a recent paper to a warning about the dangers of narrative persuasion (1983, p. 477).

As Sass and Woolfolk (1988) emphasized, Spence assumed that the narrative qualities of a patient's productions are later additions to or transformations of historical truth (something that is either less organized or differently organized). It is worth noting the contrasting ways in which non-narrative material is conceived. First, when the freely associating analysand gives a veridical account of his or her experience, the strain of transforming experience into language show as his or her words approach incoherence. Here "accuracy" is equivalent to near chaos. A second image of non-narrative material is a seeming opposite: the true memory, which is best thought of as resembling a photograph. (With a few unimportant modifications, we can treat the photograph as a place holder for a broader class of historical truth—the plain narrative, the raw material, etc.) A third image of accuracy is one level up from the immediate experience of the associative stream or memory. It is the logically forceful explanation desired by future theory, but never described in detail. This comes in two forms: the essentially descriptive, fully naturalized text of a session that includes the analysts inferences, and the genuinely explanatory scientific account of the mental forces at work in a given case.

Spence's thought needs to be seen in the context of the images just described. The first two images effectively crystalize an image of experience as non-narrative. Implicitly ignored or rejected is the possibility that the structures of untransformed, unembellished experience might themselves be narrative, so that accuracy would demand narrative form. (Of course the definition of primary process thought may itself exclude this possibility, in which case it is Freud, not Spence, who is responsible for the assumption.) Not considered is the possibility Sass and Woolfolk (1988) called a correspondence of coherences, when patient and analyst aim for a patterned account similar to the pattern of the experience recounted. Is it any wonder, then, that when Spence detected some trace of narrative organization, this was attributed to the (possibly therapeutically desirable) drive for coherence at the expense of accuracy or correspondence with the facts? When the communication of a fully accurate account of experience is an impossible ideal, it makes more sense to organize theory around the alternative values of aesthetic and pragmatic interpretations.

Less easy to understand is Spence's residual loyalty to an ideal of theory as accurate representation, expressed in the third aforementioned image—a wish for a logically binding explanation. Spence clearly acknowledged that theory, like narrative truth, is "independent of facts" (1982a, p. 292). If the imposition of narrative coherence vitiates the truth claim of the account that results, how is it possible, even in principle, for explanatory coherence to avoid similarly contaminating the claims of the "more substantial . . . science of mind" for which he hoped (p. 297)? By adopting the view that organization is a structure added to perception, and following Sherwood in his conclusion that explanations are a kind of logical addition to primary facts, Spence made his call for genuine scientific explanations weaker and less consistent than his case for the instrumental (aesthetic and pragmatic) uses of interpretations.

CRITICISM AND COGNITION

The case against narrative theory is more detailed than can be reported here, so I have chosen a central criticism that reflects a desire to rescue some standard of accuracy (which they believe narrativists to have abandoned or distorted). The heart of the complaint is that the concept of narrative mixes fact and fiction. Both Eagle (1980b) and Grunbaum (1984) pointed out that Freud based his scientific reasoning on a belief that a therapeutically effective interpretation is one that must "tally with what is real" (Freud, 1917, p. 452). Thus, Freud's view fuses the two aspirations of theory I mentioned in my introduction, accuracy and efficacy. By introducing criteria unconnected to accuracy (such as coherence, elegance, persuasiveness), narrativists split apart accuracy and efficacy.

The criticism involves two steps. First, Eagle argued that, although Spence may have said that a good narrative will need to take account of the facts (even though it will not be determined by them), nothing in Spence's position dictates this. Once anything other than accuracy has been allowed, the game has been given away. Nevertheless, the critics recognize that a fallback position is open to the narrativist: A historically inaccurate interpretation might still prove to be a powerful tool in causing change. This can only be defended by a second step, however, a step the narrativist do not take: They must test, rather than assert, the therapeutic value of narrative.

On first glance, Eagle's second step seems to substitute prediction and control (values associated with the view of theory as a tool) for accuracy (a value associated with theory as faithful representation). It does not. Rather, Eagle remained loyal to accuracy, only the issue is now the accuracy of a theory of therapeutic action, not the accuracy of a historical narratives: Therapeutic power is valued primarily as an indication that an accurate theory is being tested.

The exchanges between critics and narratives have been heated and more complex than this example suggests. The spirit has been captured by it, however. I consider now a question directed to the spirit of the narrative turn and the debate that has accompanied it.

CONCLUSION

In this section, I describe three types of context that shed light on the current narrative debate. The first has to do with psychoanalysis, especially Freud's theories. The acceptance of Freud's work posed certain moral epistemological dilemmas in particularly acute form, and narrative is well understood in the context of these dilemmas. The second has to do with the history of institutional psychoanalysis. Narrative theory has situated itself in at least two controversies that have preoccupied psychoanalysts in the last quarter century. The third has to do with the animating spirit of psychoanalytic work. Narrative is a way—one way—of addressing a quite general feature of psychonalytic work, its attempt to make sense of irrationality.

Why Narrative and Psychoanalysis?

The Context of Freud's Work. If, as I have suggested, the conflict between theory as faithful representation and theory as tool is older than psychoanalysis, one is left to wonder what it is about psychoanalysis or narrative that explains the way these have crystallized in the narrative turn. Here I offer two speculations, based on what might be called the cultural position of Freud's ideas.

First, the turn to narrative is a result of the tendency of psychoanalysis to produce a moral anxiety, a fear about the meaning of human action. Some might argue that this anxiety is only one instance of a more general modern concern that the application of scientific determinism to human action endangers a belief in moral terms (freedom, guilt, responsibility, etc.). But merely having a determinist bent is clearly not enough, for mechanistic models of the mind come and go with regularity. Recently, for example, studies of the living brain have timed electrical impulses to the microsecond—and yet no one has been tempted to give us a serious narrative theory of neurobiology. The reason no one bothered is important for understanding why narrative theory happened.

The reason there has been no dramatic neurobiological showdown about morality is that this mechanization does not seem to leave reason and action without a point, nor does it tell the ego (or whatever) that "it is not even master in its own house" (Freud, Standard Edition, 16, p. 284; quoted in Rorty, 1986, p. 1).[20] But once a personal, psychological unconscious has been described as a system with causal powers, mechanization has threatened freedom. Rorty (1986) exactly captured the difference when he pointed out how little a person finds his or her power or freedom threatened by the suggestion that his or her mind might be a brain—the two seem so different, what is lost if the former is the slave of the latter?— and how gravely threatened they seem to be by the suggestion that a belief might be caused, not by something as strange and different as electricity coursing through tissue, but by another belief, an alien belief, a belief that, because it is locked in a field of obscure but recognizable mental forces—stand-ins, if you will, for fear, desire, hatred, and so forth—functions as a cause, not a reason (see Davidson, 1982).

In this context, narrative may seem to tame the threat to freedom by rationalizing the operation of these threateningly quasi-human forces. Think of Freud's near oxymoron for the Unconscious, the "internal foreign territory." If we want to represent the influence of a belief from that zone, we can think of the representation either as a depiction demanded by a state of affairs, or as a way of constituting, helping to create or reconfigure that state of affairs. If the second approach is chosen, the way is open to domesticate the alien because, in the negotiations that draw the border, both disputing parties are the patient him or herself. If a given account is not forced on an individual by its sheer accuracy, if he or she can choose it to serve some purpose, he or she is freed of the question, Which

---

[20]The argument I give here closely follows the one made by Rorty (1986), though he is not concerned with internal debates within psychoanalysis.

belief or desire is really me? From this point of view, the great virtue of psychoanalysis is its ability to weave a personal story that includes the operation of the most alien aspects of the psyche. Indeed, as we have seen, some versions of narrative theory make this transformation of the opaque into the transparent and the incoherent into the coherent the sine qua non of narrative interpretation.

Although I completely agree with Rorty that the moral anxiety awakened by analysis is fundamental, a correlated epistemological fear cannot be overlooked. Analysis not only continues a tradition of making accurate theoretical models (of what is real), it also extends a Copernican practice that, like a turn of the screw of subjectivity in James' novel, *The Turn of the Screw*, can terminate in a whirlpool of self-vitiating relativism. The tradition is Copernican inasmuch as the practice of analysis attempts to overcome the distortion introduced by (e.g., the analysand's) limited perspective by recognizing the forces responsible for the limitation. The surface dilemma is that the new point of view is nevertheless beset by new limitations, and the whole practice can thereby be called into question.

Just as analysis is one of many psychologies to employ mechanistic explanations, it is by no means the only modern practice to push reflection to the point of challenging objective truth. The same tendency can be found in the hermeneutic philosopher Gadamer's (1976) charge that the enlightenment's prejudice against prejudice was itself merely another prejudice, or the critic Roland Barthes's claim that because all discourse constitutes its own subject, "on the discursive level . . . objectivity is as imaginary as anything else" (1971, p. 414, cited in Harries, 1983, p. 244). Though it rarely surfaces in such pure form, it is this attitude that attracts many advocates of narrative, who view it as an extension of "the perspectivist nature of . . . Freud's own technical recommendations [for clinical practice]" (Schafer, 1981, p. 3), and repels many opponents, who see it as a betrayal of enlightenment values.

Once again, the contrast between psychoanalysis and other Copernican practices is more important than the similarity. Freud's theory transformed, without abandoning, the fundamental assumption of all modern theory-making that reality and illusion can be distinguished. By making the ego the site of both cognition and illusion, by tracing the paradigmatic model of thought to the infant's hallucinatory wish fulfillment, by suggesting that in narcissism the ego effectively mistakes itself for an object in the world, Freud simultaneously relied on, and undermined, the fundamental assumption that, despite a veil of distortions, an individual's mind can be gripped by truth.[21]

Just as narrative can be seen as a response to a moral anxiety, so it can be seen as a response to an epistemological one. Although it is not clear that anything about a narrative theory requires the sort of perspectivalism expressed by Gadamer (1976) and Barthes (1971), both narrativists and their critics often assume the two go together. And the affinity is clear enough. Narrative theory has supplied a form of discourse in which the questions raised by radical Copernican reflection—Freud's own (perhaps unwitting) challenge to objectivity—can be stated in psychoanalytic terms. As Eagle (1973a) said early in the debate, adequacy and appropriateness are standards that can be applied to narratives that are not empirical. Thus, the use of a narrative framework to describe psychoanalytic data implicitly brackets traditional questions of reference and truth. Yet, paradoxically, some narrativists want narrative theories to do the work once done by theories expressed in a scientific idiom, theories concerned with reference and truth.

The Context of Recent Psychoanalytic Controversies. The development of narrative theory has been influenced by institutional factors outside the scope of this chapter. Specifically, a dispute within the psychoanalytic community (which in some ways paralleled the tensions just described) prepared the way for the current narrative debate and contributed to the central position this debate has been accorded in mainstream journals and conferences.

---

[21]If a single source of this paradoxical position is to be given, it is probably best located in the dual demands Freud made on the concept of the ego. Because Freud's ego concept is both the site of perceptual/cognitive functioning and a middleman negotiating with id, superego, and world, Freud was faced with "the necessity of representing the function of representation itself as the effect of a conflictual process, which in turn cannot be conceived of in representational categories" (Weber, 1982, p. 170). The depth of the paradox can be seen when we try to bring the primary process into focus. If we picture the primary process is as reflex action in response to a hallucinatory reproduction of a previous satisfaction, then two requirements seem to point in opposite directions. Some minimal binding of energy to a representation is required for a reproduction (a perceptual identity), yet this binding, this inhibition is an exclusive property of the secondary process (Weber, 1982, p. 38).

At several points, Weber implied that the conceptual problem raised by the representation of the mind's representative faculty pushes analytic theory toward narrative form. Because the theory makes incompatible demands on the concept of the ego, these can only be reconciled in a perverse narrative of ego formation, a narrative in which the ego overcomes contradictions by forming structures based on defensive self-deception. If true, then critics of the narrative turn might respond that this maneuver makes an already bad theoretical situation worse.

I began this chapter with an allusion to the long-standing discontent over the status of the metapsychology. A prominent spokesperson for this discontent was George Klein (1976), who insisted on the division between the clinical theory of psychoanalysis, which he saw as an important contribution worth preserving, and the metapsychology, which he saw as an unfortunate attempt to eliminate a language of purpose from the description of human purposes. (Although Klein died in 1971, he made use of arguments from the cause verses reason debate among philosophers interested in psychoanalysis, described in an earlier section.) His opponents responded with a defense of the metapsychology based on the need for a language of scientific theory construction. In this context, one can speculate that narrative explanation must have seemed to promise a theoretical, explanatory concept, closely allied with the intent (if not the language) of the metapsychology that was simultaneously close to clinical work and case studies.

The Context of Interpreting the Irrational. The turn to narrative theory can also be seen as an emphasis on the unavoidable principle of charity involved in all interpretation. It assumes that coherence is inherent in a life. Understanding a person logically requires that we assume that he or she mostly makes sense, otherwise too many degrees of freedom make it impossible to clear up the small misunderstandings. Yet the appeal of psychoanalysis, the reason psychologists have so long put up with its many logical problems, is that it offers an explanation for irrationality, for the failure of action to make a coherent whole. Davidson (1982) expressed the paradox well:

> If we explain [irrationality] too well, we turn it into a concealed form of rationality; while if we assign incoherence too glibly, we merely compromise our ability to diagnose irrationality by withdrawing the background of rationality needed to justify any diagnosis at all. (p. 303)

Narrative Theory in the Future of Psychoanalysis. Prediction is always risky, but a few generalizations can be made. Perhaps inevitably, controversies over narrative have to some extent been drawn into larger controversies little concerned with narrative per se. There has been a tendency for arguments about narrative to become entwined with arguments about related issues: about mind, about theory-making, about the knowledge claims of psychoanalysis. I suspect that the future of narrative theory within psychoanalysis will depend on its ability to sustain the tension between these larger disputes and disputes about narrative as such, without either coming to dominate the other. At present, this balance requires more attention to the latter.

In addition, there has been remarkably little argument directed to clarifying how narrative reformists differ from other psychoanalytic opponents of the traditional metapsychology (self psychologists, object relations theorists, interpersonalities, etc.). Finally, an important role may lie ahead for an aspect of narrative theory not yet fully exploited, the use of narrative theory in discussions of technique. The development within literary narrative studies has produced a diverse rigorous vocabulary for many of the nuances of ways language affects subjectivity, a language that is consequently well-suited to the nuances of intervention in psychoanalysis and psychotherapy. (It may be that this development had been retarded because it holds little promise of producing a substitute for the metapsychology.)

ACKNOWLEDGMENTS

This essay was greatly aided by the individual and collective generosity of a number of parties. Much of the reading took place as part of Jerome Bruner's research project on narrative, sponsored by the Spencer Foundation. Many of the ideas were first discussed in a memorable seminar at the Graduate Faculty of the New School for Social Research on narrative and psychotherapy conducted by Jerome Bruner, Herbert Schlesinger, and Donald Spence. Louis Sass not only served as my reader, his published work and individual discussions influenced the content of this piece.

REFERENCES

Adorno, T. (1968). Sociology and psychology. *New left review, 47,* 79–97.
Ambrose, A. (Ed.). (1979). *Ludwig Wittgenstein: Lectures in philosophy 1932–5.* Oxford: Blackwell.
Arendt, H. (1958). *The human condition.* Chicago: University of Chicago Press.
Barrett, C. (Ed.). (1966). *Wittgenstein: lectures and conversations.* Berkeley: University of California Press.
Barthes, R. (1971). Science vs. literature. In M. Lane (Ed.), *Introduction to structuralism.* New York:
Bartley, W. (1973). *Wittgenstein.* Lasalle, IL: Open Court.

Carr, D. (1986). *Time, narrative and history.* Bloomington, IN: University of Indiana Press.

Dallmayr, F. (1972). Reason and emancipation: Notes on Habermas. *Man and World, 5,* 79–109.

Danto, A. (1965). *Analytical philosophy of history.* Cambridge: Cambridge University Press.

Davidson, D. (1982). Paradoxes of irrationality. In R. Wollheim & J. Hopkins (Eds.), *Philosophical essays on Freud* (pp. 289–305). Cambridge: Cambridge University Press.

Dilthey, W. (1961). *Meaning in history.* London: Allen & Unwin.

Dray, W. (1963). The historical explanation of actions reconsidered. In S. Hook (Ed.), *Philosophy and history* (pp. 105–135). New York: New York University Press.

Eagle, M. (1973a). Sherwood on the logic of explanation in psychoanalysis. In B. B. Rubinstein (Ed.), *Psychoanalysis and contemporary science* (pp. 331–337). New York: Macmillan.

Eagle, M. (1973b). Validation of motivational formulations: acknowledgement as a criterion. In B. B. Rubinstein (Ed.), *Psychoanalysis and contemporary science* (pp. 265–275). New York: Macmillan.

Eagle, M. (1980a). A critical examination of motivational explanation in psychoanalysis. *Psychoanalysis and Contemporary Thought, 3*(3), 329–380.

Eagle, M. (1980b). Psychoanalytic interpretations: Veridicality and therapeutic effectiveness. *Nous, 14,* 405–425.

Eagle, M. (1984). Psychoanalysis and "Narrative Truth": A Reply to Spence. *Psychoanalysis and Contemporary Thought, 7*(4), 626–640.

Engelmann, P. (1967). *Letters from Ludwig Wittgenstein* (L. Furtmuller, Trans.). Oxford: Basil Blackwell.

Farrell, B. (1961). Can psychoanalysis be refuted? *Inquiry, 1,* 16–36.

Freud, S. (1917). Introductory lectures on psychoanalysis. *Standard Edition, 15–16,* 3–448.

Freud, S. (1918). From the history of an infantile neurosis. *Standard Edition, 17,* 3–123.

Gadamer, H.-G. (1976). *Philosophical hermeneutics* (D. E. Linge, Ed. and Trans.). Berkeley: University of California Press.

Gallie, W. B. (1964). *Philosophy and historical understanding.* London: Chatto & Windus.

Goldstein, L. (1976). *Historical knowing.* Austin, TX: University of Texas Press.

Grunbaum, A. (1980). Epistemological liabilities of the clinical appraisal of psychoanalytic theory. *Nous, 14,* 307–385.

Grunbaum, A. (1984). *The foundations of psychoanalysis: A philosophical critique.* Berkeley: University of California Press.

Habermas, J. (1970). On systematically distorted communication. *Inquiry, 13,* 205–218.

Habermas, J. (1971). *Knowledge and human interests* (J. J. Schapiro, Trans.). Boston: Beacon Press.

Harries, K. (1983). Copernican reflections and the tasks of metaphysics. *International Philosophical Quarterly, 23*(3), 235–249.

Hart, H.L.A., & Honore, A.M. (1950). *Causation in the law.* New York: Oxford University Press.

Hempel, C. (1942). The function of general laws in history. *The Journal of Philosophy, 39,* 35–48.

Hempel, C. (1962). Explanation in science and history. In R. Colodny (Ed.), *Frontiers of science and philosophy* (pp. 7–34). Pittsburgh: University of Pittsburgh Press.

Hopkins, J. (1982). Introduction. In R. Wollheim & J. Hopkins (Eds.), *Philosophical essays on Freud* (pp. xii–xiv). Cambridge: Cambridge University Press.

Horkheimer, M. (1939). The relation between psychology and sociology in the work of Wilhelm Dilthey. *Studies in Philosophy and Social Science, 9.*

Janik, A., & Toulmin, S. (1973). *Wittgenstein's Vienna.* New York: Simon & Schuster.

Jay, M. (1973). *The dialectical imagination.* Boston: Little, Brown.

Klein, G.S. (1976). *Psychoanalytic theory.* New York: International Universities Press.

Kuhn, T. (1962). *Structure of scientific revolutions.* Chicago: University of Chicago Press.

MacIntyre, A. (1958). *The unconscious.* London: Routledge & Kegan Paul.

Mandelbaum, M. (1967). A note on history as narrative. *History and Theory, 6,* 416–417.

Marcus, S. (1974). Freud and Dora: Story, history, case history. *Partisan Review, 41,* 12–23, 89–103.

McCarthy, T. (1972). A theory of communicative competence. *Philosophy of the social sciences, 3,* 135–56.

McGrath, W. (1986). *Freud's discovery of psychoanalysis.* Ithaca: Cornell University Press.

Meares, R. (1985). Metaphor and reality: A response to Roy Schafer. *Contemporary Psychoanalysis, 21,* 425–448.

Merleau-Ponty, M. (1962). *Phenomenology of perception* (C. Smith, Trans.). London: Henley.

Mink, L. (1978). Narrative form as a cognitive instrument. In R. H. Canary & H. Kozicki (Eds.), *The writing of history.* Madison, WI: University of Wisconsin Press.

Moore, G.E. (1959). *Philosophical papers.* London: Allen & Unwin.

Peters, R. (1958). *The concept of motivation.* New York: Humanities Press.

Popper, K. (1962). *Conjecture and refutations.* New York: Basic Books.

Ricoeur, P. (1970). *Freud and philosophy.* New Haven, CT: Yale University Press.

Ricoeur, P. (1978). The question of proof in psychoanalysis. In C. Regan & D. Stewart (Eds.), *The philosophy of Paul Ricoeur* (pp. 184–210). Boston: Beacon Press.

Ricoeur, P. (1981). *Hermeneutics and the human sciences.* Cambridge: Cambridge University Press.

Rorty, R. (1986). Freud and moral reflection. In J. Smith & W. Kerrigan (Eds.), *Pragmatism's Freud: The moral disposition of psychoanalysis* (pp. 1–27). Baltimore: Johns Hopkins University.

Sartre, J.P. (1956). *Being and nothingness* (H. Barnes, Trans.). New York: Philosophical Library.

Sass, L. (1988). The self and its visissitudes: An "archeological" study of the psychoanalytic avant-garde. *Social research, 55* (4),551–608.

Sass, L., & Woolfolk, R. (1988). Psychoanalysis and the hermeneutic turn: a critique of Narrative Truth and Historical Truth. *Journal of the American Psychoanalytic Association, 36*(2), 429–454.

Schafer, R. (1976). *A new language for psychoanalysis.* New Haven, CT: Yale University Press.

Schafer, R. (1976). *Language and insight.* New Haven, CT: Yale University Press.

Schafer, R. (1980). Narration in the psychoanalytic dialogue. In W.J.T. Mitchell (Ed.), *On narrative* (pp. 25–49). Chicago, IL: University of Chicago Press.

Schafer, R. (1981). *Narrative actions in psychoanalysis.* Worcester, MA: Clark University.

Schafer, R. (1983). *The analytic attitude.* New York: Basic Books.

Schafer, R. (1985). A response to Meares. *Contemporary Psychoanalysis, 21,* 445–448.

Seebohm, T. (1977a). The problem of hermeneutics in recent Anglo-American literature: Part I. *Philosophy and Rhetoric, 10*(3), 180–198.

Seebohm, T. (1977b). The problem of hermeneutics in recent Anglo-American literature: Part II. *Philosophy and Rhetoric, 10*(4), 263–275.

Sherwood, M. (1969). *The logic of explanation in psychoanalysis.* New York: Academic Press.

Spence, D. (1981). Toward a theory of dream interpretation. *Psychoanalysis and Contemporary Thought, 4,* 383–405.

Spence, D. (1982a). *Narrative truth and historical truth.* New York: W.W. Norton.

Spence, D. (1982b). On some clinical implications of action language. *Journal of the American Psychoanalytic Association, 30*(1), 169–184.

Spence, D. (1983). Narrative persuasion. *Psychoanalysis and Contemporary Thought, 6*(3), 457–481.

Spence, D. (1986). When interpretation masquerades as explanation. *Journal of the American Psychoanalytic Association, 34*(1), 3–22.

Stone, L. (1979). The revival of narrative: Reflections on a new old history. *Past and Present, 85,* 3–24.

Toulmin, S. (1954). The logical status of psychoanalysis. In M. Mcdonald (Ed.), *Philosophy and analysis* (pp. 132–138). New York: Philosophical Library.

Walkup, J. (1984). When a psychoanalyst makes sense, what does he make it out of? *Journal of the British society for phenomenology, 15*(2), 180–196.

Walkup, J. (1986). Order and disorder in Freud's Vienna. *Social Research, 53*(3), 579–590.

Weber, S. (1982). *The legend of Freud.* Minneapolis: University of Minnesota.

White, H. (1973). *Metahistory.* Baltimore: Johns Hopkins University Press.

White, H. (1981). The value of narrativity in the representation of reality. In W.J.T. Mitchell (Ed.), *On narrative.* Chicago: University of Chicago Press.

White, M. (1965). *Foundations of historical knowledge.* New York: Harper & Row.

Wittgenstein, L. (1953). *Philosophical investigations.* New York: Macmillan.

Wittgenstein, L. (1982). Conversations on Freud; excerpts from 1932–3 lectures. In R. Wollheim & J. Hopkins (Eds.), *Philosophical essays on Freud* (pp. 1–11). Cambridge: Cambridge University Press.

Wollheim, R., & J. Hopkins (Eds.). (1982). *Philosophical essays on Freud.* Cambridge: Cambridge University Press.

Author Index

Page numbers in *italics* denote pages with complete bibliographic information.

Subject Index